D0486611

I Believe

The Christian's Creed

We are constantly assured that the churches are empty because preachers insist too much upon doctrine—"dull dogma," as people call it. The fact is the precise opposite. It is the neglect of dogma that makes for dullness. The Christian faith is the most exciting drama that ever staggered the imagination of man—and the dogma *is* the drama. . . .

The people who hanged Christ never, to do them justice, accused him of being a bore—on the contrary, they thought him too dynamic to be safe. . . .

We have very efficiently pared the claws of the Lion of Judah, certified him "meek and mild" and recommended him as a fitting household pet for pale curates and pious old ladies. To those who knew him, however, he in no way suggested a milk-and-water person; *they* objected to him as a dangerous firebrand. True, he was tender to the unfortunate, patient with honest inquirers and humble before heaven. . . . He was emphatically not a dull man in his human lifetime, and if he was God, there can be nothing dull about God either.

—Dorothy L. Sayers

* * * *

This would be the renewal of the church—that our conscience would awaken from the sleep of death, that we would listen to Jesus, that we should be given afresh the living, present Word of God.

—Julius Schniewind

* * * *

To be a Christian means to live by the Word and the message handed down, the truth of which authenticates itself anew in life, in the realities of our own time.

—Hans von Campenhausen

I BELIEVE

The Christian's Creed

By HELMUT THIELICKE

Translated by JOHN W. DOBERSTEIN
and H. GEORGE ANDERSON

Fortress Press　　Philadelphia

BT
993.2
T543

In remembrance

of my teachers

JULIUS SCHNIEWIND

RUDOLF HERMANN

This book was originally published in Germany under the title *Ich Glaube. Das Bekenntnis der Christen* by Quell-Verlag, Stuttgart, copyright © 1965.

Scripture quotations from the Revised Standard Version of the Bible, copyrighted 1946 and 1952 by the Division of Christian Education of the National Council of the Churches of Christ in the United States of America, are used by permission.

© 1968 BY FORTRESS PRESS

Library of Congress Catalog Card Number 68-23991

Second Printing, 1969
Third Printing, 1974

4549G74   Printed in The United States of America   1-1027

TRANSLATOR'S PREFACE

In his 1961 Christmas letter to friends, Dr. Thielicke remarked that it was his good fortune to have obtained a translator "of remarkable creative power" for the English-language editions of his sermons. He went on to identify his new co-worker as "Professor Doberstein of Philadelphia, the translator of Bonhoeffer." Dr. Doberstein, who was then Professor of Pastoral Theology at the Lutheran Theological Seminary in Philadelphia, had sensed the timeliness and power of Thielicke's sermons before they had become well known in this country. Largely through Dr. Doberstein's ability, Thielicke found an American voice and an American audience. When he toured the United States in 1963, Thielicke stayed with the Dobersteins and later wrote that their cultivated home, as well as their "intellectual and spiritual affinities" with him, had enhanced his visit. A warm friendship built on mutual respect made cooperation between the preacher-professor in Hamburg and the professor-preacher in Philadelphia an easy matter.

In the same letter that announced his work with Dr. Doberstein, Thielicke noted that he had begun preparation of a new sermon series on the Apostles' Creed. Preached in Hamburg during the next years and finally published in Germany under the title *Ich Glaube*, the sermons attracted wide attention and public acclaim. Dr. Doberstein began the translation almost at once, but his sudden death in October of 1965 meant that someone else would have to finish the task. As a former student of Dr. Doberstein, I have tried to complete the translation as a token of my gratitude toward and admiration for him—and his family. I hope that the very comparison of his work with another's will accent the uniqueness of his ability to clothe profound thoughts in clear

42855

language. Significantly, the last words he translated were at the end of the chapter entitled "I Believe in God the Father":

> I can still, like a small boy saying his childish evening prayer, repeat the assurance of security: " 'This child of God shall meet no harm!' "

H.G.A.

Lutheran Theological Seminary
Columbia, South Carolina
June, 1968

AUTHOR'S PREFACE TO
THE ENGLISH EDITION

I have just returned from lecturing at the Medical Center in Houston, Texas. Although the matter under discussion there was organ transplants and the artificial prolongation of life, the real underlying question had to do with what "I believe." The questions of faith are as manifold as life itself, and this is precisely why it makes sense once in a while to take in hand the Apostles' Creed and let it lead us through a systematic unfolding of the substance of faith. For it is this substance of faith on which we draw each time we speak to the concrete issues of life.

Theologians usually present this substance of faith systematically—and I have done this too—in a scholarly dogmatics. The totality of faith, however, must also be presented in such a way that it is "proclaimed" in preaching. This is because the theological expert should not be the only one to meditate on the totality of God's mighty acts. The entire congregation should do so also. Some of us did this when we studied the catechism as children. Now as mature Christians we can do so once again—and be startled to see how much we already knew, though perhaps without consciously making it a part of our lives.

For me, another important reason for presenting the totality of faith in this way is to remind myself that preaching precedes theology. Only *after* the proclaimed word strikes home do we reflect upon what happened and relate it to the problems of life. Where theology forgets its secondary position, the result is spiritual sickness, of the kind of which traces are already at hand. We become almost completely preoccupied with ourselves, inquiring less about what the word of God says and more about who we are and the degree to which we can in our situation understand and appropriate that word.

The latter are of course valid questions. We must indeed ask whether and how far we can confess the Creed as our own and still be intellectually honest. What bothers me in all of this, however, is the priority we attach to these matters. Many of us spend all our time analyzing the situation. We get bogged down in the preliminaries—in "hermeneutical studies"—and are concerned with little else.

This is apparent in the case of the "God is dead" theologians, whose serious intentions are nonetheless not to be scorned. They concern themselves almost fanatically with the so-called situation of modern man, whom they see so locked in finitude and lacking in a sense of transcendence that he is interested solely in the practical tasks of getting on in life and getting along with others. They then go on to ask how the doctrines of the faith must be restated in order to speak to this situation, and the result is a grotesque amputation of the body of Christian doctrine.

When theology is given the nod over proclamation, everything goes wrong, for then man speaks more of himself than of the word of God which makes him a new creation. Thus it is precisely for the sake of the content of theology that we must attempt to teach the faith in the form of direct proclamation. I cannot deny that I am a theologian. In all that follows I have thought things through theologically. But what I say here I want to say as a preacher. I want to let the word of God speak. Only *after* we have drunk from the living springs of water should we begin to analyze it chemically and channel it theologically.

April, 1968   Helmut Thielicke

TO THE READER

"Do you believe that Christianity is on the rise or in decline?" In recent years I have repeatedly met with this question. The question is basically irrelevant. Where Christianity loses its public market value and no longer enjoys any prestige in the social structure, it may actually be thoroughly sound and healthy in substance; it may find expression in living, vital congregations; and the hour of promise may be imminent. Conversely, where it basks in the sunshine of public favor and perhaps enjoys the privilege of social status, it may rot, lose its dynamic, and become a liability which is carried along only by virtue of the inertia inherent in tradition.

What does this irrelevant question as to whether Christianity's stock is high or low mean anyhow? The mere term "Christianity" is in itself very questionable.

But if this irrelevant question is asked, an equally irrelevant answer may be given, for example, in terms of statistics. If we are not mistaken, worship services seem to be considerably less well attended, and not infrequently their substance and content seem to be becoming less solid and important. On the other hand, so-called religious interest is constantly increasing: theological and philosophical questions are discussed ardently. The discussion becomes quite stormy when fundamental questions thrust themselves onto the religious horizon and stir up the basic question of the meaning of life. This is the case, for example, with respect to the question of thermonuclear weapons, or the problem of the population explosion and its control, or the biological engineering of human beings and its presumed right to tamper with genes. Wherever the elemental character of problems becomes apparent with respect to their religious implications, the discussion becomes heated. And it is precisely the young people who make no secret of their concern in these discussions.

These remarkable countermovements of a diminishing or rising interest are brought about by the operation of certain contrapuntal, almost automatic, laws. In other words, religious discussion is stimulated by the fact that the basic questions of life quite spontaneously give rise to the corresponding "religious" question, namely, the question of the meaning, the horizon, of human existence. Conversely, the fact that the church's proclamation does not reach its mark may be due to the fact that its relevance to life is not recognized and, perhaps, is not made clear.

For anyone who preaches, whose vocation is theology, this is a situation that demands reflection and possibly some drastic revisions of his thinking. Perhaps, like the author, such a preacher may be dealing constantly with young people. He rejoices at the way they ask questions: by letter and orally, individually and in groups. What is more, he is delighted that, despite all the speculative tendencies which characterize the ingenuous and carefree questions of youth, it is not a purely intellectual interest that determines their passionate searching but rather the very restlessness of existence and the perplexities of life itself which are making themselves felt.

But what makes the person on the receiving end of the questions doubtful and drives him to self-criticism is this: Just where do these discussions lead us? Aren't discussions, by their very nature, endless? Do they not go on spawning new discussions? Doesn't every serious discussion end with the conclusion that this is where we really have to begin, and that we have arrived not at a period but only at a colon? Isn't this constant beginning anew the sign that we are moving in a circle, a curved line that never ends? This is disquieting, for the circle is ultimately the symbol of noncommitment.

If one examines the conversations of Jesus, one will note that they always end in an arrest, in a sudden termination of the circular. Without exception they end in a *"Hic Rhodus, hic salta."*[1] They end at the steep escarpment of a message which cannot be avoided by any detour.

[1] Here you must leap or retreat.

I believe that one can do justice to the seeker only if one leaves him under no illusions about the existence of a steep wall at which decisions must be made. He must be led to face the granite greatness of a message that brooks no evasion.

It was this consideration that prompted me to present the addresses that follow. I said to myself: If your conclusion is correct, then the wall to which you lead your hearers should be as steep as possible, and there is no forbidding wall of the Christian message that is more rugged and towering than the Apostles' Creed.

The monumental statements of the Apostles' Creed offer the extreme test of self-examination. Here we can find out whether we are willing to face the message of the gospel as a barrier and obstacle, and therefore whether we dare to put a stop to the endless circle of discussion and block up all the avenues of escape. Here it is not possible to build a road with cheap and easy grades. Here we are confronted not with the noncommittal presentation of an "essence of Christianity,"[2] but with brute facts, with statements like "born of the Virgin Mary," "descended into hell," "resurrection of the body." Either we succeed here in making it clear that this really concerns us, or we shall succeed nowhere. *Hic Rhodus, hic salta!* Here we must show our colors!

I have the impression that fundamentally it is precisely our honest and open-minded contemporaries who desire nothing more urgently than this kind of "confession" of our colors. They really do not want special tracts written for the poor neopagans and Faustian seekers in which the message is sugarcoated to make it palatable. The most alert people among us are imbued with a passion for substance. They know very well that agreements at the periphery—where, for example, it is a question of the problem of understanding or the general idea of truth or existential questions or the problem of "Christianity and . . . this or that"— lead only to an uneasy peace and an intellectual darkness in which all cats are gray. We must talk with one another about the kernel, and not merely discuss the shells. We have talked long enough

---

[2] The reference is to books like Adolf Harnack's *Das Wesen des Christentums* (*What is Christianity?*).

about demythologizing and about the thought patterns of a bygone age. The intellectual curiosity which all this has aroused in many circles (though the discoverers of this problem are concerned with far more than intellectual curiosity) may not be a bad motive, but it is by no means the only one and very definitely not the most important one. Therefore, let us talk about the thing itself and about what is possibly the most shocking and offensive form in which it has been formulated. Let us talk about the "descent into hell" and the "resurrection of the body," and not get bogged down in the preliminaries.[3]

I have asked myself whether this attempt is only an act of self-torment. I want to be honest enough not to gainsay altogether this willingness to commit an assault upon myself. For I admit that reciting the Apostles' Creed in the service is somewhat of an annoyance to me (I do not regard this part of the service as ideal). I am somewhat troubled by the fact that the Apostles' Creed seems almost to diffuse an atmosphere of misunderstandings. We must ask whether the creed is not a continual enumeration of some things which we *must* believe. Is it permissible to speak of faith at all in this additive way? Are we allowed to say anything more than the simple confession, "Lord, I believe; help my unbelief"? Is there such a thing as a minimal content of belief, the possession of which gives me the right to call myself a disciple? Didn't the people to whom Jesus attributed great faith actually believe very little so far as content was concerned, and, what is more, was not that little—as in the case of the woman with the hemorrhage (Matt. 9:20 ff.)—actually very questionable?

The fact is that I am not very happy about the erecting of this super-steep wall of the Apostles' Creed in our services of worship, nor about the many who are hungry and thirsty, the people for whom the promises of faith were intended but who suddenly grow faint and lapse into silence.

[3] Though it was, of course, merely an external indication, it struck me as significant that overflow attendance was highest after the topic of the resurrection of the dead was announced and that the attendance of young people was especially large.

And yet there is *one* good thing about this steep wall: it prevents one from sliding by too easily and makes it impossible to keep on revolving in the circle of discussion. I am convinced that many sermons are boring because they deal not too much but too little with these steep truths.

In any case, we are about to make the test. Anyone who intensively questions these truths and is prepared not to shrink from any difficulty will find that they take on a mysterious vitality. They make themselves known in a dimension where they challenge and concern us. They will be anything but boring.

The fact that the following chapters were delivered in the course of church services may have strengthened the will to challenge engagement and commitment. The preaching style does not permit one to make allowance for any extensive discussion or for the desire to safeguard one's statements by qualifications. It demands an arbitrary, "unguarded" form of statement. And it encourages one to make this venture, because the speaker, in a mysterious way, finds himself on the firing line, for now the message is no longer completely dependent upon him. What he says is embedded in the prayer, the praise, and the song of the congregation, and derives its life not from its own illuminating power but from the promise of Him who will declare Himself in His own word. The word which is here spoken aims at "teaching," and in the process a great deal of thinking has to be done. It also launches out in many different directions, for those who listened to these addresses were a mixed company—as mixed as I desire the readers of this book to be. They consisted of dock workers and clerks, students and well-to-do people, professors and tavern keepers, pietists and neopagans, converts and skeptics. Thus the *one* beam of light may be variously refracted in the countless prisms of the many questions and presuppositions in the minds of the hearers and readers. Yet what is here "taught" in connection with such a broad spread of problems will live neither by the cogency of the arguments nor by the conviction of the preacher, for this is a matter of a herald who is speaking under orders.

The author knows that preaching is a hazardous way of teaching, and he is conscious of how many breaches of style have crept in as he traversed this new way of preaching. He knows, however, that this means of stating the Christian message, the "teaching" or "doctrinal" sermon, must now be ventured. And I would rejoice if others were found who were better able to cope with this task.

As I worked on this book, I kept thinking with gratitude of the great congregation which for ten years has been coming with unswerving loyalty to hear these sermon series in St. Michael's Church in Hamburg. May many find in the message of this book that ground which "holds his anchor sure forever," just as the green spire of St. Michael's, towering high over the Elbe, salutes the sailors when they return home from distant voyages. As this spire has become a symbol of the "door to the world," so may this book become a door, a gateway to a world which is not encircled and gradually choked to death by the fateful Midgard serpent, but filled with the air of promises which hardly anyone hears.

CONTENTS

The Apostles' Creed

WHAT DOES IT MEAN
TO BELIEVE?

> Immediately the father of the child cried out and said, "I believe; help my unbelief!" —*Mark 9:24*

For years a well-known magazine has been publishing in each issue an article on the subject, "This is what I believe." In it, some more or less prominent personality, whose portrait is reproduced, tells what he regards as the ground of existence and what he would declare to be his creed.

Frequently, or even usually, what is confessed is not a "religious" faith at all, but rather some kind of philosophy of life or world view. The author seeks, as it were, to seize a banner and hold it up for all to see the message that "down underneath, the world still holds together." Some believe in the spirit, or in freedom, or in the economy; others believe in the goodness of man. Still others believe in the rules that govern the Faustian struggle of life. Now and then, someone drops the name of Jesus Christ.

If the editors of this magazine did not know that people in the subways, women under the hairdryers, and young people going home from work were eagerly reading this particular column, they would certainly have discontinued this series of articles long ago. But the series has been running on, year after year, like a tapeworm. The editors are obviously convinced that many of their readers turn to the article on creeds before they read the one on Soraya or the latest Hollywood divorce. Journalists talk about finding a "hit" when they discover such an especially attractive topic. Is it possible that the problem of faith is really a "hit"?

At any rate, it is strange that people are interested in what a politician, an auto manufacturer, or a famous movie actor believes. It is strange, if only because people today generally are interested only in the hard metal of facts. People want from the press exact information about the topics discussed by the representatives from Russia and the United States or about the scheme hatched by a group of politicians. If a reporter were to say merely, "I believe" or "I think it possible that such and such things may have been discussed," the reader would find this rather uninteresting because it was uncertain and unfounded. Conjectures, wishful thinking, and anxiety dreams produce enough fantasy as it is, and therefore the reader needs no further purveyors of "I believe" or "I surmise." As we said, he wants the hard metal of facts.

But from the this-is-what-I-believe columns these people expect something quite different, and it is well for us to reflect for a moment about *what* these people are really looking for. I think they are looking for two things.

First, what they want is not exact and verifiable information about certain life experiences but a confession of an absolute certainty by which a man lives, by which he stands or falls, yet which he cannot prove. The writer is rather like a child who believes with *absolute* certainty that his mother loves him, yet would be utterly confused if some intellectual brute were to say to him, "Now show me why you assume that your mother loves you. Do you have any evidence? What right do you have to think so?"

So when a person writes in one of these articles—I am quite consciously not taking a religious answer—that "I believe in the good in man," this is a certainty which he ultimately cannot prove at all, any more than a child can prove that his mother loves him. After all, during the course of his life the writer must surely have met some people of more than dubious character, unscrupulous social climbers, string-pullers, and other self-seekers who would seem to contradict his faith in the goodness of man. Yet, despite all appearances to the contrary, he clings to his certainty that the pearl of humanity lies hidden somewhere in the muck and mire of a demoralized psyche.

The second thing that the reader (consciously or unconsciously) expects and assumes when he reads this confession of faith is that even though this person cannot prove what he believes, he doesn't doubt it for a moment. He is willing to stake his

3

life on it; he organizes everything he does around it. Naturally, everything a person does, his whole style of life, can take on completely different aspects, depending on his conception of man as good or as evil. If he believes in the goodness of man, he will accept fairly calmly the fact that his employee is a lazy, undependable shirker. He will still be willing to give him another chance and will do his best not to be discouraged in his belief by any contradictory experiences. On the other hand, if he believes that man is a scoundrel, he will constantly be on the lookout for unpleasant surprises. He will be suspicious, will play it safe, and will never trust anyone any more than is absolutely necessary. He will use others for his own interests. If he observes someone performing a "good deed," he will suspect that there are ulterior motives behind it and will get no joy out of it.

So what I believe—no matter what it is, whether it has a religious or just a this-worldly significance—exerts an elemental influence upon my life. And even though this belief is not founded upon demonstrable realities, it nevertheless has a very real function in my life. This belief ultimately determines how I take hold of and shape my whole life; it produces an historical reality. The same thing applies when as a *Christian* I say, "I believe in God, the Creator," "I believe in Jesus Christ," and "I believe in the Holy Ghost." Hence it makes sense to use the term "faith" on two very different levels, on the religious level and on the philosophical level.

If I believe, say, that we are abandoned orphans, that the abyss of nothingness yawns before us, and that we are but the playthings of force and matter, then our life is nothing but a bleak journey without purpose or goal. Jean Paul Richter has portrayed this desolation in his novel *Siebenkäs*. Falling asleep on a quiet hillside, he has a ghastly dream-vision of a Christ who has lost his heavenly Father and who confesses that he has been wrong, that he has misled men into a false faith and lulled them into false security. "We are orphans all, both I and ye. We have no Father." Tearfully this Christ confesses that he has journeyed through the infinite cosmos, and nowhere has he found a Father.

He has met with nothing but the dreadful emptiness of the universe. Shattered and shaken, this disillusioned Christ sums up his vain passage through the cosmos: "Oh, dead, dumb nothingness! necessity endless and chill! Oh, mad, unreasoning Chance! . . . Every soul in this great corpse-trench of a universe is utterly alone! I am alone—none by me. O Father! Father! where is that boundless breast of thine, that I may rest upon it? Alas! if every soul be its own creator and father, why shall it not be its own destroying angel, too?"[1]

And so it is in fact: if I believe only in nothingness, if there is no Creator and Father, then I am not only left in dreadful loneliness ("I am alone—none by me," says Jean Paul), but I must also despairingly take charge of my own life; I must be my own creator, a self-creator. In place of an eternal authority and immutable commandments, I have: a program which I myself devise; human, all too human ideologies; and, finally, the dogma of the superman. But at the same time the man who creates himself quite logically claims the right to "decreate," to liquidate himself and others. The so-called superman has always evoked the subhuman man; he rages and liquidates as his self-devised program dictates. "If every soul be its own creator and father, why shall it not be its own destroying angel too?" asks the mad Christ. And we see the dreadful answer to this question wherever a berserk self-creator decreates and liquidates, wherever he provokes parents against their children and children against their parents and undermines the foundations of the world.

Oh, yes, what I believe—as well as what I do not believe— changes the face of the earth. It becomes my fate.

Jean Paul's terrible vision ends with the sleeper's wakening from his nightmare. He hears the evening bells ringing and finds that he is back in a comforting world which rests in the hands of the Father of Jesus Christ. And so he finds again his faith in that "boundless breast" in which beats a heart that cares for us all. His

[1] Translation from *Wit, Wisdom and Philosophy of Jean Paul Fred. Richter,* ed. Giles P. Hawley (New York: Funk & Wagnalls, 1884), pp. 197–98. (Trans.)

faith in the Father behind this world will now go with him and change his life. We must, then, try to visualize what this faith means.

The man who knows and trusts that there is One who thinks higher thoughts about his life develops a new attitude toward and relationship to the future. Influenced by the bad dream of nothingness, I was distrustful whenever I thought about the coming day: the four gray hags, Want, Guilt, Care, and Misery, who dogged Faust's path, also lay in wait on mine. I thought I knew that "haphazard strikes the lightning." And who could know what the mysterious womb of the future might bring forth tomorrow or the day after? But now that I know the Star to whom I may look and the Hand that leads me, I am certain that I have a Father who knows what I need and who will give me bread, not stones, and fish, not scorpions. I know, too, that he will be with me in whatever the future brings.

So then, I do not need to know what the future will bring, whether it be mirth or pain that awaits me. I am confident that "both spring from his hand." The faith that his will for me is good and that he considers everything that is to happen to me before he sends it, this certainty is far more elemental, far more decisive, than the uncertainty about *which* fates will be chosen to bring greetings and messages from my Father. Now, if I have this faith, I can face the future calmly. I have become, as it were, an adventurer of a higher order. Eagerly and expectantly, I look for the surprises God has in store for me; I look to see how he will let the threads run together and unravel them again. I am eager to know how he will deal with the great motif which he has given to my life, that motif which affirms that everything works for good if only I love him and remain confident that he will sustain and uphold me.

Then, too, my attitude toward my conscience will be changed. When I deeply love God, my conscience becomes more delicately adjusted, much more sensitive and responsive. Nor is this any wonder, for now my conduct is no longer determined by whether I *should* do this or that (my duty, for example), but I do it to please God. At first it is hard for me (even after I have

6

become a Christian!) to work with someone who is disagreeable or whose character is dubious. It irks me to be open to someone like that, to give him a chance, and to speak an encouraging word to him. But now (even though it still goes against the grain) I remember that Jesus Christ himself died for this man and that God grieves over him and wants to save him. Because I love God, my heart will beat with the Father's heart. Thus I cannot do otherwise than accept and be "there" for this person with whom my Father does not think himself too good to associate. And when I fail to do this, when I simply cannot manage it, then I do not merely have a sense of moral failure, but rather I am sad because I have grieved *God*. When you love someone very much, his pain becomes your own pain. This is the reason why there is no more sensitive conscience than that of a person who loves God. It registers every shadow that passes over the heart of God.

So there is nothing in my life that is not changed after I have learned to say, "I believe. . . ."

It would really be foolish to think that this affects only the so-called "religious sector" of our life. When we have found God, not one stone is left upon another in our life, including the secular area. People we meet, landscapes through which we drive, streaks of bad luck and affliction, and the bright hours of our life when we feel as though we will burst with happiness and delight —there is nothing which is not seen in a new light when the joy of faith is given to us, and our whole life is calmed because we have found peace with God. It is no wonder, then, that all of us yearn for faith.

It is not true, of course, that a person without faith is bad and that he must inevitably be a failure. On the contrary, there are splendid unbelievers who put us Christians to shame. And who knows what the Lord will do with them on Judgment Day! I believe there will be no limit to the surprises we shall have on that day. I remember a mother who was an unbeliever and who had been estranged from the church for decades. I met her again and again at the bedside of her son, who was slowly dying in great pain, and I observed how she nursed him with quiet calmness, literally wrapping him in the cloak of her motherliness during his last agonies. She betrayed not a single sign of how much she herself was consumed by pain and anxiety. One day I said to her, quite spontaneously, "I admire your attitude." Her disconcerting reply was, "Yes, attitude perhaps, but don't look underneath. I haven't a thing to hold on to."

These unbelieving and despairing, yet very gallant words have stuck in my memory for a long time. They really made clear to me for the first time what faith means. Faith means having something to hold on to and thus being grounded on that foundation which God has laid—and which is ultimately he himself. Of course, faith must not be thought of as a soft cushion on which we can self-confidently recline. Then faith would be nothing more than bourgeois religion, and the dogmas would be an air-raid shelter into which the craven-hearted would creep to escape the inclemencies of life. If faith were really such a last resort, I would find it far more decent to believe in *nothing* and stick it out in the bleak hopelessness of chance and nothingness and thus at least be able to face life without any illusions.

But the foundation on which I stand and the stay that upholds me, thank God, are something altogether different from the soft pillow on which the comfortable repose. We have only to look at the great believers portrayed for us in the Bible. Was it easy for Noah, for example, to believe God's promise that he would rescue him in an ark? Certainly it was not! If anything, Noah made himself ridiculous and brought down upon himself the derision of the people by building a fantastic ship on dry land in the blazing sunshine.[2] And was it a small thing for Abraham to leave his own country and his kin to journey into the uncertainties of a strange land, simply because he had been given the promise that the great and good hand of God would accompany him step by step into the unknown and bring him to the goal which God alone knew? Was it a purely natural thing for the psalmist to say, "Nevertheless I am continually with thee"? After all, what he was saying was this: Everything contradicts the faith that there is such a thing as justice, that a higher power rules this world, and that

[2] Cf. "Noah—the Adventure of Faith," in *How the World Began* (Philadelphia: Fortress Press, 1961).

8

there is anyone who concerns himself about me. Nevertheless, I hold fast to thee, I push on blindly through the fog and know that thou art waiting for me on the other side.

That's the way it is. The peace of God, whom I trust, is not something I have in hand, but something for which I reach out. The stay by which I am upheld and the ground on which I stand do not spare me from the depths out of which I cry. The life of God which is promised to me does not spare me from experiencing the pangs of death. And the certainty that neither death nor life, nor things present, nor things to come can separate me from the love of God (Rom. 8:38 f.) does not spare me from the onslaught of anxiety, from encompassing meaninglessness, and from the fact that tomorrow is like a mountain that threatens to fall upon me.

Thus the Nevertheless is a part of faith, just as the cup of suffering is part of Gethsemane and as Golgotha is part of the miracle of the Resurrection. Sometimes the fog grows so thick as I look ahead that I have no idea how I shall ever get through. But then I am given the grace to say Nevertheless, for suddenly He who was a man like you and me and who took upon himself the burden of this same misery is there beside me. Then suddenly, with Him at my side, the barrier is broken and I am in the clear; I have experienced the miracle of getting through.

Many people block up the entrance to this adventure of faith by thinking that they must feel something religious, that they must sense a tingling of their nerves, a religious thrill, when the experience of faith comes over them. But the Bible's prescriptions for faith will cure anyone of this delusion. The remarkable thing is that the Bible does not concern itself with the subjective experience of faith, with that religious feeling. This comes as a surprise to people of today, who are so keenly interested in psychology. Furthermore, in the Apostles' Creed there is no mention of feeling and experience whatsoever; it is composed of dry facts, a sober catalogue of events extending from the Nativity to the Ascension. The "religious man" (and who does not fall into that category?) hankers after the thrill of religious experience and instead is put off with "dogmas"!

So it *seems*, at any rate. Indeed, we may wonder whether the people of the Bible had any religious feelings, whether they ever gave way to their emotions or were simply spiritually dull. Well, of course they experienced all the emotions. But they did not talk about it! The biblical story of Joseph, for example, is far soberer and less psychological than Thomas Mann's novel based on the Joseph legends. Why? Certainly not because the men of the Bible suffered from an exaggerated spiritual chastity and were unwilling to reveal their inward experiences. These figures were not so reserved as that! If they were to step into a drawing room today, the teacups would certainly rattle. There are very good practical reasons why emotional thrills and the experience of faith play no part in this.

Let me use a very ordinary, almost trite illustration. When a boy falls in love with a girl for the first time, he is completely captivated by this lovely creature. Her eyes, her figure, the sound of her voice, the charm of her gestures and movements—all these fascinate him. Only later, perhaps, when he stops to reflect a bit, does he ask whether what he has felt is that wonderful thing called love, whether it really is like the romances that adults whisper about and that the love scenes in the movies are all about. If we look more closely at what has happened, we find that the boy actually has not been yearning for love, he has not said to himself, "I want to experience the feeling of being in love"; he simply has found the girl enchanting. That is all there is to it. And this so engrosses him that he no longer notices what his feelings are at all. He does not perceive that he himself is a lover; he knows only that he loves someone. That's the way it is. And when he tells a friend about it, he talks not about his feelings but simply about the girl.

Ordinary and worldly, all too worldly, as that is, it indicates quite simply but precisely what happens when we believe. When the unbelieving Thomas was overwhelmed by the appearance of the risen Lord and could say nothing but "My Lord and my God," he did not notice that he had suddenly become a believer and that he had experienced a redeeming certainty and a religious emotion as well. He simply saw before him the Savior who had sought and found him, who had plucked him out of the torment of doubt, and who would from now on fill his life with splendor and joy and order and certainty of purpose.

He who finds Christ becomes so filled with him that he literally forgets his faith. In the real sense of the word, he forgets himself, and he has no time to think about religious experiences. That is why the people of the Bible bore witness to their *Savior* and not to their faith. One of them was not even sure whether he believed at all (perhaps he still had no feeling), but when Jesus stood there before him he said, "I believe; help my unbelief" (Mark 9:24). May it not be that he perhaps was the profoundest believer of them all, far more believing perhaps than many a church Christian who swallows all the dogmas of the catechism whole and rattles them off at the drop of a hat? Perhaps I do not know *whether* I believe, but I *know* in *whom* I believe. The person who just wants religious experience really has no experience at all. He is the one who gets cheated. He who receives Christ *experiences* something, but he hardly notices it. The wonder of the new life, the joy of forgiveness, and the liberation from fear keep him looking constantly to this figure from whom streams of living water flow into his life, reclaiming the desert of his lost heart and working the miracle of a new beginning.

As I talk about this joy in believing, one thing troubles me. I can conceive of someone's becoming depressed by what I have described as a joy and a fulfillment of life. He may say to himself, "Yes, of course, I too would like to have this peace and I wouldn't mind having a companion like this Nazarene. Perhaps I could even grow to love him, for I don't mind saying that I am stirred by a man who loved until his love killed him, who was so present to his human brothers that he shared their life, took the burden of their guilt upon his own shoulders, and even bore their death with them. All that has a tremendous appeal for me, and I wish I could have this 'comfort in life and in death.' If it were only a matter of a noble man, I too might manage to make him my guiding star. But I can't get past the dead weight of these dogmas and all the strange stuff that is so far beyond me that I cannot accept it. 'Suffered under Pontius Pilate'—well, perhaps that I can take; the pain-wracked face of the crucified Christ is very human and I am touched by it. But all the other stuff, 'born of the Virgin Mary,' 'descended into hell,' 'rose again from the dead,' 'ascended into heaven'—well, I don't know what to do with it; I give up. If Jesus of Nazareth is to be had only by buying all this, then the price is too high for me. I'll have to go my way without him. I would have to do violence to my reason and be dishonest. And certainly he who said that he was the truth cannot expect that of me."

Well, that's the kind of depression that may overtake some persons at this point. And certainly those whose critical honesty cries a halt at this juncture are not the worst kind of people.

I want therefore to deal with all these seemingly difficult-to-understand points, one after another, in the following chapters. In doing so, we shall not evade anything. Perhaps then the scales may fall from our eyes and we shall be surprised to find that many things which have horrified us by their strangeness will turn out to be quite familiar. But possibly the very opposite may result; perhaps many things which hitherto have had a secure place in our minds will now appear steep and strange. ("Christmas," for example, may be one of these things.)

In any case, faith is not something that falls ready-made from heaven. And we certainly do not begin our life with God by subscribing to the whole catechism, paragraph by paragraph, and saying that we "regard it as true." God is far too compassionate and generous to make such a demand of us. He does not say, "If you do not acknowledge Jesus as my Son and therefore as the 'God-Man' you do not belong; you cannot be called a Christian. At most I can only put you at the end of the line, and you will have to see to it that you gradually move up to the front." A lot of human zealots may think that way, but God doesn't.

I remember what it was like when I got to high school. I had passed the entrance examination and proudly told myself that now I "belonged." The seniors seemed to me to be fairly bursting with learning, whereas I, miserable shrimp, did not know a word of Latin. They also had deep men's voices, for they were grown-up, whereas I was still afflicted with a boyish soprano. I may have been an unripe grape on the vine and the seniors may have been old, clarified wine, but I simply did not belong. There is a similar situation in the church of Jesus Christ. That Jesus of Nazareth is a man like you and me, and that at the same time he is still something else—namely, what is falteringly conveyed by the term "Son of God"—this is something that I learn perhaps after I have been in his school for a long time. But I already *belong to* him even when I have within me the first hunger and thirst for righteousness. And if I go up to him and say, "Lord (whoever you are, you know better than I how miserably I am still groping about in the dark), Lord, help me," then I have already been enrolled in his troops and I "belong."

Just let Christ's divinity, Easter, and the Ascension rest for a while. As Luther once said, every doctrine has its age, its time, and its hour. Don't hanker after a diploma when you are still a first-grader. Accept Jesus as he appears to you at first: as just a good and noble man who loved his fellowmen. Take him just the way you would take any other man whose greatness of soul impresses you. If you do this, you certainly will not yet have grasped his secret. You will be like that strange but nevertheless impressive figure in the New Testament, the woman who suffered from a hemorrhage (Matt. 9:20 ff.). She came up behind Jesus and touched the fringe of his garment in order to be healed. She still had not grasped the secret of Jesus. She saw him as just a magician, a sorcerer; she had the superstitious idea that contact with his radiations would charm away her illness. To regard Jesus as a magician is certainly a more primitive version of the same misunderstanding that results in my regarding him as merely a great and noble man, a large-scale Albert Schweitzer. And yet Jesus turned to this wretched woman and praised her faith, assuring her that she belonged, that even though she was still a beginner and even though her faith was filled with misunderstandings, she belonged.

If you take Jesus just as he is on first impression, if, in other words, you think of him in quite human terms and see him as a brother of man who loves unselfishly, who lives only by love, and who takes his mission to give men a new meaning for their lives so seriously that he dies for it—if you think of him in that way, you surely have not yet seen him face to face, but you have at least touched the fringe of his garment. And whoever holds to him, however tenuously, whoever has touched him even peripherally, to him he turns and says, "You belong to me; now come and walk with me. And if you walk with me, with each passing day you will perceive more and more clearly who I am." Anyone who has had the experience of faith knows how one progresses in its school. The Johannine writings, especially, tell us that this is not a matter of theological exercises which are designed to train our powers of cognition. Mere intellectual acuity can never enable us to pass this course. This assignment lies in a totally different direction. Only he who loves can know him who is love. "Had not the eye a sunlike nature, the eye could never see the sun," said Goethe. In order to learn to know "the Sun that cheers my spirit," in order to know "Jesus Christ my King,"[3] I myself must have something of the sunlight within me. That sounds a bit romantic, yet it is a very simple truth. That is to say, I am sunlike when I dare live for my neighbor in the name of Jesus, when I learn to grieve for another because Jesus is grieving for him, when I seek him because Jesus is seeking him, and when I conquer my antipathy because this perhaps very questionable fellow is dear and precious to the man from Nazareth.

This is the point where I must begin. It is a highly practical business. Jesus always confronts us with practical tasks. Only those who love learn to know who he is. Only those who love break out of the prison of isolation and nothingness in which they are enclosed. "Do you know what frees one from this captivity?" asked Vincent van Gogh in a letter to his brother Theo, and then replied, "It is every serious, deep affection. Being friends, being brothers, love, that is what opens the prison by some supreme power, by some magic force. Without this, one remains in prison. Where sympathy is renewed, life is restored."[4] And, we may add, there too the Prince of Life is very near, nearer than all fear and all guilt. There my life takes a turn, because he has turned to me.

[3] No. 526, *Evangelical Lutheran Hymn-Book* (St. Louis: Concordia Publishing House, 1931). Hereafter cited as *ELHB*. (Trans.)
[4] Translation from *The Complete Letters of Vincent van Gogh* (Greenwich, Conn.: New York Graphic Society, n.d.), Vol. I, p. 199. (Trans.)

The Father Behind This World

I BELIEVE IN GOD
THE FATHER

"If you then, who are evil, know how to give good gifts to your children, how much more will your Father who is in heaven give good things to those who ask him?"

—*Matthew 7:11*

Paul Cezanne, the great painter, during his difficult, for long unsuccessful, and very lonely life, used to utter a rather stereotyped groan. "Life is terrible," he said. That indictment of life did not refer to the burdens he had to bear: the lack of understanding of his work by his contemporaries; the failure of his marriage; and the contempt of his family, who had no appreciation of art. Rather, this indictment referred primarily to the meaninglessness that comes sweeping in like a chilling draft from the background of life. Why is great accomplishment not rewarded in life? Why does success so often come to those who don't deserve it, while others, through no fault of their own, are left in the shadows? Why do the cold calculators and the "realists" get the long end of the stick, while the kind, unselfish people and the champions of ideal values are at best ranked among the "also-rans"? Does life have any plausible standard by which it parcels out sufferings and gifts? Isn't the whole thing cruelly meaningless and characterized by haphazard chance?

Yes, life can be terrible because it is so enigmatic, thought Cezanne. Well, then, if that is so, isn't it simply an illusion of the weak to dream that there is a Father behind this world who thinks higher thoughts about us? Isn't all that simply a comforting fiction which has been pasted together because otherwise people could not endure life as it is?

This suggests why we human beings are always looking for the meaning of our life, why even quite naive people, and by no means only philosophical and thoughtful people, are really concerned about this question of meaning.

I remember very well how Joseph Goebbels, after the catastrophe at Stalingrad, when the German people began to feel the shock of the coming defeat, kept talking about "the meaning of the war" in articles and speeches. This shrewd judge of human nature knew very well what he was doing. He knew that men are willing to endure life, make sacrifices, and stake their lives only if they are convinced that a cause has meaning, that everything is embedded in a higher order. They want to know, they must know, that it pays to act and also to suffer in the framework of that higher order of things. Anyone who is obliged to admit that it is all meaningless and purposeless loses the courage to act and sinks into paralyzing resignation.

Faith in meaning is therefore quite simply an elixir of life. Even the greatest skeptics and nihilists know this. A poet like Gottfried Benn, for example, was literally galled by this question. As he said, he saw in history something meaninglessly "interminable," an everlasting cycle of culture coming into being and passing away, inhumanly mindless as the stars that circle around us according to mathematical laws, unmoved by anything human. But even he, for whom the world's course was so highly dubious, was unable to quench the question of meaning—simply because life without meaning is utterly intolerable. For himself, Benn answered this question of meaning by saying: Wherever creative man constructs a work of art he wrests an oasis, a tiny area of meaningfully molded life, from the desert of this futile and meaningless world. And for the sake of this tiny bit of meaning life is worth living.

Why do I mention all this when we are interested in an inquiry into faith?

I believe that Christians dare not be too quick to say: "For us these problems don't arise at all. When we say, 'I believe in God the Father,' this solves the question of meaning for us. After all, we believe that there is a Father behind this world. So, to that extent, for us there is no longer any sphinx of life nor any riddle."

Now anyone who defines faith this simply may be in for some sore disappointments, for faith is by no means such an easy solution to all the problems of life. Perhaps those who, like Gottfried Benn, struggle so earnestly and hopelessly with the question of meaning, scorning all premature consolations, are far closer to the heart of God than many self-secure, pious people. The latter's so-called "faith" is often merely a sign that they have not dared to think a problem through to its bitter end. Therefore, God's heart is on the side of the poor in spirit, the people with empty hands, for whom everything has gone to pieces and who are willing to admit it.

The fact is that faith in God cannot be misused to solve all problems in a cheap and easy way. No less a man than Job has shown us what that kind of threadbare faith looks like and how it finally breaks down (and we with it).

We recall that famous scene in heaven in which Satan gambles with God the Father for the soul of Job. It is the scene that provided the inspiration for the "Prologue in Heaven" of Goethe's *Faust*. The great Seducer wagers that he can divert God's devout servant Job from his faith.

With demonic perspicacity he has already spied the weak spot in this faith. He therefore knows precisely where he must begin his assault. Job thinks he believes in God (so the Tempter calculates) but in reality he has only elaborated a philosophy, a particular "view" of the meaning of his life and of history as a whole. That is to say, Job believes—or perhaps I should say he imagines —that justice is done in life: the good are rewarded and the wicked are punished. God is, so to speak, the principle of a just world-order. God is merely the good director behind the scenes who justly distributes reward and punishment. This means in simple practice that a man who acts rightly and abides by the directions of this Director of the world can count on it that he will pass the test of life and that in the end faithfulness and honesty will pay off. Faith pays off, thinks Job. It is a reasonable recipe for life, it is the best way to get ahead.

It was on this, then, that Satan based his strategy. This is the way he calculated:

If I succeed in upsetting this world-order, I shall also upset Job himself. This good man has worked himself into the illusion that life is meaningful and just. Simply because he believes this, it is easy for him to believe in God. In fact, it is quite obvious, isn't it (says Satan with an ironical smile), that I should believe in a good, intelligent, perhaps even a fatherly Director of the world when I see that everything in nature and history functions like clockwork and that it is really very easy and safe to live in this world as long as one accommodates oneself to some extent to this well-ordered process and keeps on good terms with its Director?

All I need to do (so runs Satan's tactical conclusion) is to perpetrate something which is totally meaningless. Then this whole pious construction will collapse. For what is meaningless, mad, and absurd will cause Job to lose faith in the one who, after all, should be the guarantor of meaning, namely, God. Once the question, "How can God let such things happen?" has lodged itself in him and begins to rankle and fester in his soul, then half the battle will be won. Then it will take only one more step for Job to regard God as unjust. Once he has gone that far, he will soon be convinced that there is no God at all, that everything is only blind chance or cold natural law. Therefore (thinks Satan) I will deluge Job with such a flood of misfortunes, setbacks, and disasters that he will no longer understand this world. And if he no longer understands the world, he will also no longer understand God, and that will make him lose his faith. *Quod erat demonstrandum*—which was to be demonstrated.

No sooner said than done, and we know what happens after that: Job's children die one after another, his cattle perish, his possessions burn to the ground. Everything that he has regarded as the blessing of God is suddenly turned into its opposite. The divine meaning of life, of which he has been firmly convinced, becomes a grotesque, grinning mask; the image of the kind and just Father seems to turn into a mocking, sardonic caricature.

It is very surprising that Job is not bowled over by this first assault of meaninglessness, that he still clings fast to the hand of God, asserting his brave Nevertheless. In other words, Job, with tremendous resolve, switches gears. Despite all these blows of fate, he refuses to admit that life consists of meaningless accidents and that faith in a just God has been proven wrong. He says rather: I must look elsewhere for the meaning of life. But where can that be?

And he believes that he has found the new answer: The meaning lies in the fact that God has higher laws and rights than those of an earthly judge whose image I project upon him. This higher right of God consists in the fact that he can take away what he has given, for, after all, everything belongs to him.

So Job finally fights his way through to a new confession of faith: "The Lord gave, and the Lord has taken away; blessed be the name of the Lord." So Job continues to believe that there is a hidden meaning in the events of life. Perhaps, he thinks, God wants to test me; or perhaps he wants me to mature through suffering. This, of course, is really a quite hidden meaning which a man cannot prove; nevertheless, one can dare to trust that it is true. One can still hope that God has his purposes in all this, even though we cannot understand them. So Job refuses to give up his faith in meaning.

Then Satan strikes a second time, and this time he employs a means that must surely shatter even this deeper and more subtle faith in meaning to which Job holds. He allows Job's suffering to go on endlessly and even increases it. Now he attacks Job's body; he smites him with leprosy, with intolerable itching, with physical and mental torments.

This is how Satan speculates: When a man is undergoing "moderate" suffering, he can say, "I am being tested and refined, I am being subjected to a severe discipline." And that can still seem to have some meaning. That need not necessarily disillusion a man about God. But this argument works only when the suffering is small or moderate.

Yet there are two cases in which this comforting of oneself with the argument that suffering is a test of faith ceases with an almost deadly certainty. First, when the torment becomes excessive. At a certain degree of pain, when the torment becomes utterly maddening, I can no longer do any mature thinking because I am no longer capable of thinking at all. Then I am simply numbed by the overwhelming pain, and all my nerves begin to vibrate. The second case in which all progress toward meaning

ceases is that in which the assault upon our faith goes on endlessly
and will not let up. Then the day comes when I say: "Now I've
gone through all the classes in this school of suffering, now I've
had my discipline, my final examination. There's nothing more to
be had from it. If I am tortured further, then it's simply meaningless. Then the only things left for me are the awful alternatives of
regarding God as a sadist or of believing in the blind spite of a
fate over which no one has any control." Perhaps the belief in the
soulless mechanism of pure process is the more charitable of the
two.

In fact, Job is finally driven to this extreme loss of faith. Anyone of us who has gone through severe and endless torment
knows what this is, having perhaps himself suffered the fate of
Job, that fate which ends in his renouncing God because he can
no longer see any meaning, because faith in a God who permits
meaningless and brutally stupid things to happen simply collapses.

What way can there be out of this deepest imprisonment of
the soul? What star can still shine over that abyss?

Many of the great sufferers have sought a way out in that
attitude which the philosophers have called *amor fati,* loving or
submitting to fate. They say to themselves: This everlasting
bickering with meaningless fate makes no sense. You only wear
yourself out doing that. The best thing to do is simply to accept
it with stoic calm and let it happen. In this way you make your
peace with life and also get through it fairly well after all. The
man who does nothing but resist and moan and say No grows
bitter and is consumed with resentment, and what fate does not
shatter he lays waste by self-destruction.

This renunciation of the claim to see any meaning whatsoever,
this willingness to resign oneself to everything without complaint
is, of course, a capitulation to fate. But perhaps for one who does
not know Jesus Christ this kind of capitulation is still the wisest
thing to do. Then at least he saves himself the fatigue of constant,
nerve-wracking quarreling with his fate. Then at least he has
again found something like a certain accord with life, even if this
accord is rather melancholy. In any case, he possesses a certain
greatness.

Externally and somewhat superficially regarded, this attitude appears to be similar to the one to which Job finally found his way and which is also demanded of Christians. Job, too, finally learned to say Yes and recovered his trust in the counsel of his God, whose thoughts are higher than our thoughts. In that Yes, Job's restless heart found a new peace. The Christian, too, says Yes, just as his Lord in Gethsemane ceased to refuse the bitter cup of suffering but accepted it from the hand of his Father. We say that Yes when we say, "Thy will be done"; let it be done even when we cannot understand it and when it goes against our grain.

Anyone who has ever uttered those words, "Thy will be done," at some very hard moment in his life, and who has won his way through to saying it, knows that a burden has been taken from him. He may have said it when the person dearest to him was taken away or when the doctor told him there was no more hope. And even though this Yes meant the end of the nerve-wracking bickering with fate (as it did for the Stoics and the pagans) it still was not a compromise, a capitulation. For he knew something that a person without Christ cannot know. He knew to *whom* he was saying this Yes and to *whose* will he was surrendering. He did not capitulate to fate, but acquiesced in the will of his Father. In saying Yes, he threw himself upon a heart that beat for him, a heart that bled with him when he suffered pain.

There is, of course, one important statement that must be made here. It is true that I can say, "Thy will be done," pious as it may sound, in a completely godless way. That is, I can say it in a fatalistic way, with the idea that what must come must come and there is nothing we can do about it. And this, of course, is precisely what this petition does *not* mean! Anybody who knows Jesus Christ does not say to God: "Do what thou wilt! There is no escaping thy will." Rather he says, "Thy will be done" with a calm and perhaps even cheerful mind. For he knows that the will of his heavenly Father, to whom he here commits himself, is a good will. He knows that it is true that his Father may not do what he proposes in his prayer, what he regards as meaningful and right. Yet that does not matter, for he knows that the Father knows his needs far better than he does. Therefore he can confidently leave the decision to his Father's will and accept what comes to him from his hand.

When we have that, we have gone through the worst of it. For now I have been spared the worst hardship: the stress and strain of quarreling with my lot, being dissatisfied and ill-humored, and losing the courage to live. True, tomorrow's events are recorded in a closed and sealed letter. I do not know what that letter contains. But I see the One who sends it, and I know how he feels toward me. Therefore I look forward to those secret marching orders with a confident and happy mind, even though they may send me in a direction which is precisely opposite from that which I consider meaningful and desirable.

Perhaps it is precisely the honest nihilists, who feel so keenly that the world is so cruel and fatherless, who will now say to me: Isn't all this merely an illusion which you have invented because without it you could not bear to face life? Is not your message about the Father's heart too beautiful to be true?

What shall be my answer to that? Perhaps this: I too have my doubts about "the dear Father above the starry sky." A man may believe in someone like that when he gazes at the sky in some exuberant moment of sentimental optimism. It is not likely that in the radioactive, tainted air of Hiroshima any of the survivors had any such dreams of that kind of God. And for the writer Wolfgang Borchert [who served in the Russian campaign of World War II and was twice imprisoned for criticizing the Nazi government] God had become an impotent old greybeard who could do nothing but helplessly bewail the misery of men.

The Father *I* believe in does not dwell above the starry sky. No, he was in a man who laughed and wept as you and I, who was tempted and who despaired as you and I, who was assaulted by meaninglessness as you and I (his last words according to the oldest witness were: "My God, my God, why hast thou forsaken me?") and who was shaken by the pangs of death as one day they will shake us. What do I care about the Father above the starry skies? He is far removed from the muck and mire in which I am stuck. And whatever he is doing in the eternal sabbath of heaven doesn't help me one bit in the sweat and drudgery of my daily, earthly misery.

But this Father of my Savior is not merely "dear." He loves. And that's something different. When a person loves, he is one with the person he loves. I once knew a convict's mother who was completely devoted in her love for her unhappy, wayward boy. And because in her thoughts she still held him by the hand as once she did when he was a small boy, and because for her there was never an hour when her heart was not full of anxiousness and care, she probably suffered more for him than he himself suffered as he endured the torments of imprisonment and the self-reproaches of his botched and bungled life.

And that's exactly what I meet in Jesus Christ: the Father who in him gave what he most loved, who suffers more over me than I myself suffer. Every evil thought and every act of hard-heartedness toward my neighbor strikes at the Father's heart just because he loves me so. He knows better than I that I am always threatening to fritter away that which he bought at so great a price. He sees more keenly than I how I keep shutting the door through which he would enter and then celebrate his advent in me, and thus blockade the road to my own happiness.

Jesus, before his entry into Jerusalem, cried out in a tear-choked voice, "How often would I have gathered your children together as a hen gathers her brood under her wings, and you would not!" In his love he suffered pains of which Jerusalem itself had not the slightest notion. He who loves must suffer because of what happens to the beloved, and often he sees that suffering more clearly than the beloved himself. Only he who remembers this can begin to see what the dying Christ suffered and what the mystery of his suffering was. His knowing love brought down upon him the whole burden of his unknowing and unhappy human brothers, while they themselves blithely tippled and played at dice beneath the cross or enjoyed the sensual titillation of a public execution. The physical pain of pierced hands and the torments of thirst were child's play compared with this knowledge of love, compared with the burden that this knowledge laid upon him. He who loves is always the one who loses, said Thomas Mann in his story "Tonio Kröger." God is the one who loses and suffers, because he loves the most. That's it! He is the one who loses—all the way to the crucifixion of his Son.

I meet this love in Jesus who suffers because of me and who shares my lot all the way to the torments of Calvary, to the ultimate of fear and despair (far more than that mother who shared the prison miseries of her son!); therefore I dare to say, "Our Father," therefore I dare confidently to say, "Thy will be done," and therefore I refuse to talk about a "dear Father above the starry skies." Only he who has been hurled into the ultimate depths can fathom what he is saying when he says these things, can understand that when he has said them he can say no more. Conrad Ferdinand Meyer, in his narrative poem *Huttens Letzte Tage* ("Hutten's Last Days"), describes how during his halcyon days this truculent knight simply did not know what to make of the crucifix, the "image of torment and pain." But when he lay in mortal illness, this is what he said:

> The longer that I gaze at it, I see
> That half the burden is removed from me;
> For two of us, instead of one, abide—
> I and the thorn-crowned Brother by my side.

The "thorn-crowned Brother" who loves me most and therefore is the loser—he it is who makes credible for me what, without him, would be nothing but romanticism and illusion, namely, that I have a Father who remembers me and whose remembering me I can believe because he suffers for me and knows me. The name of Jesus is the sign that makes me believe this and build my life upon it.

Anybody who has found his way to that faith gains a new serenity and begins to understand the exultation that the redeemed sing out in their hymns. The "dear Father above the starry skies" may, perhaps, be only the product of an overflowing *joie de vivre*, a projection upon heaven of this exuberance. But with the Father of Jesus Christ it is the other way around: fellowship with him bestows joy first of all; it grants power to sing out with that liberated and defiant laughter that resounds so infectiously in Johann Franck's hymn, "Jesus, priceless Treasure" [No. 82, *ELHB*]. He speaks of the "Lord of gladness" and of fleeing "thoughts of sadness." So, if I am in league with the Conqueror, shouldn't there be something of the humor of the Christian man in my life? Humor, after all, is always a way of overcoming the world. It is high time for us to bear witness to our Lord not only through preaching but also by our laughter.

Naturally, there are as many kinds of laughter as there are kinds of men. If I were to name the two focal points in this scale of gaiety, I would say that there is the laughter of diversion and there is the laughter of redemption.

The trick of diverting oneself works like this. Perhaps I feel depressed and melancholy. Sometimes I can put my finger on the reason why. A careful plan has gone awry or someone has done something mean to me and I have not been able to handle it. At other times, however, I cannot pinpoint the reason for my depression; I go around fighting a feeling of dejection or a vague anxiety. And the confused state of the world, with its menacing aspects, adds still more to my melancholy. Then I see an advertisement for a movie comedy starring an irresistible comedian, and I think, "This would be just the right thing for me now. A bit of cheering-up will divert me and do me good." And, as it turns out, I catch myself roaring and holding my sides with laughter as the character in the film falls into the water with his Sunday clothes on. And yet this laughter is not a real liberation. That is to say, I sense that my diaphragm and certain muscles which control laughter are functioning, but in the background of my heart the dejection still lingers like a low-pressure mass during a rainy summer. As soon as the lights go back on, the damp fog of misery creeps back over my soul.

But when I have a relationship with the Father who extends his hand to me in Jesus Christ, all this is reversed. Then, in the foreground of my life, I have to contend with exactly the same stresses and depressions that every human being has to endure. Naturally, I, too, will continue to have many occasions to be angry, irritated, and dejected, and the whole range of what is human, all too human, remains unchanged, a part of my experience. In becoming a follower of Jesus I do not turn into a block of stone; I remain a sensitive, vulnerable human being. In me, too, defiance and despondency still lie close together.

But in what I called the "background of my heart" the picture is now quite different. Whoever has fellowship with the Father in Jesus Christ knows that this part of his life cannot be touched by anybody or anything. Often I may wriggle and writhe like a worm, but in that secret part I am held firm. That is immovable, and the storms of life cannot invade this peace. "If we have thee, then neither devil, world, sin, nor death can hurt us." There I have a hold, because there I am held; there is the place where the world is overcome. There are the cheer and the calm of those whom the misery of life cannot touch, the hilarity of those who can venture the utter madness of that verse in Paul Gerhardt's Easter hymn [No. 218, *ELHB*]:

> The world against me rageth,
>   Its fury I disdain;
> Though bitter war it wageth,
>   Its work is all in vain.

One can almost hear the grave in which I am imprisoned bursting and see the smithereens flying because the Victor over the dark powers has taken possession of me. Many things, to which I had before given myself with desperate earnestness, now become a spectacle on which I can look quite calmly, and what really interests me about it is the end to which the real Director will lead the adventure of my life. "It is a joy," said Pascal, "to be in a ship on a storm-lashed sea when one is sure that the ship will not sink." The persecutions of the church are like this. Therefore God's praise is not silenced even where the church of Jesus Christ exists in the midst of the terrors of ideological tyranny. Ultimately, his church remains untouched by the myrmidons of terrorism, though the hearts of Christians may quail and cringe.

Medieval Christians, before they were petrified by liturgical gravity, knew what they were doing when, after the reading of the Easter story, they broke out into the so-called *risus paschalis*, the Easter laughter that resounded through their churches. The

42855

Eastern Church still observes this custom, even though it is a persecuted church. That laughter praises the Father who snatched his Son from the grip of death and made a laughingstock of the world and all its "fury" and "bitter war."

Why should there not be this merriment, this great affirmation of life, as we turn away from the pigsties of life and walk resolutely toward the lighted windows of the Father's house where we are awaited with love?

But to be awaited and to come home means at the same time to come to oneself, to find the truth about oneself.

> In every man there lives an image
> Of what he ought to be.
> As long as he is not that image
> He ne'er at rest will be.

And what that means is that I find the fulfillment of my life only if I have found myself. Then I shall be at rest.

But even the "worldling," the humanist, can say that. And yet something else is meant here: in order to find myself, I must know who I am and where I came from. Only then will I also know the goal of my life. But I am never anything but the lost son who seeks to make a successful life in a strange country and yet senses that he is getting farther and farther from his goal. I shall not be "at rest" until I am back home again with my Father.

One thing is sure: only he who finds God also finds himself. And when Jesus says, "My peace I give to you," what he means is that he brings us back again to the point where we are at home, where we have a Father, where we are safe, and where our rest, our peace, is full.

So wherever Jesus Christ is, there everything is changed. Where before there were grinning specters, now there is the face of the Father. Where there was unrest now there is peace, for I have found my way home. And even though I am now a "burnt child" and thus have become an old skeptic, I can still, like a small boy saying his childish evening prayer, repeat the assurance of security: " 'This child of God shall meet no harm!' " [No. 33, *ELHB*].

I BELIEVE IN GOD THE FATHER ALMIGHTY, MAKER OF HEAVEN AND EARTH

> O Lord, how manifold are thy works!
>> In wisdom hast thou made them all;
>> the earth is full of thy creatures.
>
> When thou hidest thy face, they are dismayed;
>> when thou takest away their breath, they die
>> and return to their dust.
>
> When thou sendest forth thy Spirit, they are created;
>> and thou renewest the face of the ground.
>
> *—Psalm 104:24, 29, 30*

Sometimes during vacation, when we get a little breathing space and life bubbles back into us, or sometimes as we are on the way home from a funeral, touched by the great uncertainty of life, suddenly the question about the "whence" and "whither" of life confronts us. Usually questions of this sort are quite subconscious. Only when we are especially relaxed, or perhaps shaken, do they suddenly shoot out from behind the cover of daily worries and thrust their barbs into our hearts. When that happens, a conversation can quite spontaneously take on what is called a "religious tone."

When I am thrown into that sort of situation, and my companion knows that I am not only a Christian but also a minister, I can predict with a fair amount of certainty how the first round of such a conversation will proceed. It is generally that stereotyped. The other person usually points out that he too believes in a Supreme Being—"in a God or whatever you want to call it." He announces that he can still understand the idea of a *creator*. After all, this universe with its rationally interrelated natural laws must be guided by some highest Intelligence. But he just doesn't know what to make of Christianity's talk about redemption—about the cross and atonement and resurrection and the other weird dogmas.

Often the people who talk this way are very serious. They don't speak lightly. You can tell at once whether you are dealing with an inflated windbag who is just trying to evade the real issue with small talk, or with an honest seeker who has failed in his quest and feels compelled to confess it in this way.

In such situations a counterquestion is on the tip of my tongue: Is the creator whom the unbeliever or half-believer is so willing to acknowledge really that obvious? Is the creation really such a simple thing that the religious person can grasp it with his little finger? I don't think so!

I am more inclined to believe that today when we read the hymns of creation and nature by Matthias Claudius and Paul Gerhardt we are completely at a loss, or (more charitably expressed) we look at them with an almost helpless longing. When, anymore, do the peaceful woods prompt us to praise the Creator? For whom are the clothes and shoes we remove at night symbols of mortality? Whom do they stimulate to ask about eternal things? And when the moon rises in the evening, for whom does the night-blanketed world *really* become "a quiet chamber where one may sleep away and forget the clamor of the day?" Who even looks at the moon anymore? Who even notices the change from day to night against the fiery magic of our great cities, the glare of neon signs, and the balanced comfort of automatic heat and air conditioning? Hasn't all this artificial scenery with which we have surrounded ourselves taken the wonder right out of creation?

And even apart from all this, hasn't the knowledge that we humans can blast this good old world to oblivion robbed us of the comfort we used to find in a secure and solid creation? Hasn't the ground on which we stand become shaky? Aren't the basic structures of the world beginning to totter?

Not long ago, a well-known poet visited me. We discussed whether it was still at all possible for us moderns to recapture Matthias Claudius' experience of the creation. Wouldn't it really be false romanticism to expect that gazing at the star-studded firmament would bring us peace and drive away our uneasiness? "Isn't this cosmos in which our planet swims hostile and full of death," asked my poet friend, "permeated as it is with deadly rays and antimatter?" If we ascend only fifteen miles above our allotted territory, our blood begins to boil, and we perish. Likewise, if we descend fifteen miles into the earth, our life's thread is burned up. Even just a little distance under the skin of our planet, miners can die of marsh gas. The Creator has allotted us only a very thin band between the zones of death above and below. Here he reserves a space for us men to live in, and he holds back the threatening elements of destruction at its borders. The creation story expresses this miracle of protection by speaking of God's separating "the waters which were under the firmament from the waters which were above the firmament," thus making possible the narrow zone of human habitation in between. Woe to us if these divided forces were to come together and the hostile elements collide! Then creation could be reversed and the primeval chaos break in upon us. The flood that God sent in judgment is the great symbol of such a castastrophe.

We live, so to speak, on a tiny island. We are frail, weak creatures, and our life hangs by a silken thread. Anyone who can read the signs of our atomic times knows what the Bible is trying to say here.

In any case the eternal Word does not romanticize or idealize nature, even when the tones of a richly lyrical poetry ring out repeatedly—especially in the Book of Job and in the Psalms. This eternal Word knows that we live only by God's gracious gift of preservation. Psalm 104 puts it this way: "When thou hidest thy face, they are dismayed; when thou takest away their breath, they die and return to their dust."

Therefore the psalmist does not celebrate Nature. He knows well the perilous possibilities she has at her disposal. And he knows she could unleash these, were she not prevented by God's gracious gift of preservation. This is also why the psalmist does not address the moon or "brother tree," as a modern poet would. (I am thinking of Goethe's ardent lines to the moon, "Fill once more each bush and vale silent with thy cloudy beams.") Instead he speaks to him who gives being and order to all these things, sustaining them with the breath of his mouth: "Thou dost cause the grass to grow for the cattle. . . . Thou didst set the earth on its foundations."

Only the gift of grace enables us to go on living among the threats and restrictive possibilities which hem us in on all sides. Once a person has grasped that fact, everything will depend on his coming into contact with that One by whose power and grace he lives. Then it will be an indescribable joy for him to discover that this One is not a so-called "supreme being," an anonymous "higher power," but one who has a heart, who has lighted the windows of his fatherly house in order to help us find him.

No one has expressed this more beautifully or more accurately than Luther, who begins his explanation of the Creed's article on creation with the words, "I believe that God has created me and all that exists." Now some person might ask if Luther's view of creation, being directed wholly toward man, and even more especially toward "me," is not a bit conceited and tending toward a Napoleon complex. Isn't it a bit too anthropocentric? Doesn't tiny little man take himself too seriously here? Isn't it a sign of narrow-gauge thinking, of cosmic provincialism, so to speak, when man thus regards himself as the world's navel? We can understand, in a way, if some African tribesmen consider themselves the center of the cosmos, since they have never left their native compound. They lack opportunities for comparison. But in the century of space travel, is it still possible to wear blinders which permit us to say that the heart and center of the whole creation consists in the fact that God has created "me"? Who am I, when measured against the immensity of the universe? I become so small, and my life-span so short, that no electron microscope could detect me at all, and no stopwatch could measure the fleeting seconds of my life. Wouldn't it be more accurate and proper to say, "I believe that God has created the world, that he has called the stars and planets into being, and that then, among millions of other beings, he finally thought about me (the last and most harmless member of the infinite chain)"?

It could at least sound very humble and pious if I spoke in such a way and thus modestly stepped to the end of the line. But would it really be as humble and pious as it sounds? And do I really honor God by glorifying him as the manager of the Milky Way and the mover of tremendous masses? *How does this God above the stars concern me?* What commitment can I have to him, when I think of him as some vast quantity or as a cosmic intelligence?

Whoever looks for God in nature or in the universe really encounters nothing more than an unreal will-o'-the-wisp. This God is so great and so distant that he just can't concern me anymore. If you have ever walked in the woods with the sun slanting down through the leaves, or if you have been overwhelmed at evening by the starry host which can be measured only in light years, at such a moment did you (cross your heart!) ever promise that you would change your way of living? Did you feel conscience-stricken? In such a situation, who has ever been overwhelmed by God's mercy and gone back to his family and his place of work a new man? A couple of pious thrills (which I readily admit might occur) can't switch my life onto a new track. When they fade away, I am the same old Adam. My sins smell as sweet as the flowers in May, and they flourish just as they always have. Tell me how lofty God is for you, and I'll tell you how little he means to you. That could be a theological axiom. The lofty God has been lofted right out of my private life.

It is certainly remarkable, but it is true. God has become of concern to me only because he has made himself *smaller* than the Milky Way, only because he is present in my little sickroom when I gasp for breath, or understands the little cares I cast on him, or takes seriously the request of a child for a scooter with balloon tires. He concerns me because Jesus Christ takes my speck of anxiety and my personal guilt upon himself.

Our human life consists almost entirely of trifles: of headaches or good humor, of fatigue or vitality, of our colleagues' pleasantness or lack of it, of good luck in shopping or bad luck in letting a swearword slip out. If a world war is not threatening, I am much more interested in the local section of the newspaper and the Mayor's greetings to the President than I am in the banner headlines on the front page about "The Starving Armenians."

We surely can't imagine that international power-blocs or the wide-open spaces of history get terribly far under our skin! We are much more concerned when a child in our neighborhood is run over. Even the possible threat of atomic war doesn't agitate us primarily because (let's be honest!) the lives of millions of people hang in the balance, but because we are fearful for those committed to our care, for our property, for our hometown, and ultimately for ourselves. Thus the small and the personal determine our life.

If God has no significance for the tiny mosaic-pieces of my little life, for the things that concern *me*, then he doesn't concern me *at all*. He can't upset me or become dangerous to me. Quite the contrary. He would become a comfort for my religious emotional life. For it's really rather nice to be a bit devotional now and then and to activate one's religious emotions. One should give them a lift, because inwardness stimulates the mind, and that, too, can be a pleasure. Unfortunately though, it's just froth, and my life is no different because of it. But something so basic that it could lift me off my hinges, grip me like a storm, fill me completely, *that* is what I long for deep down inside. I wait for something that is stronger than I. That is the longing of every living man, and particularly every young person.

God can become my Lord only when he is with me in the hundreds of little things which make up my life. For just this reason it is indescribably comforting that Jesus and his Father are not to be found exclusively in the immense cosmic structure. It is good to know that we should not confine our prayers to something so sublime as the "Kingdom of God," but that we may also come with the request for daily bread. And when he walked among men he didn't only tell them, "I am come to bring fire on the earth" or, "The Kingdom of God is among you" or, "Sun and moon will grow dark and the stars will fall from heaven." Beside these earth-shaking things he set completely insignificant ones: children, with their runny noses, whom he blessed; the sores of an outcast; and the sightless eyes of a beggar. It is Jesus' greatness that his love encompasses even the smallest—all the little and inconsequential people who suffer in their quiet corners—and that nothing is so small that he overlooks it.

Of course it is very easy to be a "philanthropist" and feel enthusiastic about the love of man in general. That can be just a very superficial, sham love which costs me nothing. I need only gush over Albert Schweitzer at a tea party and sing the many versions of "I love everybody." I need only give my bank standing orders to send a contribution to any good cause. But whoever really loves will use a magnifying glass to see the small and hidden details of another's need. I will be able to see that he has cold feet and I can move him nearer the fire; that he is deaf and I must speak closer to his ear; that a secret anxiety torments him; that he longs for a good word; and many more such things which usually lie, seemingly hidden, under the surface of our lives.

This is the miracle: Almighty God loves me so much that everything in my life is important to him—not only the salvation of my soul, but also my toothache and the slippery streets that I must drive, even the crocus that lifts my spirits in the spring, or a cute note from my youngest child.

If I knew only the God of nature and the "Father above the canopy of stars," I would only be able to carry on a few devout and contemplative soliloquies. Of course, that is at least something, and in a world filled with trifling superficiality we don't want to disparage it. But such contemplative moments certainly don't produce "prayer."

But if I know of Him who lovingly seeks me and whose heart is moved by everything that fills my thoughts and concerns me, then I can *talk* with this great Heart. I know that every word reaches him, and that none of the joys and problems which I confide to him will be lost, even though they are often very modest joys and very small problems. Then I may say "Thou openest thine hands, and they are filled with good things," and I can add "Thank you" and "Amen." So now even hardship cannot confront me accidentally. I receive it from this same hand, and thus it is only half as hard. When it comes like this it is accompanied by God's greeting and his grace, together with the assurance that he intends it for my welfare.

The *East Prussian Diary* of Count Lehndorff (how fortunate that a book like this can compete on the best-seller list with such books as *Lolita* and *Lady Chatterley's Lover*) is full of terror, death-agony, chilblains, bellies swollen with hunger, and corpse-filled cellars. But all at once the author sees a chestnut tree in bloom or five bright red tulips shining out at him among the ruins, and with the growls of drunken commissars in his ears the young count strains to hear the straightforward, comforting word of his heavenly Father. He knows *who* remembers him with this little message.

Thus God wraps his omnipotence in the friendly, everyday, close-at-hand things. If I am very bad off, perhaps despairing, a blooming rose can mean as much to me as a rainbow arching over the earth after a storm. It should proclaim to me that this dubious and rebellious world will survive under God's grace; that his hand will support the world and every one of us; and that no human madness, not even our demonic playing with nuclear fire, can tear it out of his protecting hand and destroy it.

How could this young Christian bear the East Prussian catastrophe with its terror, rape, nakedness, and anxiety-filled flight? How could he bear it and still find comfort in five budding tulips? Was it because he loved nature and found God there that he had strength enough to produce such lyrical feelings? If that had been the case, the five tulips wouldn't have comforted him. They probably would have made him miserable. They would only have sharpened painfully the contrast between nature's "beyond-good-and-evil" character on the one side and man's wickedness on the other. Perhaps the five blooming tulips would only have reminded him that: "The flowers don't care if I have to suffer. They are completely unconcerned about the things that are driving me crazy. They have no heart and soul." We have all had similar moments in which we took *no* comfort from the seashore or from the lonely woods, and when we fled from Nature because she was foreign to us and was not concerned about us.

The five tulips could comfort the young count only because he *already* knew the heart of his heavenly Father and had contact with him. Only in that way could the birds of the air and the lilies of the field suddenly become comforting symbols and messages of greeting from the Father's heart. If he had tried it the other way around, that is, if he had looked for comfort from nature and had searched the constellations and the forest twilight for traces of a Higher Being, he would have met nothing but an inflexible and soulless Omnipotence, an Omnipotence which passes untouched above our little human destinies, leaving us solitary and thrusting us into loneliness.

To use Luther's lovely phrase, whoever sees Christ as a mirror of the Father's heart actually walks through the world with new eyes. Only after a person has looked into the heart of the Creator of all things will he also see the *things* differently. For him the lilies and birds, the moon and the rainbow actually become messages from this Heart. But whoever comes at it differently, trying to interpret the objects, the natural laws, or the historical process in order to find traces of divine power, will always be cheated and will finally be handed over to soulless chance or to icy infinity.

The Bible refers to this sequence leading from God to his creation in telling us that God said, "Let there be. . . ." Since the world thus goes back to God's creative word, I can understand it only when I hear this same word, this word which contains the secret of the world. Only the person who accepts the words, "I will not contend forever, nor will I always be angry; . . . but I will [create] . . . the fruit of the lips. Peace, peace to the far and near" (Isa. 57:16 ff.)—only such a person understands the secret of history in times of grace and of judgment and in hours of peace or affliction.

Basically, it's quite simple. If the world is a work of God, then it is clear that I can understand this work only by starting with its author. Of course, much still remains puzzling to me. For example, I will never be able to understand why human beings who have lived lives filled with love and meaning must fade away in old peoples' homes, arthritic and horribly emaciated. I will never understand why death tears a young mother from her children or why a great artist smashes his car into some highway abutment. If I see riddles of this sort and then try to squeeze a divine meaning out of them, I will be gripped by despair, or I will take refuge in fanciful explanations because I cannot bear the dreadful harshness of reality.

However, as I said before, if I come at it from the other way, if I dare to trust that Heart which has thoughts of peace toward me, then, to be sure, I am not promised the ability to "understand" the relationship between these thoughts of God and the riddle of life or its dark accidents, but I certainly am told that I may "trust" this Heart and that, as far as it is concerned, it will always remain faithful. That is, it will always think thoughts of intimacy and not of enmity toward me. *I really don't know what God wills in this or that perplexing case, but I trust Him who does know.* I myself know only one thing: that He remains loving through everything, even the darkest times. I know it simply because of one man, Jesus Christ, who never had an unloving thought.

If we begin in this way with the heart of God, we not only walk through the world with different eyes, but we also handle things differently. God both changes our view of life and, through us, intervenes in life itself. He wants to transform it through us. He wants his Christians to be the world's revolutionaries. I shall pick out just a single viewpoint from the many which could clarify this idea. If someone bases his life simply on the creation and does not know the Creator himself but knows only Nature and her laws, he obviously cannot avoid exploiting all the possibilities with which Nature is endowed. He will develop a great Promethean passion to mobilize the entire physical and biological potential of Nature. He will want not only to learn about all her slumbering powers, but also to utilize them for technical purposes and make them subservient to his will. Man as the lord of nature and the manager of her powers; man as the great director of natural laws; man as the goal of all things—that will become his pride and his passion. His dream is to have everything in the world be "possible" and to have all the world at his disposal. He not only operates within physical nature, conquering the immensity of space as an astronaut and getting the smallest particles to dance to his tune through atomic physics, but he also manipulates biologically the life around him: he attacks genes; he controls the system of endocrine glands; and he develops contraceptive pills. He can alter character through pills and treatments. He can produce depression or exuberance through the use of chemicals.

Is it only that he *can* do all this? Isn't it rather that he *must* do it as long as he is confronted simply with nature, as long as he does not stand under the discipline and the will of the *Author* of nature and does not inquire about His purposes?

As a matter of fact, this is the sinister thing about political and ideological atheists. The things that they physically, biologically or technically *can* do, they *must* do. They *can* change the orders of creation (family, society, and the bonds of love); therefore they *want* to do it, they *must* want to do it. Therefore they interpret the creation to conform to their ideal of "we can do anything."

Doesn't this titanic *will* which wants to topple the foundations of the world grip all of us, even those of us who inhabit the so-called free world?

Whether or not this frightful and destructive will gains power over us depends on *one thing*. This one point may be made through these questions: "Are we ready to ask about the Creator's purpose and to place ourselves under his command? Or do we see ourselves only apart from the creation and therefore desire ourselves to be the Almighty, thus becoming little gods who wheel and deal with the things at our disposal, blindly reducing them to their technical properties and using the work of the Creator as though he had no rights to assert?"

Today we face the frightening and exciting fact that knowledge is indeed power, and that we men have actually become very powerful. But the problem is that we are not mature enough for our own knowledge and ability, and that (as in Goethe's "Sorcerer's Apprentice") the unleashed powers of nature threaten to outgrow us. *God is also Lord in the world of knowledge and technology*. We must learn again to recognize that. Really. Not only is God involved in our eternal blessedness, but, since he is involved with that, he is also concerned with laboratories, test tubes, and computers.

The disobedient man is one who provokes the judgment of God by his unrestrained will to power and knowledge, not because he is stupid and naive, but precisely because he knows so much and can do so much. It is none less than God himself who has given us talents of scientific and technical knowledge so that we might live under him and "profit" to his glory. But these talents can blow us sky-high. This is the meaning of that passage from Isaiah, "the wisdom of their wise men shall perish, and the discernment of their discerning men shall be hid" (29:14). *This* is why God has turned the wisdom of this world into foolishness.

Even the way I look at television is involved. Does my craving for it seduce me into giving myself without restraint to this wonder of technical ability? Is every thought, all peace of mind, every idea, thus to be sacrificed? Or do I maintain control over myself? Even this quite everyday relationship to television has to do with my obedience to God. Do I utilize technology in his name or do I play fast and loose with his gifts?

Far be it from me to express here general thoughts about the technological era which change no one and which call no man to the peace of his Father's house. That is why I have used this short and very common example of television. If God wants to accomplish something through us, if his Christians are to be the world's revolutionaries, then his work will not begin with great ideas about or programs of criticism of culture. It will begin within my own four walls. It will start with the way my household and I behave toward those things with which technology confronts me: what I do with television, with my car in city traffic, and with the medicine I take, be it tranquilizers or pep pills. God is involved with all that. Whether I sit in front of the set or behind the steering wheel, I am in the presence of God. He is not only in pulpits and on altars. His word is not just in sermons and hymns, but it is mixed into the most everyday things. He is at the movies and on the street, on assembly lines and beneath the neon lights. The presence of God is limitless. It is the heart of everything.

Yet I don't *find* this Heart in the things themselves. Rather, *once I have found the Heart, then I understand the things.* And then I walk through the world with new eyes. My hands and my thoughts receive new plans and new tasks. I become literally a new man, full of new joy and new drives. Then it becomes clear to me what life could be like. The heart of God is the strategic point from which I can master my life. There it is decided whether I will succeed in that life, whether I will succeed even in failure and defeat.

I want to quote the *East Prussian Diary* once more. I don't do this just because it is an especially fine and cheering witness to the fact that a man can have peace amid torment and trouble. The main reason is that all easy chatter dies away under the extreme pressure of sorrow and need; all illusions burst, and only what is authentic in our words remains. Then this metal rings true: "Don't we live out our days like a disconnected series of chords and 'dischords'? And yet there is a melody in it! God alone knows it, and if he sets the first pitch, then he already can hear the final note. And sometimes he lets us sing along for a little while."

Don't words like "omnipotence" and "omniscience" become empty concepts and baseless speculations when we overlook the fact that hidden behind the higher thoughts and melodies runs the theme of a great fatherly and seeking love around which all the other melodies revolve? The wise men and philosophers are frustrated when they try merely to think through the concept of an almighty God. Ultimately this concept of theirs disintegrates into the elements of fate or chance. Then there is no longer any security or refuge.

But a child who prays to the loving God for a hobbyhorse or for good picnic weather makes fools out of these wise men. With his little hands he points to the greatest good, the *heart* of the heavenly Father.

It was in a child that this Heart revealed itself, a child lying in a manger. Here again God is in the small things. Therefore, it may be that He lives most often not in the perfected prayers of the liturgy, but in the moans of the dying and in the mute gaze we turn toward him in our greatest need. And the deeper the chasms that engulf us, the nearer are the hands which never let us go.

AN ADDITIONAL QUESTION:
DO MIRACLES REALLY HAPPEN?

> "For truly, I say to you, if you have faith as a grain of mustard seed, you will say to this mountain, 'Move hence to yonder place,' and it will move; and nothing will be impossible to you."
> —*Matthew 17:20b*

Up to this point we have been dealing with the creation. In so doing we must keep the question of God's relationship to the world constantly in mind. One side of this question concerns the laws of nature and how, if at all, they depend upon God. Another involves the problem of God's lordship of history: Is our human life simply the playground of chance, or does it move along methodically and according to plan under the direction of God's higher thoughts? Finally, there is the question how one can seriously maintain that God cares about our little life and its concerns. How dare we bother him with such microscopic problems as our next meal or our toothaches or our examination jitters?

All of these questions revolve around one theme. How does God influence the course of our life and the course of the world in general? Is he (if he exists at all) the Great Unknown in the background who does not intervene directly but merely makes sure that the gigantic ball of world history rolls according to the laws of nature and of cause and effect? Or does he himself really intervene when I call on him for help? Does my life run its course according to eternal laws, such as those the astrologists ascribe to the stars and their influence? Does my marriage simply run its course mechanically, according to the laws of attraction and repulsion? Finally, is the East-West conflict merely the inevitable result of power politics and rocket technology? Shouldn't God be present here, too, not only guiding the hearts of men and world leaders "like streams of water" but also helping to heal an illness and performing something new and unexpected in my life and yours?

42

All of these questions come to a head, as it were, in the problem of miracles. For when a man acknowledges that God can perform a "miracle" he is saying that this world of ours and this life of mine are not simply left to themselves. He is saying that God stands on the conductor's podium, setting the pitch and giving the cues; that he "has a hand in everything"; and, what is more, that we can call on this hand and entrust ourselves to it.

So, when we begin to talk about miracles, we encounter the basic question about what is to become of us. And this question is so passionately debated precisely because it concerns a fundamental decision of our life. It goes without saying that tempers don't flare over the simple question whether it is "possible to conceive of" something like miracles. Such rational problems do occur, but they don't usually release the flood of passionate discussion that the debate over miracles has always unleashed. The real excitement in this question arises from the fact that we are dealing with a theme that lies at the very root and center of life: Dare we count on God's caring about us? Suppose for a moment that he did. Then there would actually be some possibility for faith and trust. Then I could even pray. In an especially dangerous moment of my life, I could calmly and cheerfully say to him: "Your will be done; you will make it come out all right."

But if God *doesn't* care about us, then the world is left to itself and the historical process just rolls along according to its own laws. Everything becomes meaningless. I can only bow before my fate; there is no remedy.

In any case, one thing becomes clear. The problem of miracles is not a theoretical one, like the question of human life on other planets. The latter is certainly an interesting and perhaps even exciting question. But it doesn't really get under our skin. Whether Mars is inhabited or not has nothing at all to do with my personal life. Whether it turns out that there are skyscrapers and football stadiums on Mars or that there are only vast stretches of ice, stone, and craters, nothing changes for me. The problem of miracles, however, hits closer to home, once I decide to think it through seriously. For then I am involved in nothing less than a search to discover if I can "count on" God. Will he come to me, walking on the billows in the fourth watch of the night and take me in his arms? Or will I drift helpless and alone on the waves? Will wind and waves have the last word? Everything depends on our understanding from the very beginning that the question of miracles is a basic question of our existence, and not simply a rational problem. That is the first thing that we have to clarify for ourselves.

If we now apply ourselves to the question itself, we must first bring some semblance of order into our use of terms. We must realize that the concept, "miracle," can be used with three entirely different meanings. Let me briefly identify them.

First, the belief in miracles can show that I am unenlightened and have not yet found out about natural laws and the way they operate. Let us assume that an explorer is the first white man to come into the deep African bush, and that in the evening he turns on his portable radio to hear the news. It would certainly appear highly peculiar to the good bushmen to hear a grown man's bass voice booming forth from a small box. They would wonder how a hundred-and-fifty- or two-hundred-pound man, or an entire orchestra, could be charmed into such a dainty little cabinet. In this situation, the bushmen would certainly be willing to believe in a miracle that enabled a grown man with a bass voice to reduce his size to that of a tiny doll and still keep his sonorous tones. But just as soon as one of them learns a few fundamentals of physics from the nearby mission school, this sort of miracle is swept away, and what once was supernatural magic dissolves into normal, natural, and calculable concepts.

Were the biblical miracles perhaps of this same type, as people have so often thought? Weren't they, possibly, believed and retold by people who, like our hypothetical bushmen, were not "in the know" because they were still completely naive about physics and biology? After all, these people had not yet learned to explain a thunderstorm, for example, in terms of voltage relationships in the atmosphere, so they considered it the discharge of divine wrath.

We shall hold this question for now and turn to a second sense in which men speak of "miracles." This consists in saying that the miracle is not a supernatural event in the outer world at all, as it appeared, for example, when Jesus healed a sick person. The miracle consists rather in a quite special way of contemplating nature. It lies in the subjective act of seeing. Goethe said once,

> If you would step into the infinite,
> Just probe the finite in every direction,

for in this finite, in this world about you, you find all secrets. You find the band that "holds the world's heart together." Then you find the primeval miracle in a flower. Then you also find that God who pleases "to move the world from within, hiding himself in Nature and Nature in himself." It all depends, therefore—and this is the upshot—on the perspective from which I view nature. I can view it, say, in a religious sense—"divinization" is the technical term for this approach. Then a snowcapped alpine peak, glowing in the reflected sunset, will become a parable of the Creator's glory, a miracle of his greatness, a liturgical message, so to speak. But if I view the same phenomenon, the alpenglow, through the eyes of a natural scientist, the alpine peak appears as a fold in the earth's crust covered with frozen water and refracting rays of light under peculiar atmospheric conditions.

Both times, then, I see the same object, but I see it in each case with different eyes. Consequently, the miracle here seems to depend not on the object but on my eyes. In essence, it becomes a certain way of looking at things. In one case I see the things themselves, regarding them as objects of natural science. In the other case, I see them as a parable of this whole perishable and passing world.

If I speak of such "miracles" (miracles of earth's beauty), then I do not say, "Here we have a supernatural intervention by God." More probably, I only want to say, "Here we have something quite ordinary, yet I *see* something extraordinary in it." Thus through my eyes an event or object becomes transparent, revealing an entirely different reality—perhaps the majesty of the Creator, perhaps even the fascinating order of the universe, which is "beautiful" in itself. One need only possess a certain religious talent in order to see things this way. It is exactly the same with music. One must be musical in order to respond to music as a statement in sound rather than as noise. A dog may howl when it hears a Bach fugue. But a man, at least a "musical" man, "gets something out of it." In the same way I can "get something out of" scenery or nature through the help of my religious "talent." Things may suddenly become transparent to me and turn into parables of a deeper reality.

When this concept of miracle arose (it happened principally in the Romantic era), it was received as a greatly liberating idea. Suddenly all the intellectual difficulties with which we must struggle when we want to believe in supernatural interventions by God were swept away. The uninterrupted validity of natural laws and this religious way of looking at the world could be combined without raising any difficulties.

But is that what the New Testament means by "miracle"? For *are* the disciples such religiously "talented" men at all? Are they artists and poets? Aren't they really levelheaded, simple people, even perhaps somewhat primitive? Have we ever heard that they admired a sunset?

Their fellowship with God—let's throw caution to the winds and say *feeling* for God—springs from entirely different ground. It arises from the absolute attention they pay to what Jesus of Nazareth says or does. They watch how he acts and what goes on around him. They know that everything depends on what happens there. For there it is decided whether or not God is stronger than the chain of crime and punishment. So they observe whether he can forgive sins and relieve burdened consciences. Moreover, there it is decided whether or not God is stronger than death. So they despair when Jesus seems to succumb to death on Good Friday. Finally, there it is decided whether God rules the world only in a general way or whether even the smallest and least significant life with its big and little problems is still important to him. So they are alert as hunting dogs, noting whether Jesus of Nazareth is interested only in the strategically important personages, such as King Herod and the higher clergy, or whether he has time for the woman with the hemorrhage, the lepers, and the blind beggar. (None of these could be of any use at all to him. Each of them should have been uninteresting to him, humanly speaking.)

That is what the disciples are interested in, because that alone holds the key, because that alone determines what will become of them; and only there do they see who God is and what place he wants in their lives.

This brings us to the third sense of "miracle." We need only recall a few of Jesus' miracles in order to discover immediately that they have a decisive character which sets them apart from all we have said so far. That is, this form of miracle is an event initiated by God. Quite simply, something happens. Thus the biblical miracle is not at all limited to my world of vision, to my way of seeing things. It is an event out there in the *world*, caused by God's creative power. Something "happens."

Furthermore, the people who witness such an event do not feel themselves religiously elevated and inwardly edified, as in the case of the alpenglow. Instead they are shocked and frightened, so that they ask in complete bewilderment, "How can he do these things?" They can even suppose that Jesus is in league with the dark powers of magic. Thus it is not edification but shock that results from a miracle; not insight into higher worlds but a claim of God that pins one down and forces a decision. *That* is the effect of a miracle, and we can observe it time after time.

Then what has happened?

Here again, for the sake of structuring our thinking somewhat, we must first ascertain that the Bible speaks of two different types of miracles.

One type occurs when God guides the laws of nature in such a way that his activity becomes overwhelming and, so to speak, demonstrative, forcing me to confess, "God has spoken here. Here he has acted in my life or in the life of my people."

When Hitler's dictatorship collapsed in 1945, and the sun of a new day brought millions of murders to light, the conviction grew upon many of us Germans that God had spoken in this collapse. Now his judgment was breaking in upon us. The biblical archetype for this sort of divine intervention is the Book of

Job. The evils that afflict Job involve both meteorological phenomena and historical processes: fires, tornadoes, and Chaldean enemies see to it that Job's property burns up, that his cattle perish, and that his children and his servants die. It all occurs quite "naturally," yet Job says that it is the Lord who has given and who has taken away. In the midst of these natural and historical processes none other than God himself had acted. Of course, meteorology is involved in all of it. The tornadoes are actually triggered by a low-pressure center. But the real point of what happens here has less to do with meteorology than with theology. Here God himself is in the whirlwind. Here God himself has erected a sign.

Perhaps I ought to clarify what happened here by permitting myself to use a personal experience.

I had been paralyzed for many years, and the physicians had done all they could for me. Then suddenly came the news that a medicine had been discovered which could render this disease harmless, although not cure it completely. And, in fact, the medicine pulled me out of supposed incurability and at once made me able to move about and work again. I don't believe that anyone would consider it extravagant if I said, in the joy of this unexpected recuperation, "This is the Lord's doing; it is marvelous in my eyes." My physicians said it with me.

What happened here?

Of course, I was critically enough attuned to tell myself that, basically, things went in a quite natural way. Several chains of cause and effect had simply intersected. On one hand there was my illness, progressing relentlessly toward its final stages. That final point was both physiologically calculable and, one might say, certain, according to the laws of causality. But somewhere else in the world another, completely different, chain of causation ran entirely independently of this one. In some laboratory somewhere some researcher, who knew absolutely nothing about me, was feverishly at work combatting this illness. Then at the crucial (if not the last) moment, these two chains of causation crossed. But, even though everything went so naturally, I could not help saying, "This is the Lord's doing." He was the one

who arranged these chains so that they had to cross at that moment.

"Who is it who has wrought such desolations in the earth?"
asks the psalmist, even though politically there are plenty of
causes to which war and desolation can be ascribed in terms of
the law of cause and effect. Who gives growth and increase?
Who opens his hand and satisfies the desire of every living thing?
(Ps. 145:16.) Destruction and construction, war and peace, separation and reunion, sickness and healing—all are natural and interrelated. The name of God isn't likely to appear on most hospital charts, even in church-related institutions. But even though
these processes seem so natural and are related to one another so
persuasively, I can still confess the miracle of God's presence.
"The Lord gave, and the Lord has taken away; blessed be the
name of the Lord" (Job 1:21).

Still another, completely different, sense of "miracle" may be
found in the Bible. The first, as we saw, is imbedded in the laws
of nature. The second consists in the fact that the laws of nature
are broken. The freedom of God asserts itself by defying nature's
laws, standing in opposition to them. We see a faint resemblance
to this latter usage when we talk about our own wills in charac-
terizing ourselves as free and knowing ourselves as responsible.
When Jesus says, "Rise, take up your pallet and walk!" and
paralysis is swept away in that moment, one cannot call that a
natural process of healing. Rather, at this point a will power from
outside breaks into the natural sequence.

In the next chapter I should like to treat a miracle that is almost
too clearly of this sort in order to show as fully as possible how
events and the interpretive proclamation of those events are interwoven. But first let us turn to some preliminary questions.

One question runs like this: Don't these miraculous supernatural
interventions belong to an obsolete world view in which heaven
and hell were thought to exercise an active influence upon human
history, whereas today we know that nature's powers operate
within a self-contained economy? No physicist today can reckon
with miracles and interventions that come from outside the
closed cosmic system and break it open! Don't narratives of this

sort stand as alien elements, like fairy tales, in the brightness of our modern world? Aren't they as strange as a fetish from the South Seas which suddenly turns up in a modern glass-and-steel laboratory?

Now we neither could nor would dispute the fact that the history of Jesus was wreathed in legends, just as his road to Jerusalem was wreathed with palm branches and covered with garments. For Jesus grips not only our heart and conscience, but also our imagination and our powers of thought. Those for whom he had become the Lord of life praised him with all the means of expression they had at their disposal. One might say that they improvised on the real events, expanding many details of Jesus' wonderful life in somewhat the same way that a curve is extended by using a dotted line. Even the imagination did not want to be excluded, and it too joined the hymn of praise.

Yet this first question is in no sense decisive. More important is the *basic* question: Do the miracle stories *really* belong to the figure of Jesus? One could even ask if he wouldn't perhaps be greater without this wreath of supernatural marvels. If I may express myself somewhat heretically, the question could be formulated as follows: Isn't it a very questionable procedure when a man who makes the outrageous claim that he is "unique," that he is "the Son of God," does not confirm this claim simply through his message and the overall radiance of his person, but is compelled to go beyond that and—again to put it very pointedly—bring in all these miraculous goings-on? A great actor is great even without stage properties. To depend too much on the use of masks, costumes, and technical refinements is to betray a basic mistrust of the performer's powers of suggestion.

Now isn't the case of Jesus similar? Must there not have been *other* ways for him to make his importance as Savior believable? What further use to us moderns is this whole miraculous spectacle? Gotthold Lessing, the most honest and inexorable of all doubters, has bravely blurted out our own innermost misgivings: "It is one thing to experience a miracle yourself, and another only to hear reports that other people purportedly have experienced them." But we ourselves have not experienced them! So honesty presses us to deepest mistrust. Where can these alleged miracles from long ago possibly find their root and their place—and their meaning—in my life? This is the decisive question!

In reality, this relationship of miracles to our own life may be specified exactly. I can state it as follows: Apart from miracles, prayer has no meaning. It degenerates into a mere conversation with ourselves. We then start from the assumption that God can never hear our prayers, and that in fact he doesn't possess the power to intervene in our lives. For, logically, we can pray to God for specific things or changes in our lives only if we may assume that everything is not already determined and that for him the future is still open. But what would God be if we couldn't speak with him about our needs, like beloved children with their loving father, or if he gave us stones for bread and scorpions for fish simply because he just didn't know and couldn't even hear what we needed? Then it would doubtless be more honest to be an atheist or to assume a tragic world view and worship destiny or fate.

In recent philosophy there has been a view of nature called the Kant-Laplace theory; it holds that both past and future events in the world are completely fixed. If life still appears to us men to be a little elastic, and if things seem to be able to go along in this way or that, then, according to this theory, the fault lies in the limitations of man's vision. A "highest intelligence," as Laplace calls it, could survey the whole panorama of world history from the past to the future in all its inexorable fixity.

A film analogy can clarify this view. As a movie unfolds on the screen, I know that the whole story lies ready on reels in the projection . booth. There can be no unforeseen incidents. Whether or not the romance will turn out happily has been determined, and it has been inalterably printed on the celluloid strip. Now, if we view history in the same way, there cannot in fact be any fortuitous occurrences—and naturally that goes for interventions of God, too. God can neither break through the natural law of cause and effect (as in the story of the paralytic), which is the usual sense of "miracle," nor can he guide the laws of nature to certain ends (as in the case of Job or in the example I gave from my own life). Any prayer would be senseless in the face of the fixed, unfolding film of world history and of my little life, because, of course, a real intervention would be completely out of the question.

Now I won't go into the fact (as I have repeatedly done elsewhere) that this Kant-Laplace theory has been superseded by contemporary physics, and that modern natural scientists make a reconciliation of faith and science much easier than it may have been in the eighteenth and nineteenth centuries. That is certainly important, but it is not decisive. It is much more essential that we come to know the *message*, the peculiar *theme* of the miracle stories. The theme is that God still has power over his world. He does not leave his own all alone, like dust particles in a turbulent world; he is with us. He not only "comforts" his followers who are at the point of capsizing in their little boat, but with sovereign freedom he also commands the waves and all the elements. Since Jesus Christ lives in innermost communion with his Father, he too participates in his Father's royal freedom. Therefore he is equipped with authority to set up the signs of his Father's victory along his way, and to break the chains of guilt, sorrow, and death. This secret participation in God's royal freedom becomes the more apparent by way of contrast to the powerlessness of the disciples. When mighty works of God are demanded of them, they fail time after time, precisely because time after time they do *not* have this ultimate union with the Father's will, and because their faith in terms of size does not even amount to a grain of mustard seed. This is the explanation for their remarkable question, "Lord, why could *we* not cast out this spirit?" (Mark 9:28). And Jesus answers very obscurely, but nevertheless in such a way as to point to this missing unity of the disciples' wills with the will of the Father, "This kind cannot be driven out by anything but prayer and fasting."

Thus, wherever Jesus speaks and acts, he not only teaches, he does something! The kingdom of God which he proclaims does not consist in talk, but in power and in deed. This means that Jesus does not use a textbook to explain to us that there is a loving Father, a Creator who watches over life and keeps it in order; Jesus *acts!* He doesn't merely inform us that God can forgive sin, crossing out our past and letting us begin over again. What happens is this: He speaks a word of efficacious power, which in the very speaking becomes a deed. "Your sins *are* forgiven!" He says it in the same way it is still expressed today in Holy Communion, where forgiveness comes to me so assuredly that I can actually take it up in my own hands. When Jesus comes to a man, Jesus acts; he transforms him and leads him onto an entirely new level of life.

Now it is in this sense that miracles testify that the encounter with Jesus amounts to a transformation, a re-creation of life. He speaks an efficacious word. The man who lay powerless can now leap to his feet. And the man who lay in chains is loosed and free. The man who has experienced Christ knows that it happens today and every day exactly as it did to those who saw Him face to face.

One more thing must be said in conclusion. In the New Testament, sins, sickness, and death are unnatural intrusions into God's creation. They are all like a curse which lies on mankind. Therefore Jesus is not only the pastoral counselor who helps a man get right with his conscience. Jesus is at the same time the physician who heals wounds and to whom we may entrust even our bodies and all the things we need and worry about, whether internal or external.

And yet, all of this healing and forgiving that he does in miracle and message is limited to individual signs which, so to speak, flash in the dark like Morse-code messages between ships. Millions of men have lived out pitiful lives, before Christ and after Christ and even when he was on earth, and this signal flashed upon only a very few, who then went away as new men. Individual signs! Yet the New Testament understands these individual signs as heat lightning, so to speak, that discloses the Kingdom of God on the horizon, heat lightning that announces daybreak. And in that kingdom which lies over the horizon, betraying its presence by those flashes, guilt and sorrow will come to an end. Even death will be no more. Therefore, when things go hard for us, when darkness falls upon us and we don't know how we can get through the coming night and the following day, then we are commanded to look toward that kingdom which already announces itself in the heat lightning of Jesus' miracles. God has his hand in things and is with us always, to the close of the age.

That, then, is the message of the miracles. It is the message of heat lightning in the dead of night, a signal that suddenly illumines the thick darkness shrouding my path. Once again I know where I am, who is with me, and where the path is that will lead me to my goal. This is why we don't need to take cover when, time after time, we get blocked in on all sides. We have spotted our Lord's signals; through a tiny crevice we have seen the kingdom of the Father, where there is no more mourning or crying, where tears are wiped away, and where death shall be no more. But the Lord who receives us at that goal of our pilgrimage is also the Lord of the paths that lead there. He accompanies us with his miracles and his presence. We need only call and he is there. That is the message of the miracles.

ONE MORE QUESTION:
WHAT IS THE POINT OF THE MIRACLES?

And when he returned to Capernaum after some days, it was reported that he was at home. And many were gathered together, so that there was no longer room for them, not even about the door; and he was preaching the word to them. And they came, bringing to him a paralytic carried by four men. And when they could not get near him because of the crowd, they removed the roof above him; and when they had made an opening, they let down the pallet on which the paralytic lay. And when Jesus saw their faith, he said to the paralytic, "My son, your sins are forgiven." Now some of the scribes were sitting there, questioning in their hearts, "Why does this man speak thus? It is blasphemy! Who can forgive sins but God alone?" And immediately Jesus, perceiving in his spirit that they thus questioned within themselves, said to them, "Why do you question thus in your hearts? Which is easier, to say to the paralytic, 'Your sins are forgiven,' or to say, 'Rise,

take up your pallet and walk'? But that you may know that the Son of man has authority on earth to forgive sins"—he said to the paralytic—"I say to you, rise, take up your pallet and go home." And he rose, and immediately took up his pallet and went out before them all; so that they were all amazed and glorified God, saying, "We never saw anything like this!"
—*Mark 2:1–12*

These four men picked a somewhat strange and strenuous way to bring their seriously ill friend into Jesus' presence. Before they would plow through to a miracle doctor in this way, they must have been completely convinced that a decisive and healing operation could occur. When the crowds blocked the doors, they slipped around to try the window. When that didn't work either, they followed the foxy suggestion of some especially clever person and hoisted the stretcher onto the roof, worked around up there until they had made a hole, and then used ropes to let the sick man float down over the heads of those assembled below. Then the friends jumped down after him. There probably was a dramatic pause while this performance took place. I know that I would certainly be nonplussed if that happened to me while I was making a speech.

So now they stand before Jesus and look at him expectantly. Even the man on the stretcher watches him. Presumably it is very quiet, because everyone knows that something sensational is about to happen. Even the crowd holds its breath. Each person's heart pounds for a different reason. The man on the stretcher thinks, "All my torment will soon be over." The people who have brought him are dead sure that this Nazarene can cure him. Otherwise they wouldn't have gone to all this trouble.

Presumably the crowd is of two minds. There are some skeptics who think, "Now we'll see that all this buildup about his being a miracle-worker is simply propaganda and that he is really a charlatan who will make a fool of himself." He certainly has the opportunity to make a fool of himself. Others think, "If the healing works, we'll have to consider whether we should take him seriously and join his cause." Still others feel a pleasant shiver of excitement in anticipation of witnessing an unusual event.

But Jesus always reacts differently than men expect. Instead of healing the sick man, he now says something that certainly no one expected. When he observes the faith of the sick man and his companions, he says only, "My son, your sins are forgiven." To be sure, nobody had asked him for anything like *that*, and it must have been a deep disappointment for the lame man. He had to learn that Jesus had heard his prayer for healing, if he had heard it at all, in a sense different from the way that the sufferer had meant it. He had to learn something about prayer that we all are expected to learn and are even promised. He had to learn that God doesn't always seem to hear our personal petitions—for example, the healing of a disease—but instead he acts in a quite different, totally unexpected way. The hard part of this hearing or not hearing our prayers—and we all know about the latter, too—is that we can't find any connection between what we ask for and what God actually does in our life. This lame man is in the same situation, and he is certainly disappointed as Jesus begins to talk about forgiveness of sins instead of healing him. This is because the poor fellow cannot yet see that, in some subterranean way, his illness and his guilty life are bound together. He cannot yet understand that sickness, pain, and need are the great "disturbers of the peace" within the creation and that God neither intended nor created the world to be like this. This has all happened since the picking of the forbidden fruit.

But Jesus knows about this obscure connection; that is why he starts out by laying bare the deeper roots of the illness. His first step is to rectify the guilt problem in this broken life. The lame man, however, gives up. His only diagnosis is, "He didn't hear me. They could have spared themselves all that bother with the roof."

The people, too, standing around this scene in great numbers, must be really surprised when Jesus, instead of performing his usual healing miracle, starts talking about the forgiveness of sins. Who knows, there may even be some malicious grins, especially among the representatives of the church, who also were the medical experts in those days. Doesn't that seem only too likely at this point? Hasn't Jesus backed down in front of everyone? A cure would be objective proof. It would be an exact test where he could show his colors and demonstrate *what he had*. Here he would put himself up against scientific criteria. But when he says, "Your sins are forgiven"—sure; unfortunately one can't check up on that! That is an inner or even metaphysical occurrence. Anyone could say a thing like that.

The critical theologians who are included in the picture have a further objection. This man must certainly realize that by being so bold as to pronounce absolution he is claiming a monopoly that belongs to God alone—and that is nothing less than blasphemy. But apparently Jesus is ready to settle for this charge of blasphemy if it will only get him out of the disgraceful role of an ineffective miracle doctor.

In any case, the thoughts of all the witnesses of this scene run in the same direction. But now, says the report, Jesus himself ascertains all these private conjectures and suddenly throws this gem of a sentence into the evil play of their thoughts. "Which is easier to say, 'Your sins are forgiven' or 'Rise, take up your pallet, and walk'?" "Naturally," think the onlookers, "that's the whole thing in a nutshell! Obviously it is much easier to say, 'Your sins are forgiven' because nobody can check on it. But to get a lame man back on his feet—that is something else again." And yet Jesus actually says, (what a truly unusual and unexpected moment!) "In order to convince you that the Son of man has power to forgive sins . . . rise, take up your pallet, and go". And now it happens. It *really* happens. The paralytic takes the very bed that had carried him before and carries it himself. The effect is indescribable. Panic almost breaks out. Among the murmuring of the crowd, one can hear bits of prayers praising and thanking God.

What is the point of all this? At first one might suppose that Jesus wanted to prove his identity and silence his critics by performing the healing miracle. He seems to have used the opportunity to obtain a sort of medical certificate which attested his supernatural healing gifts and which witnessed indirectly to his qualifications as the Messiah or Son of God.

If this first impression were really correct, then we today who read or hear all these things would be in a painful predicament, for that which had a certain power to prove something to the eyewitnesses of that scene no longer possesses that power for us. I am reminded of what Lessing said about there being a difference between seeing a miracle with your own eyes and only having other people—and distant, far less enlightened people, at that—report that *they* had seen something of that sort. Then we would be in precisely the situation of doubting Thomas, to whom his fellow disciples reported that Jesus was risen from the dead. He could not and would not believe it unless he himself laid his hands on the nail-prints of the risen One.

Stated simply, in an absolutely crucial matter like this, it would be simply irresponsible to trust mere hearsay evidence. One must be convinced for oneself. But today we cannot prove to ourselves whether or not Jesus did in fact produce this miracle to authenticate his authority to forgive sins. Unfortunately, we know of it only through hearsay. And we can never establish for certain that this was not a case of mass suggestion, hallucination, or superstition, because we don't know personally the people who function here as eyewitnesses. In any case, they have a mentality completely different from our own. Thomas, at least, knew his fellow disciples personally, and even then he remained skeptical. If we are to stay honest and realistic, we must concede that using a healing miracle as proof doesn't carry any weight with us. I don't see any real possibility of getting around this fact. The question is, what consequences do we draw from it?

Does this conclusion mean that we slam the Bible shut and admit, "Well, there's nothing to *that*. We have to 'wait for another' "? Doesn't it, rather, involve a demand for further critical and unremitting questioning? Doesn't it drive us to a close examination of whether Jesus really intended this miracle to be only a proof or whether the meaning of this event is to be sought in an entirely different area?

The first alternative, though, would raise a puzzling question for us. If the miracle in this case has the force of a "proof," then that means that Jesus no longer lays claim to the believing trust of men, but that he has substituted "seeing"—the proof of being an eyewitness—for "believing." Thus the problem would look somewhat like this: A person must "believe" in Jesus' forgive-ness. One must simply "trust" in his authority—on the mere basis of his word. Yet in contrast to this, anyone could "see" the healing of the lame man. If the point of the miracle is to be a proof, then that would actually mean that a person didn't need to "believe" any longer; he would have only to "see."

This momentary reflection shows us that the miracle cannot have been meant to be just a proof. The basic tone of the New Testament message is that we live by *faith* and not by *sight*. Faith will not be permitted to see what it has believed until we are called out of this temporal order and the form of this world has passed away, until the curtain has fallen on the theater of our world. Until that time comes, God's secret remains hidden from us.

If the question depends on what we can "see" and "look at," then the evidence seems to witness *against* God. Think of wars, mass graves, crippled children, flood disasters, and everything that we in our own lives see as meaningless cruelty. Not being able to see the sense of it, we can only have faith in him who knows its meaning. Here we have only the "Nevertheless I am continually with thee" which lets us grasp for the Father's hand through every darkness. And as the hiddenness becomes deeper, this faith must grow stronger. Every one of us remembers that precisely in the darkest hours of our lives, when no human being could help us and the deepest agony of being forsaken ate at our hearts, precisely *then* we felt the miracle of this Nevertheless, and God sent his stars to rise over us. That is why it is precisely these most difficult hours that we don't want to do without, not because they are so difficult, but because it is at such times that we experience that faith which can break through steel and stone.

And is Jesus now to sweep all this out the door with one single word? Is he really to lay aside this gift of grace, with its poverty and its promise, and replace it with a cheap "Take a look; what do you say now?" Is God all at once to be so cheapened and demoted to the bargain basement that a person has only to open his eyes in order to see him? That certainly can't happen.

Therefore we must be on the wrong track when we interpret the miracle as a proof that would make faith superfluous.

This hypothesis is supported when we look at Jesus' attitude toward miracles at other times. At every turn, one conclusion is obvious: Jesus carried on a passionate battle against the concept of miracle which was then popular and which is still widespread among us.

One time, for example, the people came to him and said, "Give us a sign. If you give us a sign we can believe in you." But Jesus rebuffed them brusquely, even roughly, and promised them instead, "An evil and adulterous generation seeks for a sign; but no sign shall be given to it except the sign of the prophet Jonah" (Matt. 12:39). What did he mean by this rebuke?

We can understand him only when we draw out the meaning of another of his sayings (see John 7:17): "If any man's will is to do my Father's will, he—only he—shall know whether the teaching is from God or whether I am speaking on my own authority, and thus whether I am the Christ of God or whether I am putting on airs in my own name and am therefore a braggart and a charlatan.

"Only he who does the Father's will finds out—no one else. Only he who gets involved and puts everything on this one card can recognize what is going on here—no one else. But you, you who demand a sign, you want God at too cheap a price. You want him without risk and without anything at stake. And the reason is that you don't want to risk the experiment of discipleship, because then you would have to change your life. You want a sure thing and a proof of Christ 'without obligation.' That's why you want me to perform before you like a magician, turning stones to bread, suspending the law of gravity, or staging a few yogi tricks, just to prove to you that I am something special. If I did that, then you would say, 'How about that? The man must have something.' But it would be just as though you had been to a vaudeville show—you would go home and act just as you had before."

You'll have to admit that no one has yet been converted by a vaudeville show, no matter how impressive it may have been. So

Jesus recognizes these proof-seekers as an especially bad sort of malingerers who, despite all their curious carrying on, just don't take the question of his messiahship seriously. Jesus is recognized only in action and in involvement. That is, in faith and in deed. Otherwise you draw a blank.

At this point Jesus differs from other men. When Nehru had to decide whether or not to become a follower of Gandhi, he started out (as the stories clearly indicate) to discover what sort of man Gandhi was. He observed how Gandhi handled people and situations. And when he had become convinced of Gandhi's authority, he went to him and said, "I shall follow you; I am your man. You can count on me."

But it is exactly the opposite with Jesus. First I must entrust my life to him. I must begin by daring to say, "I want to try you out, Lord; I am willing to risk the experiment with you. In your name I am willing to put up with a person who really gets on my nerves. I am willing to forgive a person who has wronged me. In your name I am willing to say, 'Our Father, who art in heaven,' I am willing to stake absolutely all I am and everything I have on this experiment with you, and then we'll see how it all turns out." And in fact only in this way, by making common cause with him, will I discover what he has to offer.

Perhaps now we understand why Jesus described the sign seekers as he did. He always refuses to perform a miracle where people want to use it to dodge a personal decision or to avoid becoming personally involved. He dispenses with any cheap miracle propaganda because he knows that in the long run you don't win people with this sort of fake advertising. Sure, when something startling like that happens they are shocked and amazed for a moment, but the skyrockets in their souls quickly fade away and the night shadows once again fall over their hearts. But Jesus wants faith from the heart. He wants the very center of our being and not just a couple of nerve-twitches from the threshold of our ego. Therefore he wants a miracle to be anything but a visual proof which makes the commitment of faith superfluous.

But then what is his point in healing the paralytic? It is certainly a significant event, but where does it lead us? That is the question now before us.

In order to find out, we must note once again what Jesus does in the first act of this healing account—he pronounces the forgiveness of sins. Characteristically, he doesn't say, "You with the paralysis, listen here. None of us men is without sin, and God is the judge. But in certain cases God can issue a verdict of grace rather than justice. I would like you, you poor wretch, to be such an exception, so that you are removed from the law of guilt and expiation."

If Jesus talked like that, he would represent a philosophical world view that held that God was ultimately to be identified with the cosmic moral order, with the law of guilt and expiation. Didn't someone write, "all guilt is avenged here on earth"? God would be the cosmic bureaucrat who carried out this law of expiation and vengeance. He would stand behind all the world's tragedy.

But Jesus did *not* talk like that. It happened entirely differently. When he says, "Your sins are forgiven," he is not *teaching* something, as we have already indicated, he is *doing* something. That is, if we analyze what is going on here, Jesus makes it clear that in this case it is still true that the sins of the fathers are visited upon their children. It is actually true that the principle of retribution rules in the world and that God applies this principle, acting as a judge and avenger toward the guilty. The law of guilt and punishment holds sway. "But look here, you poor man, now you have met *me*, and I have the power to take your hand and lay it back in the Father's hand. By my word I can spring open the locked door of the Father's house for you. Look! It is opening. I say to you that it is opening, and you are once more at home."

That's what Jesus does. Or, changing the emphasis, that's what Jesus *does*. With his mighty arms he grips the spokes of that crushing guilt-and-expiation juggernaut which rolls over us all. He brings it to a halt. And he does this right in front of a man who looks to Jesus with eyes full of faith, trusting that he really can bring that tremendous force to a halt. Albert Schweitzer once expressed it in a grandiose and shocking way by saying that when Jesus tried to stop this cosmic wheel by force, he himself was left, a lacerated corpse, hanging in its spokes on Golgotha.

Thus we have established that Jesus is not giving a lecture about the nature of sin and its forgiveness. He *effects* this forgiveness. He doesn't lecture about all the possible restraints and chains that bind us; he shatters them. His word *accomplishes* something because he has authority. Only when we have understood that do we strike the deepest vein in this account and suddenly come to know the meaning of the miracle. By healing the paralytic, Jesus is not trying to offer express proof of his authority to forgive sins so that he can establish his own identity. Rather, he wants to use the miracle to bring something quite different to light. He wants to say, "Just as my ending a sickness is an authoritative intervention in the course of natural law, so my saying 'Your sins are forgiven' is an authoritative intervention in the law of guilt and expiation. Your past is gone. I let you become a new man. God has embraced you now as a returning son."

Thus the point of this miracle is to demonstrate that both healing and forgiveness are *actions*, that they are both encroachments on the power of iron-clad law. Behold, a mightier one is at work here; the Son of God himself is on the scene—*that* is the point of the miracle.

It can be reduced to a terse sentence. The miracle is intended not to "prove" the word of forgiveness, but rather to "interpret" and clarify it. It is intended to demonstrate for all to see that the word of forgiveness involves a deed and not a moral philosophy or a world view. Your sins *are* forgiven; rise, take up your bed! Healing and forgiveness of sins are merely two sides of the same authoritative accomplishment.

Many of the miracle stories may have offended us because they seemed to demand too much of our credulity. But once we have grasped the fact that this miracle is not intended as a proof, many of these other remarkable accounts appear in a completely new light. It becomes clear that the miracles of Jesus certainly do not relieve people of their need for a personal decision about their lives in relation to Christ. On the contrary, the miracles demand such a decision. We can recognize this in the fact that the miracles remain ambiguous and, one might say, within an enigmatic code, instead of proving something crisply and clearly. But once we have taken a position in relation to Jesus Christ himself, we can interpret the miracles correctly, because then we understand them through *him*.

There are impressive examples of this process. Sometimes Jesus effected a miraculous healing and yet the people were not convinced. They could not deny that something extraordinary had happened, but they remained skeptical enough to ask, "By what authority are you doing these things?" (Matt. 21:23). They considered it possible that, instead of divine strength, occult powers —devilishly sinister powers—were being brought into play here. One time, the clerics blurted out this hypothesis with unblemished frankness and clarity. It was true that he had just healed a man possessed of a demon, but, they proposed, he himself was possessed. He drove out the devil through Beelzebul. He cooperated with the power of the underworld, and only by this demonic help could he drive out other demonic powers (Matt. 12:22 ff.).

A whole geography of hell was hauled in to explain the darkly magical background of this miracle. Granted, the ghost of an antiquated and superstition-ridden world view haunts these accounts. Nevertheless, the spirit-oriented interpretations of Jesus' contemporaries continue to have importance for us and are interesting in two respects.

First, the miracle does *not* act as the proof of Jesus' identity. In the old days it was not much different from what it is among us modern-day skeptics. Even then, people almost never believed simply on the basis of a miracle. That is, miracles have always demanded a very personal decision from people. People have to make up their minds about the person of Jesus himself. Everyone, and this includes the Pharisees, the skeptics, and all the spectators as well as those who today read the account of such a healing, has to clear up whether or not this Jesus really stands in a special, unique connection with a higher world. Each one must clarify (or, quite simply, "decide") whether or not he will see in Jesus the Lord to whom all power in heaven and earth is given, so that he commands the elements and smashes the power of fate and destruction. Each has to clarify for himself (once again, "decide") if he will see in him the heat lightning of that coming kingdom where there will be no sorrow, no weeping, and no more death. Each must become clear on whether he will see Jesus as the representative of this kingdom or as a magician who is gifted with dark, demonic powers—or even is possessed by these powers.

We cannot make this very personal decision with the help of a precise "miracle analysis" or by ordinary observations. No matter how incontestable the miracle—and those people of long ago, particularly the critical churchmen and the physicians, were not fools enough to let themselves be taken in by every fakir's trick; they certainly had a full measure of realism and skepticism in their makeup—no matter if the miracle is attested to the *n*th degree, the really decisive question, and therefore the one that puts us to the test, still remains open. That is the question whether this miracle stems from *God* or from *demonic* powers such as Beelzebul or Mephistopheles. "By what authority do you do that? For heaven's sake, whom do you represent?" *That* is the sinister question that persists and that no miracle can answer. Thus people face the frightening contingency of having to take Jesus for God or for the devil.

A second observation goes along with this. The miracle remains ambiguous. People of those days, as we said, faced the possibility of confusing God and the devil with one another as the originator of the miracle. We today, living in the age of space travel and atomic physics, have a world view widely different from theirs, yet we face basically the same question. We confuse what God does for us in miracles with nature's laws of cause-and-effect. I have already pointed this out in recounting my own cure. If we are shielded from an accident, if we get a check for exactly the right amount to meet a tight financial situation, or if a new medicine that can save us is discovered at the last moment, the conclusion is more than obvious: everything has happened "naturally"; it just happens that two causal chains fortunately crossed in a striking way. We somewhat saucily call on the name of a pagan goddess, Fortuna, to describe our situation. We were "fortunate." That's all. And thus we once again face the question —the decisive question—of who we take God to be. Is he the Lord, *our* Lord, who is with us in everything and who is always there for our good? Or is he some sort of Principle and First Cause which means less than nothing to us?

So then, miracles belong to the mystery of Jesus' own person. He exposes himself to that confusion and that misunderstanding in his very person and not just in his message and miracles. He can be confused with a wandering preacher, the founder of a religion, or a very noble man who, with his ideas, finally suffered shipwreck. And Jesus himself did nothing to dispel this ambiguity of his appearance. He wanted to remain "encoded," so to speak. He wanted to keep us guessing and trying.

Of course, once there was someone who wanted to help him out of ambiguity. He offered him glory and power and the wealth of this world. He wanted Jesus to leap from the temple in order to put on an immense propaganda campaign with him (Matt. 4:1 ff.). Then there would no longer have been any ambiguity, and everyone would have shown him due reverence. But the one who wanted it that way was, unfortunately, the devil; and Jesus declined his offer. He wanted to remain ambiguous. He wanted to stay in the picture-puzzle so that we would have to search for him with all our powers of mind and heart fully engaged and totally committed. He didn't want to be cheaply bought when he himself paid the highest price. He wanted, as Kierkegaard put it, to release "the infinite passion of our inwardness." That can't be done by an objective certainty such as a mathematical theorem.

Jesus goes about incognito, wearing the mask of a servant and a failure, because he wants it that way. The only ones who can find him behind his mask now are those who come to him ready to make a decision, saying, "Here you have me, you have become too much for me." No one finds him like a penny in the street, no one experiences an earthquake that miraculously reshuffles his life, no one is overwhelmed by the cadence of twelve legions of angels—no one! The only one to recognize Jesus is the man who stands before him, holding his life in his hands as an offering. For that man, Jesus wondrously steps out of his disguise as the crucified and reviled one and for once stands before him as the bearer of an authority that empowers him to heal wounds. Jesus Christ does not come without obligation, and his miracles don't, either. Only the man who seeks him in commitment will find the tracks and traces of his miracles, even in his own life.

> The path of God is in the rivers
> and the great torrents
> yet you do not detect his feet.
> Therefore God also hides his path
> in the sea of sorrow so that
> we must search for him.

To search; to search in commitment, that's the thing. "When you seek me with all your heart" (says God's own commentary on the matter) "I will be found by you" (Jer. 29:13–14).

The Salvation of Man

I BELIEVE IN JESUS CHRIST, GOD'S ONLY SON

Inasmuch as many have undertaken to compile a narrative of the things which have been accomplished among us, just as they were delivered to us by those who from the beginning were eyewitnesses and ministers of the word, it seemed good to me also, having followed all things closely for some time past, to write an orderly account for you, most excellent Theophilus, that you may know the truth concerning the things of which you have been informed.　　*—Luke 1:1–4*

Where should one begin, in an attempt to comprehend Jesus or at least to sketch in his silhouette? By recounting the stories which the New Testament tells about him? Or how about those for whom he became everything: their only consolation in life and death, the person for whom they were willing to die? And they did die—in Nero's arena, at the hands of stone-throwing fanatics, or by a hangman's noose in the gloomy dungeons of some totalitarian state. Could we tell of him by describing their encounter with him? We would have to recite a thousand years of history, from Stephen the Martyr to Dietrich Bonhoeffer, in order to discern his consoling and carrying power as it is reflected in the hearts of his most faithful followers. Or should we tell about how our life is lived in his mighty shadow?

It is he *himself* that we are trying to comprehend, not just the reaction that he prompts among us men.

But how can we get to him? As in the case of many old frescoes, hasn't the real picture of Jesus been painted over by centuries of dogma and legends? Was he really the same person who meets us today in Sunday school and in the preaching of the church? In fact, is there anything left of his real portrait at all, or is everything just untrustworthy repainting and alteration? If that is the case, then isn't the "portrait" simply a product of human fancy and, therefore, a human creation?

These questions have been asked before. In a very famous book, Albert Schweitzer pointed out how many scholars in the course of history have set out on great research expeditions to "capture" the historical Jesus, not with "swords and clubs," but with spatulas to scrape beneath the overpainting so that, bit by bit, through shrewd detective work, the mosaic of facts would be reassembled.

But, remarkably, all these expeditions failed to reach their goal. It was just as if this mysterious figure sought to evade every grasp, as if no one could lay hold of him in quite the same way as *other* historical figures like Hannibal and Napoleon could be captured by scholars.

Sometimes they discovered a noble man who seemed to unite in himself all the perfections that corresponded to the ideal humanity of their own day. In such a case, an honest man would have to confess that he was certainly not looking at the real Jesus of history but only at his own (somewhat foolish) reflection in a mirror.

At other times, when the last layer of extra paint had been removed and they looked forward with the greatest excitement to seeing the actual, real Jesus as he must have looked when he walked the earth, they backed off in dismay. They found themselves face to face not with the awaited Savior in his calm and masterful greatness but with an unreal specter, an apocalyptic rabbi standing in the sulfurous and lurid light of the cosmic catastrophe, proclaiming the imminent collapse of everything and the end of the world. And in order to hasten this end, as Albert Schweitzer put it, this monstrous man seizes the spokes of the wheel of the world "to set it moving on that last revolution which is to bring all ordinary history to a close. It refuses to turn, and He throws Himself upon it. Then it does turn; and crushes Him." But the hoped-for end does not come. "The wheel rolls onward, and the mangled body of the one immeasurably great Man, who was strong enough to think of Himself as the spiritual ruler of mankind . . . is hanging upon it still."[1] What a classically

[1] *The Quest of the Historical Jesus,* trans. W. Montgomery (2nd English ed.; London: A. & C. Black, Ltd., 1926), p. 369.

71

grandiose, vast picture Schweitzer has conjured up here! But what shall we do with this unfortunate mover of the great cosmic wheel who ends as a sacrifice to it? What shall *we* do with him? How can I bring my sins to this ancient mythical figure? How can I entrust my children to him for time and eternity? In my last hour, how can I let myself fall into these strange, unearthly hands? Weren't the disciples right when they saw a *"ghost"* coming toward them over the waves in the fourth watch of the night? (Matt. 14:26.) What has happened to the comforting voice of the Good Shepherd? Where is support and security any more? It is almost inconceivable that anyone would have said to this oppressive figure, "Lord, you have the words of eternal life!" or, "Only say the word and all will be well," or even, "Lord, help me."

It is quite remarkable that all of these attempts have failed to lay hold of the figure of Jesus by means of historical reconstruction. It is unusual that his trail has been discovered everywhere, so that one cannot deny that someone has passed by, yet no one has met Jesus himself in this way.

And yet it is also clear that he has not been sought out of pure curiosity. The search has, in a way, been conducted with hearts aflame. The scholars who have set out on this track have said, "We feel that some mighty figure who once walked this earth must stand behind the ecclesiastical dogmas and doctrines and all that has been said about a 'Son of God' and a 'Redeemer of the World.' But we cannot base our whole life, our confidence for time and eternity, on these human interpretations or on the whole apparatus of theological concepts which this figure has set in motion. When we come to the point of staking everything on one card, we want to entrust ourselves only to the original figure of Jesus. Therefore we must scrape down beneath all the overlying layers of ecclesiastical tradition and find him as he was and perhaps still is."

Yet, as we have said, all of these attempts ended in failure. No one can get beyond the trail which the figure of Jesus left in the hearts of his disciples. The disciples themselves had to be content with saying that their hearts overflowed with him. Even if they had been modern men interested in an historically accurate biography in the contemporary sense, they would still have been in no position to capture this unfathomable life in a true-to-life portrait. What is more, they lacked neutrality. They simply were not in a position to be coolly objective, for their lives had been lifted right off their hinges. Today, when a traffic accident is reconstructed, the eyewitnesses seldom agree. The reason is very simple—the participants can't be objective. They are far too moved and influenced by what they have experienced. They are much too "involved" in it to be able to reproduce the scene with photographic precision.

That is only a very distant analogy to what has taken place with the disciples. They report what their dazzled eyes saw and what their ringing ears heard. They confess that their hearts were overwhelmed by a figure whose words could fell a man to the ground. For what they heard was unheard-of and what they had to tell was unspeakable.

How could one write an objective account of how men were freed from burdens of conscience, or of how the multitude in the wilderness was mysteriously satisfied because he was there, or how the powers of guilt, grief, and death had to retreat like a beaten army when he arrived on the scene? How could this be scribbled into a biographical record complete with commas and periods? How could even *one* man do it? Didn't the pen begin to run away with the hand that was supposed to guide it?

The reports about Jesus which we have are testimonies of the faith of people who had been overwhelmed by him. There is no other way to speak of him than by means of testimony—whether for or against him. All who met him were drawn into the charmed circle in which they had to show their colors—the disciples and the women at the cross and even the centurion on Golgotha who stammered out, "Truly, this man was the Son of God," not to mention the executioners, the higher clergy, and Pontius Pilate. Only one thing was impossible—to remain neutral and uninvolved. In a situation which froze the blood in one's veins, impartial reporting was out of the question.

The testimony of the overwhelmed—that is what we have before us. We can't get beyond it. For from our position on this side of the events we can't go through the testimony with undisturbed objectivity and try to extract the so-called historical Jesus from it. We can only say "yes" or "no." The only possible reactions are either the confession of a Thomas, "My Lord and my God," or the equally vehement resistance of an Archimedes, "Get away from me and don't disturb my circles."

Even people who resolutely turn away from everything bearing the name "Christianity" can be touched by this testimony. The great and quite respectable atheist Albert Camus said Jesus was so humane "that I think pretty well of him, my friend." And the Soviet poet Evgeny Yevtushenko confesses, "Not that I am a follower of Christ, but I like his manner: 'If you are struck on the cheek, turn the other one.' " They, too, have touched his garment, and who knows when he will turn to them and call *them* by a name which they themselves do not know? For as long as his hand of blessing is hidden from them they do not yet know who they are and to what they have been called.

Although it is therefore impossible to keep him at a distance and speak about him objectively, and although there is no historical portrait of him, the question of who he was cannot be silenced. Who was it who walked our earth and lived his life between Bethlehem and Golgotha among us? If we were to give up this inquiry about him, his picture would immediately become unrecognizably distorted, because then there would be basically only two possible interpretations of him.

On the one hand we would have to say, "In the final analysis it doesn't matter *who* he really was. The main thing is that we have his words and his teaching, like the parable of the prodigal son or the golden rule. That is enough. It lets us see God as our father, it changes our picture of mankind, and it gives us creative impulses for our life. Is it really important to know who Pythagoras was, or even if he lived at all? The important thing is that we have his teaching, the Pythagorean Theorem. So we don't have to worry if there are no objective findings on the life of Jesus." But the question is, does the analogy between Pythagoras and Jesus really hold up? Could, for example, the parable of the prodigal son really be cut loose from the Savior who told it, so that it would have a life of its own? Suppose we found this tale, about a young man who went to seed in a foreign country but finally found his way home, in the works of some poet. What use would it be to us? Would we then dare to say, "Well, then, God will also be a kind father to *me* and will receive me with open arms when I have failed and appear desolate before him?" No matter how lovely the poem or how beautiful the story, would I really dare to believe, on the basis of it alone, that instead of all guilt's being avenged on earth there is something like forgiveness, that a heart beats for me and does not abandon me, and that I am given a new start? It's far more likely that I would call it the fairytale of a poet who was dreaming his way out of a hard, merciless life.

The conclusion is obvious. If I am really going to take this parable seriously, then I can accept it from only one person. I can accept it only from Jesus Christ. Only through him can the fairy gold become real coin. I can even explain why it has to be he and no other. I notice, according to everything that is reported about his acts and sayings, that he knows this father who embraces the prodigal son on the threshold of his home. I detect that it is *his* father, and that he speaks out of a very intimate fellowship with him. Such things can be known only through the innermost harmony of two hearts. This is the one and only reason I believe it. I know that the *witness* is trustworthy and that when he tells about the wonders of an eternal Heart he is not like a blind man describing colors. Jesus does not only proclaim the good news; he himself is part of it.

In this sense, it is really crucial that this one man *did* walk the earth once. If that is a fraud, then the message, no matter how heartwarming it may be, is of absolutely no use to me. Therefore I cannot help asking repeatedly who he was. But now I ask in a new way. That is, I am asking as someone whose whole life's meaning and even whose fate depends upon the answer to this *one* question. And the more I mature in this sort of questioning, the more a cool "historical" interest in Jesus of Nazareth appears irrelevant and grotesque.

There is a *second* possibility that remains open when I give up asking if he was a figure in history who really walked this earth. This is to consider him a *mythical* figure like Apollo or Thor. In this case, I tell myself that this man never actually lived; he is only the projection of all our longings, a visionary savior-figure found in other myths as well. He is a figure into which we have packed all the saving forces that we men long for when fate's masked visage confronts us and roots us to the spot, or when death alarms us, or when the problem of guilt shakes us. Thus we are thankful that someone once dreamed up a Savior and that people had sense enough to clothe him in the warmth of living flesh and blood, so that he became a living figure who endured all the heights and depths of life just as you and I do.

But—and here again is the problem—will this flight into a myth hypothesis really get us off the hook of the question of *who* Jesus was and whether he really lived? The oldest accounts of him (Paul's report of the Resurrection, for example) were written barely a quarter-century after his death, and a respectable number of witnesses who had been Jesus' companions were still alive. Myths don't develop in such a short span of time. At best, the memory of a dead hero is adorned with a few legends and transfiguring anecdotes. The creator of a myth chooses the dim, distant past, beyond the reach of memory. In 1968 he doesn't invent a divine being who, he maintains, lived in New York and died on Lexington Avenue in 1940. Of all the theories about Jesus which have been propounded, this mythological explanation is by far the least likely.

The one thing remaining—and how grand it is that it worked out this way—is to inquire who this individual was. But we must remember to pose the question so as to approach him from the direction pointed out in the accounts of those witnesses who were overwhelmed by him.

According to the unanimous testimony of the accounts, it was always Jesus' *acts* that solved the question of his identity. The clergy ask, "By what authority are you doing these things?" (Mark 11:28). Another time they say, "It is only by Beelzebul . . . that this man casts out demons" (Matt. 12:24). That is to say, "He upsets natural laws because he is in league with demonic powers and avails himself of black magic." Then who is he, runs the question. Is he a messenger of God, or does he come from the underworld?

It is rumored among the crowds that he is John the Baptist come back to life. Still others, desiring to maintain their balanced view, try to explain away the extraordinary impression Jesus has made on them. They point out his commonplace origin: "Is not this the carpenter's son? Is not his mother called Mary?" (Matt. 13:55). "Doesn't he live around the corner there, at such and such an address? Has the good Lord really gotten the notion to establish a branch of the Kingdom of God at Smith's or Schneider's? Why should we get excited?"

In contrast to this, the men in that boat threatened by wind and wave ask the question in such a way that it has almost turned into a prayer: "What sort of man is this, that even the winds and the sea obey him?" (Matt. 8:27). He himself says nothing about who he is, except at the end of his life (Luke 22:70; 23:3). But wherever he goes, the question of his identity arises and refuses to be put down. The masses run after him, wanting to make a political leader out of him. Perhaps he is a world conqueror, or at least the top ideologist of the Jewish people, who provides new slogans and initiative. But then why does he waste his time with a blind beggar or with a "gypsy" from Samaria? Why doesn't he evaluate people according to their political potential? Why does he go in secret to speak with his Father instead of rushing into the tumult of the struggle for power? If he wants power, why does he preach and practice compassionate love? Indeed, who has ever found power and love combined in one person?

Question after question! The mystery of his person fascinates and repels at the same time.

And yet another side of him is quite human. He walks with his followers through the fields, speaking about the lilies or the birds of the air, who are not anxious but let their heavenly father care for them. That is something that anyone could put into practice. And time and again one has to nod in agreement, because this man talks about things that one has unconsciously experienced, but he puts them in such a crystal-clear way. "No one can serve two masters." Therefore it is necessary to choose; one must make up one's mind. That is a statement that anyone can understand. Or again, "Is not life more than food, and the body more than clothing?" Or, "Where your treasure is, there will your heart be also." Sometimes, hearing these things that sound so plausible, one thinks that the Kingdom of God is the most natural thing in the world. He describes it so clearly, like someone who has just come from there and who sees it as plainly before his eyes as I see that olive tree over there beside the road. One can hardly feel, anymore, that the things of God's Kingdom are transcendent and otherworldly, or that they lie in some other dimension, because he talks about them just the way he would discuss events and things which everyone has experienced. Recently, a blowhard ordered an architect to build him a very pompous structure. But then the wherewithal ran out, some checks bounced, and the half-finished facade stands there, a daily laughingstock to everyone and a public witness of its builder's would-be greatness and ultimate failure. Jesus uses this sight to tell the people that if they want to be his disciples, they should first count the cost and see whether they have enough to carry through (Luke 14:28 ff.). Better not start out with me at all if you're not ready to invest everything; don't think that I may be had cheaply or at a bargain! You must be ready to pay with your lives. Be clear about that. Otherwise you are better off not starting out to follow at all. A lukewarm half-Christian is worse than an ardent heathen; he is neither hot nor cold. He will eventually pull back from entrusting himself to me, and in the end he will present the same deplorable sight as that half-finished building.

Isn't that clear? The simplest heart could understand it and realize suddenly, "I must make up my mind. It is a question of success in life; and I know that the passport to success is not tossed to me for nothing. It costs something. But I also know that even if it costs my own life, it is worth it."

Sometimes people think that Jesus speaks just as pious people always have. But then something cutting, something sharp, suddenly appears, slicing through all pious regulations and all religious commonplaces like a knife. Then it sounds like this: "Of

course your catechism teaches thus and so, *but I say to you. . . ."*
When he starts opposing all the authorities like that, going
against Moses and the prophets and claiming the authority of a
witness for God beyond that of any other man and a unique right
for himself, then comes the moment when one has to face the
upsetting possibility that he has developed a Napoleon complex
or that his popularity has gone to his head.

In the next moment, however, these blasphemous thoughts take
their leave. Something in his words seems to come from another
world. And that appears to indicate that the speaker *himself* has
come from another world, from a realm beyond all the lilies of
the field and the birds of the air. This impression of the "totally
other," even when he is ever so human, crops up precisely when
he begins some especially important sentence with the words,
"Truly, I say to you." This introductory word, "Truly," stands
for "Amen" in the original text. A very peculiar procedure,
wouldn't you say, to introduce a sentence with a final flourish
like "Amen"? Everybody knows you say "Amen" at the end, but
Jesus says it at the beginning.

Listeners in those days noticed this peculiarity, too. The temple congregation used to say "Amen" after the reading of God's
word or after the priest recited the prayer. They then confirmed
what they had heard with a "So be it. I have heard this word and
I want to enlist under it; I will belong to this word completely."

Then what did this Nazarene mean by beginning his speech
with an "Amen" instead of concluding with it? Was it another
way of expressing the reappraisal of all values that took place
because of him? Was this his method of letting it be known that
he was the revolutionary who exploded everything that came
before him? In any case, he again provoked the question of who
he was—he who seemed to evade all the current formulas, making it impossible to fit him into people's categories and concepts.

It is precisely this placing of "Amen" at the beginning of his
words that does more than anything else to point up the mystery
of Jesus' person. By putting the concluding word at the beginning, he gives us to understand that "I have already spoken with

my Father before I even begin to speak to you. And what I now repeat to you is what I have received previously from him." Before Jesus opened his mouth to speak to men, he had already had a conversation with his Father and had concluded this conversation with "Amen"—with a "yes" to the Father's word, a "yes" that showed his submission to his will. The people who heard Jesus speak got in on just this last word. They heard him end the conversation with his Father, turn to them, and repeat what his words, "Yes, Father," had confirmed.

And so it happened that the first thing they heard was "Amen" when Jesus disclosed to them what the Father had prepared for them and what they had to do to participate in all those waiting riches, experiencing what blessedness is and what life could be.

So then, Jesus was a colossus, trusted and near, yet at the same time foreign to his hearers. He was near to them because he was full of compassion and because he always saw them as human beings and as children of God, even when they lay in the gutter and went to ruin far from home. A lonely person could say, "Here is someone who understands me." And a sufferer could say with certainty, "This man will stay with me when everyone else turns away. At his word, sorrow and death must depart."

In the same moment, he was also distant. He came from a fellowship with God which we men have lost, although perhaps we struggle for it and try to regain it. But he possessed this fellowship and came forth from it. He lived in continual conversation with his Father and he let us overhear that last word, "Amen."

Who was there, or is there, who could speak and act as he did? Who was there, or is there, who could enjoy the lilies in the spring with us, suffer pain, loneliness, and anxiety with us, be a human being with us, and die as we all must die—only more horribly? Who could do all of this and yet be able to say of himself, "Where two or three are gathered in my name, there am I in the midst of them." Who was there, or is there, who is able to say that? Could it really have happened? Could he really have lived?

If the answer were "yes," then he would change our life. All the presuppositions of our former life would be swept away. The people in the news, the powerful political figures of East and West, would be seen to play a role different from that which we had previously believed them to play. All at once everything in my life would have a different meaning and a different priority. Suddenly I would have a new theme for my life. It wouldn't be so terribly important whether or not I got the house I wanted or the job I tried for, because for once I would know that someone was with me who had given some thought to the road which he had marked out for my life. I would know that he himself had borne the hardship which he had imposed on me, and that he had strength to match all burdens. He would be with me when the little ship of my life had to battle the waves, and then he could command those waves with authority. "What sort of man is this, that even winds and sea obey him?"

That question both frightens and blesses us. We have posed it now, and we want to meditate further on it.

It is possible—and God can arrange it this way—that no stone of my life will remain on another once I experience who he is. No one who has met him can go away the same. So it may be that we too learn to say our Amen—the Amen of happiness in having found ground that supports us, peace that secures us, and a new meaning that opens up fresh and enticing horizons for our lives.

CONCEIVED BY THE HOLY GHOST, BORN OF THE VIRGIN MARY

And the angel said to her, "Do not be afraid, Mary, for you have found favor with God. And behold, you will conceive in your womb and bear a son, and you shall call his name Jesus.

> He will be great, and will be called the Son of the Most High;
> and the Lord God will give to him the throne of his father David,
> and he will reign over the house of Jacob for ever;
> and of his kingdom there will be no end."

And Mary said to the angel, "How can this be, since I have no husband?" And the angel said to her,

> "The Holy Spirit will come upon you,
> and the power of the Most High will overshadow you;
> therefore the child to be born will be called holy,
> the Son of God."

And Mary said, "Behold, I am the handmaid of the Lord; let it be to me according to your word." And the angel departed from her.   —*Luke 1:30–35, 38*

Around the twenty-fourth of December there are people—and by no means the worst people—who do not allow uncontrolled emotion to well up within them. Instead, they force themselves to the sober and hardheaded conclusion that the real message of Christmas doesn't concern them. The message that God became man, that the Word became flesh, and that their life's destiny is tied up with that babe of Bethlehem doesn't touch them at all. Every honest person is bound to take this message seriously and to be wary lest hard and inexorable questions such as "What does it mean?" and "What about it?" be dissolved into nothingness by clouds of emotional steam. He takes it seriously, and really wants to know what there is to it. And since this question leaves him helpless, he is torn by the contradiction between his Christmas emotions and the questionable *fact* which prompted these emotions. "Conceived by the Holy Ghost, born of the Virgin Mary" —do we realize what we are saying here? And even if we think we know, which one of us hasn't felt that slight hesitation which comes over him when this phrase crops up in the creed?

If it should turn out to be more than a fairy tale, then the whole course of the world would naturally take on a meaning different from that which I had previously imagined. My personal life, too, would center on themes completely different from those I had formerly held to be true. My bank account would get a quite different (and very much lower) priority, while the market value of daily prayer and a little bit of love for my neighbor would suddenly skyrocket.

That brings us to the subject for our meditation: what does "conceived by the Holy Ghost" mean?

To start out by putting it in dry words, this says that the man Jesus did not originate from human generation, but that God himself entered the realm of history through him. That may sound somewhat like a textbook definition, but it is good to start out by setting up the exact statement, free of all accessories. Even the operation of the atomic bomb can be presented in sober mathematical formulas, although the effect of its explosion is the fall of a world, with children burned to death, future generations ravaged, the earth scorched, and the song of birds stilled. The same thing is true here, but in the opposite way. That sober Christmas formula conceals a rise instead of a fall and life instead of death.

If I may draw out the meaning of this formula for the future, of our lives, two key points can be recognized at once.

First, God himself has come among us in Jesus Christ. That is a bit different from what the ancient myths tell us about Zeus or Apollo, when they took a little tour of the earth in human form in order to take a close look at this remarkable human race. The immortal gods risked nothing in taking the trouble to come down from Olympus. They touched the world only as a tangent touches a circle, and then they headed back to the safe world of Olympus.

But Christmas tells of one who left his base in heaven, came into our front-line trenches, and shared with us the ultimate in forsakenness, the hells of human anguish, and the agonies of hunger and thirst. Finally, he even exposed his heart to the great temptations which beset us: the temptation *not* to drink the cup of suffering, but to seek a painless way out instead; the temptation to choose the line of least resistance and then to call out the power of twelve legions of angels so as not to fall into the hands of men. For Christ it became a temptation to be a "god," to disengage himself, so to speak, at the decisive moment from the crucial scene on Golgotha and withdraw to Olympus. Therefore the showdown came at Gethsemane and Golgotha. When guilt, suffering, and death began their painful encirclement, he could have broken out, he could have been spared all that humiliation just by a wave of his hand. But, although it was possible for him to do it, that hand never moved. Instead, he let himself fall, living and dying, into the hands of his Father. He loved, literally, until it killed him. For that reason, and for that alone, we have the unbelievable chance to count on God's loving us, knowing us, remaining true to us, and never abandoning us.

Isn't love much more than what a person feels on his wedding day, when the heavens ring with music and the honeymoon beckons? Then even the heart of a would-be Casanova is brimful of what he is sure is love. But whether or not it was really love becomes apparent only as the rice-showered couple creep year by year through the prosaic pages of daily life—when illnesses or problems with the children occur, or when one hurts or disappoints the other. At these times, a really loving person does *not* leave the scene. On the contrary, the worse it gets, the tighter his loving hands hold on. One partner does not want to have it better than the other; if one lies sick in the hospital, the other suffers every pain too, at least in spirit.

For this reason, we may believe that God's heart belongs to us. He doesn't give us a friendly nod of goodwill from heaven, but he suffers the fate of a refugee with us as an inhospitable manger receives him and the flight into Egypt stretches before him. That is why, in the temptation in the wilderness, he suffers in his own heart what happens to man—to you and me—when we are promised every glory on earth—power, influence, prestige, and all the world's riches—at the price of just a little disloyalty, a small step "somewhat out of line," and a little twisting of our orders. *That* is the extent to which God becomes man, the extent to which he loves us and wills to experience unconditionally what it means to be human. Therefore we can believe in this love of his and be sure that he is completely for us.

Now, is it still a dry, bloodless formula when we say, "The Word became flesh"?

Second, the phrase "conceived by the Holy Ghost" means also that Jesus Christ came not from below, but from above. But here again we have a mere formula. If I might develop it somewhat and make it clearer, I would say that the figure of Jesus cannot be explained merely from his biological relationships. He crops up right in the middle of these relationships. He, too, has a mother who bore him and a line of descent of which he is a member just like the rest of us. However, this attribute of belonging to a family tree does not say everything about him. It could be said with some truth that something equivalent to the creation happened here. God called into being something that had not been there before, not even in the form of a seed or a stamped-out mold. To be sure, he placed it in the middle of relationships, right in the continuity of the historical process. Thus it is actually possible to specify with apparent exactness the historical date on which Jesus was born and even the geographical spot, the one-horse town of Bethlehem, which became famous only because of him. Thus everything is quite down-to-earth, not at all "spiritual" or superhistorical. Yet everyone who has been touched by the figure of Jesus has noticed that in his nearness he is still "totally other" than we. He comes to us from a realm that lies mysteriously outside everything we know as the setting of *our* life, that setting where we are begotten and born, where joy and sorrow are prepared for us, and where we finally lay ourselves down to die.

Thus the Christmas story, pointing to Jesus' origin in its reserved and modest way, is arranged somewhat like a musical score: its upper and lower lines must be read simultaneously. On the lower clef are concrete earthly events. There is an over-packed little town to which people stream for the taking of a census. There is a shortage of accommodations with all of its miserable side-effects—exorbitant prices and hearts hardened against the financially weak. There is an expectant mother who will have to go through her difficult hour in a stable and then shortly thereafter flee with her newborn infant because she and the child are threatened with becoming sacrifices to overall political expediency.

All that is like an outline of how our human life runs along, caught up in the greater events of the time. Is there anything more human than a young mother? And yet what could be more typical than the equanimity with which the course of world events rolls right over her? What do a worried mother and a whimpering baby matter in a situation that is determined by statistical questions, general laws, the persecution craze of a tyrant, and, finally, by overall political expediency? What do the mighty of this world care about the fates suffered by refugees whose flight is a result of their policies? The sequence of notes in the lower clef is just that down-to-earth and human. But it is not the whole melody.

Above it, in the upper register, sing the angels; above it heaven is open. Whoever fails to read this upper clef has not understood the whole score, for *both* lines harmonize: God comes into our life completely human and near us; nothing human is foreign to him, but nevertheless he breaks in on our life from a totally different realm. Thus there is harmony between the upper and lower lines, and we have a two-part score, with the story of the birth in a manger and the hallelujahs of the angels overhead.

The phrase "born of the Virgin Mary" points in the same direction. In symbolic language, it tries to clarify the fact that here something happens to mankind, something before which we can only keep silence and become passively receptive. Thus the husband, the symbol of "what makes history" or what creatively masters life, doesn't enter the picture. Rather, the focus is on the virgin, the symbol of silence, listening, and acquiescence. Medieval Christian artists tried to express the fact that nothing sexual was involved in this conception by portraying Mary receiving the creative word of God, as brought by his angel, through her *ear*. This organ of *perception* is in this case the organ of *conception*.

When confronted with this ultimate mystery, who could say where reality leaves off and symbol begins? Who would assert that God couldn't also have come to us through the *normal* processes we know as conception and birth, and so tabernacle among us, using *that* way to bring about the miracle of Jesus? Questions like "How could it happen?" or "Where is the boundary between the testimony of faith and the subject of the testimony?" die on our lips wherever the ineffable miracle takes place; wherever the glory of God is suddenly among us in the slums of life, and we have him with us; or wherever he shares my joy, my care, and, finally, even my last short hour on earth. We can only stammer out what has happened to us and say that now someone has seized control of our life. His love is very close to us, so that we acknowledge, "You are a man like me," and yet his love is so basic, so unswerving, and so incomprehensibly faithful that at the same time we must confess, "My Lord and my God" and, "You are different from what I could ever be, and I'm yours for that very reason."

The shepherds in the fields fell to the ground when the overpowering divine light blazed around them. They weren't able to look up in order to make observations or "studies" any more than the disciples could sweep the heavens with telescopes when the one who had become their destiny set out to return to his Father. The only thing that the shepherds and, later, the disciples, knew for sure was that they bore a great joy in their hearts and that they had to give vent to what was new, creative, and pivotal in their lives by glorifying God. They didn't know precisely what it was that had worked such a transformation in their lives. They knew only that they had been transformed. When they nevertheless volunteered to describe the actual catalyst for this amazing alteration, they could do it only haltingly and in pictures, using, as it were, symbolic language. The usual patterns of thought and language are not adequate to tell of such unprecedented events.

By this time one or another of us may be thinking, "I almost envy a person who can see things that way. I can well imagine that such a viewpoint would give my life an unparalleled impetus, but can I honestly see it that way? It all depends on whether I can make it a part of my consciousness, whether I can accept the message that God has become like a brother to me, following me along the misleading paths and dry stretches of alienation and signaling to me by a hundred different signs, 'I am with you; I know about you; I care about you.' Ultimately, doesn't it all depend on whether I can believe just one thing? Can I believe that this man Jesus, whose greatness even the atheists admire (and so do I) was the Son of God? The message, yes, I hear it well; alas, I don't believe it."

During the last war, a young German soldier in Russia wrote me, "How quickly now it can all be over for me. This is why I would like to be clear about what may be relied upon to the end. Is it Christ? He is an ideal for me, of course, and I have often imagined what might have happened to me if I could have met him in person. But no matter how much I admire him, can I build my life on him? He is still only one among many who have walked this earth before me, even if he is the greatest. But I have to be able to believe that he is the 'Son of God' if he is to be my savior. And the trouble is right there; at that point I am quite helpless."

How many of you could say exactly the same thing right now? What good does it do me to establish that the shepherds in the fields and the disciples in those days left the scenes of the events of Jesus' life with burning hearts and new, richer lives? What good does it do me when I don't share the *presupposition* that would enable me to re-create those reactions, and when this strange, mythological concept, "Son of God," only serves to widen the gap between them and me?

If you are among those who control their longing for peace and their ability to believe like this, or if you can't get away from your honesty and alert self-criticism—praise God!—then right now I can tell you something very encouraging. Even the people that Jesus encountered while he was on earth, who had an immediate confrontation with him and for whom he then became the Lord of their life, even these people were not immediately certain that this Jesus of Nazareth was "the Son of God" and "of supernatural origin." Becoming clear on this point was by no means the initial act of their faith. On the contrary, they slowly grew *into* this certainty. A lot of water had to flow down the Jordan before they got that far.

But how did they start?

They started by being struck with something quite *human* in Jesus. They couldn't get over the fact that here was someone who could love so selflessly and unconditionally, even embracing the poorest and most depraved with that love. But just when they felt themselves touched by this love and knew that they were secure in his heart, right then they may have been struck by the aloofness of his figure and his alien majesty. Was this love they so happily found in Jesus really the same as the love they felt in their own best moments? Was it only an increase or a higher degree of that love whose fragments and wretched rudiments they themselves produced when they felt a little sympathetic or when their hearts occasionally filled with compassion? Wasn't the love they observed in Jesus mysteriously different? He went so far as to love the unlovable. His heart went out to the very rowdies who were causing such a scene around his cross, sneering at him with their dull, senseless barbarity. He prayed that his Father would even forgive *them*, and he himself still remained close to them.

How was that possible? How could something like that happen —something that the disciples themselves could never manage to do?

It may have been only gradually that they caught on to the reason. Jesus didn't look at his persecutors and tormentors through the eyes of an underdog, feeling himself trapped and unable to react with anything but hatred and contempt toward those enemies who wanted his life. Rather, he looked at the faithless judge, the intriguers, those who wanted to trap him, and the executioner through his Father's eyes, and sorrowed over his erring children. He looked at them as the father in the parable looked at his younger son fleeing into a far country, and as that same father later watched him coming home, disgraced, ruined, the black sheep of the family, coming to stand again before his father. Jesus didn't see the *dirt* in which the men around him were stuck fast; he saw the *pearls* that lay in the dust. He didn't see the deluded, the sadists, and the plotters; instead, he saw in them what they were intended to be but had unfortunately failed to become. He could love even his enemies naturally, without striving for an effect, because he saw them in this other light. In his love for someone he brought out that which was peculiar to a person's life, even though it lay hidden under layers of dirt; he *loved* it out. Therefore many who knew that he saw them and loved them became new persons and experienced the great transformation. His love was not simply a reaction to something lovable, as our love is. His love was creative. It called a "new creature" into existence.

That was the lofty distance felt by everyone who met him. No other man had yet been able to love like that. But he could. And he could do it because, in some mysterious way, he stood at his father's side. He came from another direction than we. He was more humane than it was possible for humans to be. One has to speak in paradoxes like that in this case, because our concepts begin to blur when we try to explain in human words something that surpasses or fulfills everything human.

Even the words "Son of God," with which we finally try to speak about the unspeakable, are a stammering attempt of this sort.

Thus both the near and the alien are always tightly interwoven in Jesus. Nowhere does this combination come to such razorsharp expression as in the miraculous catch of fish (Luke 5:1 ff.) Jesus has just exercised his power in order to help his followers in an emergency. He has saved them from a night's useless labor by having them make a great catch. He is as close to them as a brother and is, so to speak, a "good buddy." But now Peter doesn't reach out to shake hands, as one normally does with a good buddy, nor does he say, "Thanks for pulling us out of that one." (Think how a hockey team hugs the happy goalie after he has made an amazing save!) The scene is quite different. Peter loses his composure. He falls before Jesus and says, "Depart from me, for I am a sinful man, O Lord." All at once, there, in the midst of the most human closeness, appears that separating "otherness." Shock at the immensity of the act crowds close upon joy at being helped. You are different from me; I can't bear your nearness; I feel myself shrink by comparison, with all my weaknesses disclosed. Depart from me, I can't bear that otherness, that majesty of yours.

So it is always something quite *human* about Jesus that strikes people at first. But precisely when they thus cling to the near and dear, they suddenly become aware that there is still something enigmatic and "totally other" at work in the background. Jesus never imposes his divinity on them. With him the story always starts with the understandable, the simple, and the human.

Of course none of those who believed in him came up with the idea of saying that there must be something like a "Son of God" in order for us to be saved. Such an absurdity can, at best, have been hatched in heads accustomed to Christian tradition and dogmatic concepts but without any encounter with Jesus himself. Without exception the people around Jesus came looking for something different from what he really was. They wanted a miracle-worker, a physician, a teacher of wisdom, or even only a good man. Some wanted a word of advice, and others only touched his robe with a superstitious thrill. Nevertheless he didn't send any of them away with the warning, "You are looking in the wrong direction; I'm not any of these things; let me introduce myself: I'm the Son of God." Instead, every one could seek in the most normal human way for that in Jesus which his own limited judgment understood, or even misunderstood. When people confused Jesus with the ideals of their own longing, he put up with it. And then when one of them did break through to the realization that the Son of God stood before him, and when he felt that grandeur of the Almighty sweep over him, Jesus would tell him to keep quiet. He didn't want the people to be hypnotized by a grand title, such as "Messiah," or to come under the spell of a "dogma." It was enough for him that they took him quite simply as a man, a man "like you and me." But by thus reaching for the outer hem of his garments—notice that it never was the *hand* of the Savior which they stretched to touch—they began to plunge more deeply into the encounter with him until finally, amazed and frightened, yet blessed by the great renovation in their lives, they learned to say, "My Lord and my God."

For a long time I couldn't get anywhere with modern expressionistic and abstract art. I thought it was chaotic nonsense, just as many of us may have considered such Christian dogmas as "divine sonship" or "the Holy Trinity" to be remote and absurd. Then I read the letters of Franz Marc and studied the biographies of Emil Nolde, Kandinsky, and other modern artists. Suddenly I met men who somehow impressed me by their passion for their work, by their character, or even by their readiness to sacrifice for what they wanted. These were quite simple, human instincts that I could understand and that seemed plausible. Of course that wasn't the essential thing about these people, but still it was something. It had a very simple result for me personally. I told myself that if what I could understand of these men on the human level was so sincere, solid, and perhaps even impressive, then their art couldn't be nonsense. Then *I* must have been the one at fault if their art didn't speak to me. Starting from there, I began gradually to grope around in the work of these artists until the first stage of alienation and skepticism passed and their art became more familiar. Finally it began to speak to me.

That is only a poor (and also only halfway fitting) parallel to our experience with Jesus. We should quietly leave aside everything that appears dogmatic and mythological to us and hold on to what we understand: that here is someone who has spoken words about sorrow, anxiety, and freedom that get under our skin; that here is someone who is totally identified with his life's work; that here is a man who loved until it killed him, because he took love seriously and did not hold back any reserves for his own safety. If I held on to all of that, it would still be only a *hem* of his garment. That wouldn't be Jesus *himself* at all. Perhaps it would only be the ideal picture of a noble man and therefore somewhat deceptive. If I grasped him at *this* point and held on—

if I tried to understand him from my point of view as if he were like me—then I would soon come to the place where he mysteriously eluded my grasp and simply could not fit into my psychological and ethical table of values. But I would have come to the key point precisely when I made that discovery.

I must start by walking this road of natural, human togetherness with him.

I can do that with the excitement of an experimenter, realizing that the road I dare to travel in association with Jesus may be the road that leads me into life. It may be that I will experience the reality of the promise, "him who comes to me I will not cast out." It may be that Christ holds me more than I hold him.

Everything that we know about Christ or experience with him is built up from below in this way. It begins with the most human level. If we try to gulp down dogmas prematurely, we may choke on them. The God who became man at Christmas and who has come to us on the front lines wants us to receive him as a man. He wants us to say to him, "Good evening. Who are you? May I walk along a little way with you? I don't know you, but something about you draws me." Even the Soviet poet Yevtuschenko may have spoken to him in that way when he said that of course he was no Christian, but something about Christ "pleased" him. Perhaps God laughed at the innocence of that remark, but if so his laughter was kind and full of promise. Perhaps on *my* way home, when I am once more alone, I will repeat the words of the disciples from Emmaus: "Didn't my heart burn within me as I spoke with him?" My heart already knows more than my understanding; as is often the case in life, it is one step ahead of my intellect.

What if I tried it once and "started small"? Faith in Jesus is also human enough to grow. It does not presuppose a perfect dogmatic framework.

Ernst Juenger said in *Radiations*, "The decision . . . to begin by holding to a law of faith, even without an inner call, is not at all as senseless as is generally thought. In fact, it is the proper opening for the metaphysical game. For then God must make the countermove."

Actually, learning the faith is so human that it can be presented in the form of a game. God will follow if only I am ready to open. We live on this promise. And if the game then goes further, I begin to notice that God was already at work while I was sitting down to make the first move. The Holy Spirit is always on the scene before my decisions. But if those who play and wager can count on God's cooperation and his carrying through the game to the end, what about those who are in dead earnest? How much more is this same promise true for those who hunger and thirst after righteousness (and who shall be satisfied) or for those who call out of the depths and those whose restless hearts desire peace, or for those to whom the nothingness of their lives is repugnant and who long for streams of living water, for the springs of life, and for the "one thing needful"? Heaven opens above us as on Christmas Eve, and we are called to a paradise where no angel stands barring the way.

We need only turn around, for God already stands behind you and me, watching us, long before we have caught sight of him.

SUFFERED UNDER PONTIUS PILATE

Surely he has borne our griefs
    and carried our sorrows;
yet we esteemed him stricken,
    smitten by God, and afflicted.
But he was wounded for our transgressions,
    he was bruised for our iniquities.   *—Isaiah 53:4–5*

When we read a novel or a biography, the author tends to make us share in all the dimensions of the life he describes. Bumbling and fumbling, love and hate, fulfillment and disappointment march past us, half revealing and half concealing secrets of the human hearts that reflect them. And usually a great display of psychology is involved in an attempt to make these human fortunes understandable.

By comparison, the Bible is much more concise. Sometimes it seems as though it describes only the skeletal structure of life, and is just plain uninterested in colorful details, scents, tones and shadings, character fluctuations, and even excitement. A reader of the Old Testament will come across long stretches where individual kings are noted with the brevity of a telephone directory: "He was born, did what pleased or displeased God, and died." Period! Contrast that to what the confession magazine reporters can dig out of the lives of monarchs, past or present! Do the biblical writers suffer from a lack of imagination or literary anemia? Obviously this peculiar style of narration rests on the fact that the Bible considers other things essential. It seeks the pivotal point of life in a spot quite different from the place we would look. If it says, "This king did what pleased God," then that establishes the decisive outline of a life. Then, in God's shorthand, everything else—down to the last detail—has been said. It means, for example, "This king had his emotions, but they could not become his master, because he stood under the discipline of another Lord. He had successes and triumphs, but they didn't lead to prodigality. He received them as blessings and knew how to give humble thanks. He also had to suffer and bear his burdens, as we all do." But more important than an exciting psychology of suffering, as far as the biblical writer was concerned, was the fact that this king knew from whose hand his affliction came and knew therefore that it would cleanse him. For readers who can understand its implications, the meager phrase, "He did what pleased God," becomes a vessel from which the spirit of a living person arises. The reader can see every act of that drama which unfolds in the course of a human life.

The Apostles' Creed has profited from this extremely austere style. Could anything really be briefer, more stenographic, than its speaking of Jesus' life as: "born of the Virgin Mary, suffered under Pontius Pilate"? That is no novel about a life; it is only the framework of birth, suffering, and death. Not that his life had lacked all those experiences which fill our daily lives. His eyes, too, had seen springtimes and sunsets; he too had breathed the scent of flowers, had hungered and been filled, and had known the refreshment of sleep. There were times of loneliness in his life, as in ours, but certainly there were also hours filled with friendship and human companionship, even the wedding joy of Cana.

The remarkable thing, though, is that whenever anyone tries to reconstruct the story of this life it slips through his fingers, and he ends by merely projecting his own life onto the surface of that unfathomable one.

Therefore the brief phrases, "born of the Virgin Mary, suffered under Pontius Pilate," do not try to capture what we would call the "fullness of life" (and, if possible, the "full" life!); they try to grasp the bond which holds this fullness together. And this bond consists in the fact that Jesus of Nazareth has *suffered*. If this key word doesn't ring in our ears, then all the scenes of his life are shuffled into the accidental designs of a kaleidoscope. At the same time, we miss the whole point of his life. This point is called suffering. I said that he too had seen flowers and had followed the flight of birds. But no poet should lyricize that or try to construct a romantic relationship to nature. The truth is far different. Since Jesus was filled with apprehension over the lost state of humanity, and since he was driven by a passion to rescue men and help them, there could be no aesthetic of nature for him. On the contrary, even the brightness of a spring day must have saddened him because it contrasted so oppressively with the darkness of man's destiny. The flowers and birds about him lived carefree under God's sun and were sheltered by his care without thought for the morrow. But man, with whom he was most deeply concerned, had slipped away from trust in that divine care and now worried about himself. Man was haunted by anxiety for the future, by the passage of time, and by the prospect of a lonely death. He could not get free of the curse which he brought upon himself the day he craved control over his own life. Even when his eye penetrated the parables of nature and discerned behind them traces of his Father, Jesus' joy in this understanding was swallowed by the tormenting knowledge that his fellowmen floundered deaf and unknowing through God's world, and that they *overlooked* all those messages from God which the lilies or the flight of birds should have spoken to them.

To anyone who loved as he did, everything, even gazing into a spring sky, must have led to suffering. For he could see everything only in the light of that one theme of life: that God sought man and that man would not let himself be found, but instead overlooked and disregarded all of God's messages and signs. Now he, Jesus of Nazareth, had been put on the trail of the prodigal, at the cost of his own life.

From the beginning, this suffering for mankind is the keynote of his life's melody. Even as he enters this world, there is no room at the inn. We men have no use for him. The first night of his life he sleeps among animals. The manger in which he lies is of the same wood as the cross on which he dies. Even as a baby he is robbed of peace and security. Not only does he have housing problems in Bethlehem, but he also becomes a political scandal. Herod, the representative of the state, senses that there is a power in the child which is rooted in the world's foundations and which will unleash discord and set the world on fire.

He walks as an alien upon our earth, without house or home, and has nowhere to lay his head. And if they shout, "Hosanna!" to him, then it's certainly a mistake. As soon as they discover *who* confronts them, they roar, "Crucify him!"

Later, toward the end of his life, he breaks into tears (Luke 19:41) when he looks upon Jerusalem, the city which has closed its heart to him and which fails to notice the birds of ill omen already circling overhead. "How often would I have gathered your children together as a hen gathers her brood under her wings, and you would not" (Matt. 23:37).

That is his suffering: knowing—and having to watch as those he loves run obliviously toward their ruin, disregarding all warnings and failing to take hold of the lifeline.

Nietzsche's Zarathustra says: "He has not yet suffered enough, for he has not yet suffered on man's account." But here is someone who has suffered because of man. In another place Zarathustra says, "Love for mankind is God's hell." Here is one who walks through this hell.

Finally the last, incomparable loneliness closed over him as even those who had been his companions deserted him. When Socrates drank the cup of hemlock, he was surrounded by his faithful followers. Their veneration supported him, and he died in the midst of philosophical conversation. But Jesus hung between criminals, the soldiers bellowed below him, and snatches of a conversation that was far from philosophical reached him there on the cross. Only a couple of women stood before him crying quietly, and even they cried for the wrong reason. They were not shaken by the fact that a man was here suffering through the last agony of *their* (and of our) alienation from God. No, they sniffled only over the pierced hands and the pains of his death-struggle.

All this could almost sound like the text of a tragedy in which the hero, who wants the Absolute, is rejected by society as though he were an alien substance and then is crushed by the relativity of this world. This course of fate is familiar to us. And many a person falls for this tragic tone (especially if he has seen the Passion Play at Oberammergau or heard the St. Matthew Passion), even from only a musical or literary standpoint. But, if that is the case, he has been tuned in on the wrong frequency.

We begin to grasp what is happening here only if we ask what it is that *constitutes* this suffering of his.

His suffering can be expressed in a simple formula: He suffered because he acted the way he loved. If someone loves another completely, he will want to share everything with him. He doesn't want to avoid the dark valleys and abysses, or the loneliness and anxiety, which have been allotted to the beloved. Therefore Jesus never stays, as we said, back at headquarters—in the safety of heaven—when he whom He calls his brother is sent to the front in the battle of life.

This is why we can believe this love of his. How easy it is to play the role of "Friend of Man" when making speeches before management and labor and to say, "The whole point is the human factor." How easy it is to be socially concerned or to transfer sums of money from one bank account to another as tax-deductible contributions. Basically, that costs a person little, and generally it doesn't hurt a bit. But Jesus Christ transferred himself from security with his Father to the abysses of guilt, suffering, and death. Suppose that you attend a charity ball, enjoy yourself with glasses of sparkling champagne, and spend several times as much on evening clothes for the occasion as you do on your contribution to charity: the latter almost becomes a by-product of the event. Then you shouldn't be surprised that the unfortunate are not impressed by this charity and are so ungrateful as to strongly suspect that this well-manicured, giddy Society just wanted to concoct a moral alibi for having fun. A pleasure, after all, is only half as great when it is accompanied by a bad conscience! Therefore one must procure the extra luxury of moral self-satisfaction—in just this form of charity entertainment—in order to drown out the voice of inner criticism. And somewhere at the end of this long bowling alley (you can't see it any more, but still . . .) the coin rolls into the kitchen of a refugee or into the XYZ Old Folks' Home.

But here, between Bethlehem and Golgotha, someone walks by our side for whom we are not anonymous recipients. Instead, he calls us by our *names*. The man who gives up his life, who transfers *himself*, and not merely an impersonal bank balance, *is the man who will also know for whom he is doing it*. In this situation I know that I am seen by someone who is involved with me and who will not let any darkness separate me from him.

One of my friends was a military chaplain with the beleaguered troops at Stalingrad. Since he had a large family, was frostbitten, and was also in great pain, he was among those who were to have been flown out of the doomed area along with the wounded. But he refused to be rescued because he wanted to remain with his comrades, with that congregation of the condemned. We heard nothing more of him, and we don't know if he died in that battle of Stalingrad or somewhere in Siberia. But we do know one thing. Even if he could only whisper, and even if his weak words had lost all their rhetorical skill and flair, they nevertheless penetrated hearts as messengers of life and were able to comfort the despairing and gently accompany the dying on their last journey. Here was a man who was in earnest, a man whom one could believe. For he had let himself be closed in with the besieged troops in Stalingrad. In doing that, he had lived up to the word of his Lord: no man has greater love than to lay down his life for his friends.

This is why Jesus is found on all the battlefields where we are hard pressed and in all the besieged areas where we are in distress. And it is a very glib and trite expression to say that nothing human is foreign to him.

Nowhere does this solidarity with us, this standing at our side, come to deeper expression than in the account of the temptation in the wilderness. There in the wilderness he, the pure, the sanctified—we may say this without striking a false note—he let his heart be thrilled by temptation equal to that which we human, all too human, fickle and feeble creatures have to experience every day. We, too, in our little niche, know something of the wild possibilities which the Tempter called up before Christ in this encounter: to win all the nations of the world, to gain prestige, to make a career for oneself, *and* to do it all at the cost of only a little betrayal of our task. (We have already spoken of this in the preceding chapter.) We also know about the fascinating possibility of taking the path of least resistance and acting out of faithlessness and opportunism. Here again Jesus of Nazareth has stood at our side. He, too, has held out on this front line of life's battle, where we must struggle to make decisions between unclear alternatives, and where the Tempter's art of beclouding the issues makes it easy for us to become disloyal and to excuse ourselves with biblical quotations, ethical arguments, or "loftier viewpoints." Jesus put himself in all these situations because he loved us. And men who sit in some black hole need no longer look upward to where a crack admits light and fresh air. They need only look down to the bottom of their abyss. *There* is Christ, there where the border runs between despair and disintegration. *Therefore we can trust him.* And therefore it is no empty phrase to say that he is there for us and that he is our brother.

Mere feelings, even feelings of love, are certainly cheap. They depend to a great extent on the state of our nerves. Some people have such watery foundations that a touching newspaper account can activate their tear ducts. Yet a minute later they are once again eating their ham and eggs with apparent gusto. But in the biblical account there is nothing about "*feelings.*" Only twice does the Bible mention Jesus' tears flowing when he was struck by human misery. Love in this case does not mean being moved spiritually (this element is certainly not absent, but it isn't the characteristic motif). It is, rather, love in its unsentimental and realistic sense: being there for the other person, entering into his situation without holding anything back for oneself. More precisely, it means to transfer *yourself*. It is in this sense that this man loved.

The negative image of this attitude becomes clear to us in the prodigal son's elder brother (Luke 15:11–32). His mistake (it was his only one, too, but it became *the* sin in his life) was that he could not love. Otherwise he was, morally speaking, perfect: he had loyally served his father; he had had no escapades; he was serious and was considered an honorable man. But when his brother returned, miserable, from the far country and his father welcomed him with open arms, overflowing with mercy and forgiving love, the elder brother remained cold and loveless, consumed with jealousy.

The father had followed his unfortunate son over that road to the far country, just because he loved him. He had suffered all the agonies of homesickness with him. His own heart had gone through all the despondency and all the bitterness of self-reproach which his son had faced. Now he was happy that the young failure had found his way back and had returned to the shelter of home.

The brother, however, who was moral in a vinegar sort of way, had looked down with disgust on that lost life. *He* certainly had not been dragged into any depths, and the temptations of that wild, restless heart were foreign to him. He sat in the center of a well-fixed, middle-class life. And since he didn't "love," he even lacked the imagination to visualize how anyone could come to be imprisoned for murder, robbery, or moral crimes, to say nothing of feeling any oneness with unfortunate creatures of that type, or of hearing the wild wolves that had broken loose in *those* lives howling in the cellar of his own heart. But just because he was so frightfully untouched and so entirely without love in the crucial moment, his heart could not beat in tune with his father's. As he withdrew from his brother, he also, unwittingly, withdrew from his own father. And, finally, *he* was the one who, in a very subtle way, went to a far country. From this foreign land, however, there was no returning. The loveless cannot find a way back. But the homesick, those consumed by an unhappy love, those who are harassed by a hunger for righteousness—they can come home again. Which of these two, then, was the "lost" son?

Jesus Christ waits for a tiny spark of yearning to answer him when he lets us know that he has permitted himself to be trapped in Stalingrad [or on Corregidor!] with us. He wants to kindle fire on the earth, to be sure, but it will be sufficient for him if this little glimmering spark in our hearts is fanned until a very slight flicker from one single splinter appears. This is the same flicker that the prodigal son must have felt when he suddenly realized that his father had not given him up. "There is someone who does not rave at me. There is someone who stands at my side—even at the swine-trough. I have an 'alter ego' in my pain."

But Jesus Christ's self-forgiving love brought him suffering for still another reason.

Sometimes we have an unpharisaical moment and are ready to forgive a colleague or neighbor if he does something wrong or, possibly, maligns us. Then we readily say "we want to spread a cloak of Christian charity over the matter and forget it."

Of course that is a little self-deception. For we just can't forget it. At best, we can repress it. And therefore something remains between us, just under the surface. Everything hangs in the air, so to speak. We watch our step, as though we were walking on eggs. It remains secretly between us. It has an almost hypnotic power. If we examine ourselves ever so slightly, each of us recognizes that. Yet we find ourselves being drawn to that hidden but still present offense.

Jesus Christ rejected this cloak we have named after him, this "cloak of Christian charity." He sees quite clearly what is wrong with us, and he suffers the pain that it causes him. This pain is very great, because his suffering is not solely the result of the wrong mankind does him. In Gethsemane his disciples fall asleep or betray him when he needs their presence the most. Men intrigue with false witnesses against him. The shouting people who acclaim him one minute scream for his death the next. He is vilified and abandoned by everyone to an agonizing execution—that certainly is suffering enough. And yet, in his life, *that* is not the particular nerve that twinges. The center of his agony lies elsewhere. It lies in the fact that everything evil that men do to him is doubly terrible because he must measure it all against what men were *meant* to be. The lights in the Father's house were lit so that all men would find their way home. The table was set for all of them; the Christmas peace was proclaimed for all over Bethlehem that night. They might have been children in their Father's house, yet they roamed about in a far country. They preferred servitude under foreign masters. The great estate of freedom was intended for them, and instead they entangled themselves in dark passions. They were to have walked confidently in the clarity of the eternal word, but instead they knocked about aimlessly, without guide or goal, in the twilight zones of life. They didn't claim the homeland prepared for them, but remained shelterless and driven by anxiety. As Jesus scanned this distance between what men were meant to be and the state in which they in fact found themselves, he sorrowed for them, not on *his* account, but on *theirs*. He knew more about them than they knew about themselves.

This is why the artist has given the portrait called "The Christ of Sigmaringen" that unfathomable, knowing expression. While his disciple lies sleeping on his breast, Christ gazes at the world with this knowing look, without dream or illusion. He sees more than we men see. He sees even the unborn thoughts and desires within us. He sees that we are potential murderers. He sees the fearful delusions of mental patients and suffers through the despair of the suicide. He knows us as no one else does, not even we ourselves. "One must watch," one who sees all this must watch and stand fast—that is the theme that Manfred Hausmann sees in the knowing face in this portrait.

Goethe said once that a person can understand only what he loves. Here is someone who loves as no man has ever loved. That is why he understands us as no one else does. That is why he collapses beneath the burden of this understanding. Do we sense what it means to say that he has borne the sins of the world, that we all lie upon him like a burden? And, to the extent that we lie on him, he carries us.

In the final analysis, then, can we have a greater comfort than to know that there is someone who knows all about us and still will not throw up his hands in despair? Perhaps we are people who are honored and looked up to in human society. Our clean moral slate is respected. But, now and then, don't those among us with more delicate sensibilities think, "If they only knew what I dream about sometimes! If they only knew what a hypocritical disguise my public countenance sometimes is, or what a morass of envy and jealousy is within me as I turn on my smile and congratulate my more successful colleagues or competitors with apparent honesty! If they only knew how many mental murders I already have on my conscience, what a liar I am, and how little concern I have for my neighbor! If they only knew how, back in the Third Reich, I could have been quite precisely informed about the extermination of Jews and mental cases. But I didn't *love;* therefore I didn't *understand,* either, and I didn't *suffer* with them. I even protected myself from loving and from being in the know, because it would have gotten on my nerves and maybe I would have had to do something."

It is just as well that they don't know all this! If they knew it, they would be upset about me. Therefore I hang out my shingle, the clean slate.

But there is one who knows all this about me and, despite it, is not angry with me. Instead he says to me, "I have come for precisely such people. I sorrow *with* you, if you sorrow over yourself."

That is the comfort that is spoken to us here. Someone sees through me, but he is someone who loves. I am known inwardly, but by one who suffers with me. Here another takes over my burden. "Surely, he has borne our griefs and carried our sorrows." Do we understand what the prophet meant by that? Basically, he has spelled out nothing less than the secret of love:

In all other cases in which two people meet and strike up a friendship or fall in love, they want that "other" in order to make life easier, fuller, and more beautiful for themselves. *This* is the only case in the world in which one so loves that he wants only the burden, where there is such self-forgetting love that it is concerned only for me.

With that we come across one final secret. There is a somewhat artless hymn verse which, with that oversimplification that sometimes characterizes the banal, articulates a real problem:

> If salvation's joys were clear,
> There'd be many a Christian here.

Yes, that *is* really the question: Why isn't the joy of salvation clear? Why don't people know it? Granted, they are busy with completely different questions, with installment buying, with their chances for promotion, with their salary increases, and sometimes with the world situation—if it becomes critical. But nobody says a word about the man of Golgotha. Elemental passions seem to break loose in a football stadium when a pass is completed or fumbled and the crowd screams and shouts. But would anyone be so elementally gripped about the matter of his temporal and eternal destiny? Do such passions ever break loose in the pulpit or pew when a sermon dares to speak the monstrous fact of One who loved until his love killed him, who committed the madness of seeing through men with his love and then lifting the burden of the world's sin onto his own shoulders? Wouldn't it drive a person crazy to study the way suffering and slumbering are apportioned in this odd world?

Yes, if the heavens parted and God descended, or if Christ landed in our city in a spaceship with a great display of fire and smoke, then he would fill the television screens and the headlines. Wouldn't that even be the merciful way, perhaps, if he made himself visible and hearable, commanding twelve legions of angels to roll their drums for an announcement? Then it would be impossible to overlook him, and even the most phlegmatic lazybones would notice what hour had struck. So why did he care so little about "reaching" men? Why did he wrap himself in silence? Why could men abuse him and he not be moved? Why could they silence him and he not "speak up"?

In fact, why was the whole undertaking from Bethlehem to Golgotha carried out the way it was, with the public excluded? Why did it all end in a public hush-up even though our destiny was involved? Why? How can a person avoid becoming upset once he understands what is going on here? Why is God silent? Here we encounter the last secret.

If he were to come to us with a pomp of world prominence, then we could not believe his love for us. Whoever wants to be known as great in this world keeps his distance. He marches past us behind cordons. The privileges of the great create distance.

But here is someone who wants to be one of us, a comrade of the outcasts, a brother of the blind, and a companion of the lonely, the suffering, and the dying. He appears among them *without* privileges, sharing their fate, the Savior of the world —incognito.

But precisely this love which he practices in oneness with us makes him unrecognizable. This is why he can be confused with a founder of a religion, with a teacher of wisdom, a rabbi, or even with a provincial figure on the border of world history. For the same reason, he has done nothing to call attention to himself through a messianic title, nor did he follow the Tempter's suggestion to jump from the pinnacle of the temple as a demonstration of his power.

He even consciously kept the miracles he performed ambiguous in order to prevent a type of mass hypnosis. This mass suggestion would not have produced faith but rather would have eliminated it. Jesus was not to be picked up casually. He wanted to be found by the heart, not by titillated senses.

To find Jesus of Nazareth with one's heart means, however, to hear *his* heart beating. It means to let myself be touched by the fact that I alone matter for him—that I matter so much that it is as though I were the only one on earth, and that he loves me even to the point of giving his life for me. Then suddenly, if this touches me, the incognito is lifted and I stand confronted by the majesty of the Son of God. Then my chains are broken, and for the first time I realize in what bondage I have lain. Then I experience what life can be. Then I discover what it means to be free of burden, dazzled by a new-won liberty.

CRUCIFIED, DEAD, AND BURIED

"Greater love has no man than this, that a man lay down his life for his friends."   —*John 15:13*

We have said that Jesus loved to the point that it cost him his life. We reached that conclusion not out of sentimentality but from an objective diagnosis. To say that his love cost him his life means, in plain words, that he was so much for us, and that we meant so much to him, that he suffered through our human lot with us and that he wanted to be at our side precisely when we were guilty, and when we must suffer and die. In that way there could not be a deathwatch where he would not be standing by us so that we too might say at the end, "When hence I must betake me, Lord, do not thou depart" [No. 201, *ELHB*]. There isn't a man living who wouldn't sense the human importance of knowing that there is someone who wants to share our fate and who will not let any depths separate us from him.

Here we have a simple picture of a life linked to ours by bonds of love. Why then do we obscure it by talk of an "atoning death" and a "vicarious sacrifice"? Why can't we leave that life in the simple framework where it is so obvious and overwhelming in its humanity? No sooner are our hearts moved to similar acts by the message of that self-forgetting love than our intellects have to rebel and defend themselves against something alien. A mythological and poetic concept threatens to stifle what was so human and close to us. These hot and cold showers to which the church exposes us seem to be entirely too irritating!

And yet men have drawn sustenance from this message of atonement. They have found strength in it to sing hymns of praise out of the depths of human life. For its sake they have let themselves be stoned and thrown to the lions. They have become springs in the desert for their fellowmen. And now I am naive enough to preface what I am going to say with a very simple statement. Anything which was once taken seriously remains serious for all time. That is, anything that was once a support, a comfort, and a foundation in the borderline situations of life deserves our most serious consideration. We ought to look at it from all sides. This is obviously not a case of any old idea that simply occurred to some people at some brilliant or mystical moment. Where would we be if we took all random occurrences seriously or even tried to consider them at all? But in this case it is obvious that we are dealing with proven truths which have stood up under the most extreme test of strength that life has to offer. For a person just to shrug them off and go on about his daily rounds is nothing less than contempt for those who lived and died for those truths. It would make charlatans out of the martyrs and declare that the children of God are orphans who live on grotesque illusions.

If we are going to meditate a little on these ultimate questions of the faith, it will be good to begin by making an observation which may be so obvious that it sounds trivial: if the cross of Golgotha is a sign of atonement, then that presupposes an antithesis between God and man, a basic conflict which it removes.

We are stuck already! Who considers God his opponent? Or who has experienced even the mere resistance of God? When someone tells me that he finds God in nature, then I am quite sure that God is pretty innocuous as far as he is concerned. Do you remember some critical viewpoints that we met in discussing the relation of God and nature? The sun slanting down through the woods may thrill a person; the starry host of the winter sky may teach a person about the greatness of the creation—and I have all due respect for such feelings. But there is certainly one thing that doesn't happen. This God of the stars or of the springtime doesn't accuse me; he doesn't block my path as an opponent; he doesn't become a serious problem in my life, setting his barbs in my conscience. As we put it earlier, the lofty God of nature has been lofted right out of my personal life. He never becomes a crisis in my life; he lets me go along unmolested. I don't suffer because of this God, and when things don't make me suffer, I don't take them seriously.

And in other respects, if I am honest, "God" is a pretty pale word. So when I am confronted with the *realities* of my life, the little bit of religiosity I had dissolves like a puff of smoke. How do I solve problems like my vocational advancement, the writing of a very delicate love letter, or getting out of a touchy situation without losing my hide? Who thinks anything about God at times like that? It's only in moments of calm and reflection, when we stop to catch our breath, that we haul out thoughts about God.

The remarkable thing is, however, that if God isn't in my office, my kitchen, or my children's bedroom, then he isn't around when I stop for breath, either. If I banish him from the center of my life, I can't find him around the edges. This harmless God of religious emotion is a very breezy fellow. No wonder he is really nothing more than a lot of "wind" to me. He neither resists me nor holds me, to say nothing of frightening me.

Consider how the "idea of God" usually develops (the very phrase is characteristic and speaks volumes). We make a diagnosis of life and come up with the conclusion that it is unfair, it is meaningless, it is a battle; and we have our doubts about the way things turn out. *C'est la vie*—that's life! And from that I draw the conclusion that if there is a God I can charge him with having made life the way it is. If, therefore, I conduct myself in accordance with this way of life, I am also in harmony with him who created this sort of world. Quite apparently it is *he* whose voice sounds in my racing blood and who approves when life urges me to pamper my "sacred ego" and to be sure that I get my slice of the pie. That's life—and consequently that's the kind of *God* who created this life.

In actual fact, this so-called *"God of living,"* whom I have found in my own image and tailored perfectly to suit myself, is just a bubble of pure religious froth. He is not a boundary that I meet, nor is he a barbed-wire barrier in which I remain caught.

It is quite the reverse with all the figures in that great drama of God and men which the Bible unfolds before us, because God was *not* that sort of bubble for them. Noah and Abraham, Isaiah and John the Baptist, Paul, and, later, Luther could accept the message of atonement as though they were prisoners in a death cell receiving a pardon. It was like new breathing space to their souls. That was because they had rubbed themselves raw against him and discovered that, at bottom, it is frightening that there is a God—at least it *can* be frightening. The more seriously I take him, the more completely I shatter myself against him. My life is a failure when measured against what he meant me to be, what he expected of me. I die of shame before that knowing look of his that pierces me. In me I have the makings of a murderer, an adulterer, and a thief. That's what God meant to those men of the Bible. They had to endure the holiness of those eyes that would not let them go, and out of their experience of the eternal majesty they could have repeated with redoubled intensity the conclusion of Goethe, an unrelenting observer of himself, when he wrote in *Wilhelm Meister*, "Had not an unseen hand re-strained me, I might have become a Girard, a Cartouche, a Damiens or any wretch you can imagine. The tendencies to this I traced too clearly in my heart. Heavens, what a discovery! . . . what a monster lies in every human breast."[1] Yes, what a dis-covery, and we can add that this repressed secret of ours is seen by a witness outside and above ourselves. That witness once re-leased us intact from his hands, and someday we must return to give an account of ourselves.

Whoever has made this discovery knows that God can arouse terror and can burn in our bones, more like a devouring fire than a bubble of our religious temperament. He knows how unen-durable God can be, and he comes to understand Peter's cry, "Depart from me, for I am a sinful man, O Lord. I cannot endure your presence." He learns why we prefer to invent harmless gods, made in our own image, to approve our actions, or why we prefer to push God aside entirely and scornfully call him a hob-byhorse for bigots. He also knows that this complete silencing of

[1] Johann Wolfgang von Goethe, *Wilhelm Meister's Apprenticeship*, trans. Thomas Carlyle ("Harvard Shelf of Fiction"; New York: Collier & Son, 1917), Bk. VI, p. 395. (Trans.)

God, this unceremonious running right over him as though he weren't there, is not a sign of something clever in humanity or of mankind's final conquest of this present world. Rather, this very act is the most frightful judgment and uttermost darkness. And where men think that God has been silenced, he has merely withdrawn. *"Dieu se retire*—God withdraws," says Leon Bloy. Where they think they have liberated themselves and God has become nothing, he holds them in the court of their own nothingness— they are alone in the "wide open grave of the All" (Jean Paul).

Naturally, anyone who understands or even has an inkling of this hidden judgment will hear the message of atonement with ears quite different from those of people with a bit of banal religiosity or nihilistic illusions. The understanding person knows what an abyss there is to be bridged, what sort of peace is involved, and what a miracle it is that God himself is the one who reaches over to us and proclaims the Christmas message of peace on earth.

Yet, even when I can get a little sense out of all this and try to make clear to myself—perhaps only theoretically—that this discord between God and man is *the* problem of our life, the question about the connection the death of Jesus is supposed to have with it becomes all the more pressing. How can someone else set things right for me? Why can things be set right only if Jesus dies an agonizing death for me? Can't God come to me in some *other* way? Can't he bring something new into being in some way that has more majesty and elegance than this dismal method that reminds one of an archaic sacrificial cult? Why can't it happen in some simple, human way as it does in the parable of the prodigal son? All it takes there is the father's clasping of the returning son to his bosom. All strangeness and alienation would have to dissolve before the superior power of this love. Why interpose a theology of wounds and blood? Why this frightful detour by way of the gallows of Golgotha?

I certainly can't explain why it had to happen this way. We can grasp it with our hearts, of course, but never with our reason. Here someone else steps into my shoes and bears the punishment that I ought to suffer. I cannot explain it. But I can give the reason *why* I cannot explain it.

I would like to clarify what I mean by using an analogy from mathematics. The squaring of a circle—converting the area of a circle into the area of a square—is geometrically impossible. But, even though the mathematician draws a blank here, he is by no means excused from the task of pondering the problem. Instead, he applies all his ingenuity to the question of why this geometrical problem is ultimately unsolvable.

The same is true here. When I said that it is only with our hearts that we understand the meaning of forgiveness of sins through the blood of Jesus, and that we can die secure and at peace in that knowledge, I did not mean that we had to switch off our minds and proceed only by "faith." There is never a moment when God excuses us from thinking, much less forbids it. But he gives us subjects for our thinking which are different from those we propose to ourselves. That is the case here, for when it comes to this central theme of our faith, the subject we are to think over is: Why is the atonement a mystery of faith that we cannot clear up with our reason? Why does our thinking break down here? Paradoxically, this very question demands the most strenuous thought.

In this chapter I can make only a few suggestions about the problem. Our ability to think and to conceptualize, of course, does not begin to break down when it is confronted by the mystery of the cross; that process starts with a much earlier question. The very question of God is impossible to think through to the end.

Let me formulate the problem at issue this way: What happens when I try to think through the nature of God? If I were to review the classical solutions to this question as they appear in the history of ideas, they would lead back to two basic types.

One may say that God is holy and just. He sees to it that "on this earth all guilt is punished,"[2] as the elderly harpist in *Wilhelm*

---

[2] Johann Wolfgang von Goethe, *Wilhelm Meister's Apprenticeship and Travels* (New York: A. L. Burt, n.d.), p. 126. (Trans.)

Meister puts it, and that world history, therefore, is world judgment. Taken absolutely seriously, this attitude would mean that man is condemned to death, that he must perish for his offenses. He sets himself up in place of God and wants to transform the earth into a man-made paradise; this megalomania must end in his creating hell instead. And since we today know what technical possibilities for destruction—both biological and physical—have fallen into the hands of this self-important man, we sometimes think we catch a horrifying glimpse of what the final consequences of this conceit will be. If God is merely just, then man's experiment can end only in failure—by explosion.

The second solution to the question of God's nature seems precisely the opposite. One may say that *God is Love*. That means that whatever happens, be it the devotion of an Elsa Brandström to the care of war prisoners or the insanity of playing with atomic fire, the love of a Bodelschwingh for the epileptics or Hitler's killing the mentally ill—God encompasses it all with his everlasting arms of love. Everyone, good or bad, philanthropist or rascal, remains equally close to him. In God's love one stands above the roles of good and evil: one is the point of indifference between all contrasts. Then God becomes a giant pair of parentheses around life, and in principle no one can run afoul of him or fall out of these parentheses. But I can't warm up to this love, because it doesn't come from a *heart* that beats for me and suffers for me. This love arches over me like the coldly sparkling firmament of a winter's night, indifferent to what is happening beneath it—indifferent to marital love or adultery, to the work of a midnight mission or a holdup on Main Street. I can no longer be comforted by this love "as one whom his mother comforts." It could never be more than a way of expressing general optimism about life.

Basically, both ways of thinking about God, whether I understand him as justice or as love, come to nothing in the end.

And that is just the reason why, when it comes down to it, the message of the Bible exceeds all human thought and why the peace of God (what an odd phrase!) "passes all understanding." For here I am told something inconceivable: that God is *both*. He is just, and therefore must condemn what is unholy and sacrilegious, *and* nevertheless he has a heart full of compassionate love which would rather console than condemn and which overtakes the lost and brings them home.

This mystery of the divine heart is beyond the comprehension of our intellect. It can touch only our *own* hearts. And there, in our hearts, we quite definitely feel and experience this mystery.

Since this is such a delicate and ineffable mystery, only the language of the Bible itself is adequate to contain it. For example, the psalmist says, "God be gracious unto me according to thy goodness, and forgive my sins according to thy great mercy," and he fears that he must perish before the face of God because he cannot bear God's holiness. He must take cover as the shepherds did on Christmas Eve when the brightness of God burst upon them and they trembled to see themselves penetrated by that light. But when, faced by God's high and holy power, the psalmist thus breaks down before his eternal judge, he can still say in the same breath, "Comfort me with thy help! A broken and a contrite heart, O God, thou wilt not despise." Similar thoughts must have occupied the mind of the prodigal son there in the pigsty when he was farthest from home. (How often we come back to this parable! It is as though it always had the last word—as though it were full of "last words"). The unfortunate stray presumably said to himself, "My father is a just man. He is strict and precise, and no one puts anything over on him. I couldn't face him. When I think of his righteousness and his hallowed seriousness, I die of shame." But at the same time he thinks, "Nevertheless my father *suffers* from my misery because he loves me. He won't give me up, because I am his child. He has surely put a light in the window as a signal of his love! He is telling me I may come home!"

Thus *both* of these voices blend in the heart of the prodigal son. One says, "My father is good; I am ashamed to appear before him in my depraved condition." The other voice says, "My father is kind; I may come home." Both of these voices speak together in *our* hearts, too, but no intellectual formula can combine them. That is because my heart alone can comprehend what goes on in the heart of God.

At this point it becomes clear what the death of Jesus means to us. God himself reconciles righteousness and love. He himself steps into the breach and gives his most beloved. But what does all this mean?

What happens here may be expressed by the quite simple and yet unfathomable word, "forgive." What occurs when I forgive another person? It does not mean, as we mentioned in the previous chapter, that I can "forget" what he did to me. I just can't do that. No, when I forgive another, I myself step into the breach and say to myself, "The same thing that made the other person mean, hateful, and guilty toward me is in my heart as well. Ultimately we are two of a kind." If I tell my neighbor, "I forgive you," and I say it from the bottom of my heart, then, in a manner of speaking, I take over the burden of his guilt and place it on my own heart just as though it were mine. Then I don't tell him, "Oh well, it wasn't so bad, I don't take it seriously." No indeed, forgiveness isn't that light a matter. Rather, I say, "Yes, what you did to me was very wrong; it was even shocking. But I know from looking at myself how fickle and wicked the human heart is. Therefore I could do exactly what you did. It's coiled up in *me* too. So I'll suffer through it with you. I'll put myself in your place. I'll share your burden." When I forgive another person, I share the burden of his guilt. I become his brother and his sister, a burden-bearer at his side.

This is precisely what happens on Golgotha. In the suffering, crucified Jesus Christ, God himelf steps up beside us. He himself bears all the perils and temptations of our hearts. He takes everything human upon himself in all its doubtfulness and infirmity—suffering and anxiety, loneliness and the fear of death. He does this by taking upon himself the weight of human history and entering into finitude and forsakenness. God takes our burden upon himself because he forgives us. Golgotha hurts God.

So we are not dealing here with a cheap love that merely pretends or stretches a point.

This is the holy God, for whom our lost lives are an unspeakable hurt, and who nevertheless says Yes to us. He lets the father in him conquer the judge, and he takes our burden upon his own heart. God himself suffers there where the Crucified hangs. That is what all this means. When he cries, "My God, my God, why hast thou forsaken me?" the eternal Heart abandons itself to all the forsakenness and despair that a man suffers in his separation from God. Nothing more stands between God and me, because he has become my brother. At the bottom of every abyss he stands beside me.

God stands (or, better, Jesus Christ hangs) at the point where judgment must fall upon me. Let him who *can* understand this; I don't. But all the martyrs' songs in praise of it rise to the skies, and all who have experienced the forgiveness of their sins and through it have become new men know that it is *true*. It is a *truth* that one can live by and that can transform a person, giving him the joyful gift of a new start. You all know it, and I know it too; yet no one has comprehended it. It can be said only in a song of praise. When our intellect tries to talk about it, we begin to stammer, just as I have been doing, because what I had to say was simply too difficult.

A child can understand in his heart when his mother forgives him, even though something happens there which the wise of this world cannot explain.

Gottfried Benn quotes a very deep, although also a very heathen, phrase from Andre Malraux's *Psychology of Art:* "On the day of judgment, *statues* rather than a former way of life will be humanity's advocates before the gods." What Malraux means is that when the final judgment bursts upon mankind an advocate will be needed because mankind cannot defend itself. Malraux pleads, therefore, that the gods may not regard man in the wretchedness of his murders, lies, and base thoughts, but that instead of viewing man himself they may consider his statues. In these man presents his essence in a supreme and matchless way in which, freed from his failures, it may pass the test and count in his behalf.

In this sense, Jesus Christ is the statue of true humanity. When I have to appear at the last judgment, God will see me in him who has bound his fate with mine. We have discussed this scene of the final substitution with one another once before. When the hour of my defense comes and the eternal judge calls out my name, he will ask, "Who are you?" And before I can answer the Prosecutor will take the floor and reply, "Who is this? He is one who has done this and that. Because he has no sympathetic love, he has overlooked the loneliest colleague of his who worked right beside him. He is a slave to his ambition and has only a pitifully small amount of love for others. He has always been his own best friend. He has never noticed that people right and left of him cried for his help, for a kind word, and for just a little mercy. He has been too self-centered to be able to give that or even to begin to try."

And, when the Prosecutor says that, my whole past will rise up before me and I will have to admit that he is right, difficult and painful as that will be. For, indeed, I *am* my past. When I want to know who someone is, I certainly ask about his background, because a man truly is what he has behind him, what he accomplished and what he failed in, what he did and what he left undone. Every businessman who hires an employee asks about his background, because he instinctively says to himself, "This man is what he has been up to now." When it becomes a serious matter about what *I* have in my background—and before the eternal Judge it is awfully and inevitably serious—then there is no escape; I am at the end of my rope. I cannot avoid this identification with my past.

But then my attorney, my defender, Jesus Christ, steps forward and obtains the floor. He says, "Mr. Prosecutor, everything you have said is correct. And yet it is completely wrong, because this man no longer is what he has in his background; that is *really* behind him. I have crossed it out and taken it upon myself as *my* burden. I have blotted out the accusation and nailed it to my cross" (Col. 2:14). Then he turns to the throne of judgment. "Father and Judge, if you ask who this is, I answer that he is the one for whom I died and that I have suffered *with* him and *because* of him. I have become his brother, and he has let me adopt him. He knew that his hands were empty. He knew about his stained conscience. He knew that there was no escape from his wretchedness. And he was pleased when I said to him, 'Be clean!' He accepted my offer to bear everything for him and with him. He stood beneath my cross and said, 'I want to stay here by thee. Despise me not, I pray.' Therefore, Father, he is yours and mine, and I bring him to you now. As he has looked to me with eyes full of trust, look upon him now as my brother and let him be with me always in your peace and in your glory."

That is the miracle of transformation. I am no longer identified with my past ("I live, yet no longer I" [Gal. 2:20]); I am the companion of my Savior. Nothing can ever tear me out of his hand. Now, when anguish grasps for me, *he* takes my place with *his* anguish, and he is there with his death when I set out upon my last journey.

"Statues will be humanity's advocates before the gods"—this heathen surmise doesn't understand what it is really saying.

My being accepted by Jesus in this way means that nothing can ever tear me out of his hand. The honor of divine sonship which he thus confers upon me can never be taken away. Everything else, of course, fades away. Old age is a dreary thing for those who are looking only for beauty and charm. Those who are looking only for happiness and self-fulfillment must kill crippled thalidomide babies just because they are unfortunate. Those who care only for ability and the capacity to get things done consider the incurably insane and the mentally retarded to be unworthy of life. How dreary and dismal life becomes when we humans want to decide what is worthy and what unworthy. We Germans know where that leads—we have lived through it.

But since Another has laid his hand upon me and has bought me dearly, my life has an imperishable value. Now I am made holy through his suffering and death, so that nothing and no one else, not even I myself, may ever lay hands on me again.

In Graham Greene's novel, *The Heart of the Matter*, Police Commissioner Scobie despairs completely of himself and, oppressed by failure and his great guilt, decides to commit suicide. Then he feels compelled to enter a church, although he considers himself an unbeliever, and, even more, unworthy. As he sits there in despair and quarrels with himself, the voice of Christ chimes into his disconsolate monologue from the altar. "You say you love me, and yet you'll do this to me—rob me of you for ever. I made you with love. I've wept your tears. I've saved you from more than you will ever know. I planted in you this longing for peace only so that one day I could satisfy your longing and watch your happiness. And now you push me away."[3]

But Scobie cannot push him away, because he who became his Savior holds him fast. And if even then he committed the great sin of casting this dearly won life away in despair, this One would still remain true to him in the uttermost reaches of hell. Where we are too weak or too much in despair to reach out for the eternal hands, they hold us fast and catch us when we stumble. They reach out to us as they did to Peter when he was sinking into the waves. They reach out to us even when we do not keep faith with ourselves and when everyone else forsakes us. They cradle my head when I can no longer do anything but groan, lost to all the human sounds which still reach me. Death itself dare not come between us. I am that safely in his possession.

I have been given a security that shelters me now amid all turmoil and that will still be with me in the future when the Eternal Judge lays his robe aside and tells me as my Father, "Well done, good and faithful servant . . . enter into the joy of your master."

> Here I will stand beside Thee,
> From Thee I will not part;
> O Savior, do not chide me!
> When breaks Thy loving heart,
> When soul and body languish
> In death's last fatal grasp,
> Then, in Thy deepest anguish,
> Thee in mine arms I'll clasp.
> [No. 201, *ELHB*.]

---

[3] (New York: Viking Press, 1948), p. 289.

DESCENDED INTO HELL

"There was a rich man, who was clothed in purple and fine linen and who feasted sumptuously every day. And at his gate lay a poor man named Lazarus, full of sores, who desired to be fed with what fell from the rich man's table; moreover the dogs came and licked his sores. The poor man died and was carried by the angels to Abraham's bosom. The rich man also died and was buried; and in Hades, being in torment, he lifted up his eyes, and saw Abraham far off and Lazarus in his bosom. And he called out, 'Father Abraham, have mercy upon me, and send Lazarus to dip the end of his finger in water and cool my tongue; for I am in anguish in this flame.' But Abraham said, 'Son, remember that you in your lifetime received your good things, and Lazarus in like manner evil things; but now he is comforted here, and you are in anguish. And besides all this, between us and you a great chasm has been fixed, in order that those who would pass from here to you may not be able, and none may cross from there to us.' And he said, 'Then I beg you, father, to send him to my father's house, for I have five brothers, so that he may warn them, lest they also come into this place of torment.' But Abraham said, 'They have Moses and the prophets; let them hear them.' And he said, 'No, father Abraham; but if some one goes to them from the dead, they will repent.' He said to him, 'If they do not hear Moses and the prophets, neither will they be convinced if some one should rise from the dead.' "

—Luke 16:19–31

It is easy to argue about heaven. There are many unsolved questions, among them these: Is what we call heaven included in a great Beyond where we shall find a fulfillment that we have been denied during our earthly life? Or is this hope of a great Beyond merely the cowardly excuse of those who hesitate to face social misery or to help hungry children in India here and now? Doesn't this view seem to lead to a refined soul-strategy—to comfort the unfortunate with a great Beyond when one is not ready to help them here and now (where they are in trouble!)? Can't revolutionaries be kept down and uprisings prevented by feeding people with such hopes?

We should ask, in fact, whether heaven has not actually had to put up with being used again and again to stupefy the masses, diverting them from this world and drugging them with illusions. It is not at all difficult to understand why militant Marxism is so critical of so-called Christianity and why it promises the losers and the exploited an earthly paradise instead of heaven. We know what enthusiasm its claims can produce: "We are bringing the heavenly great Beyond to you on earth. We don't put you off with hopes; we act. We don't feed you with the opium of heavenly illusions; we give you bread you can eat right now."

No wonder millions bite. And yet, on reflection, it is true that many who have promised heaven on earth have in reality made the earth into a hell. Time and again the promised paradises turn into dictatorships of terror.

As we said, it is easy to argue about heaven. It is a favorite topic of discussion. The idea of *hell*, however, seems to be painful and even proves fatal to discussion. Didn't Nietzsche have some justification for criticizing the terror which Christianity awakened when it played upon men's imaginations with threats of infernal fire, glowing pincers, and eternal pain? If earthly authorities time and again utilize the false hope of heaven as a trick, then isn't the threat of hell its negative side, so to speak? Doesn't this terror of the Beyond help clerical authorities who try to throw *their* saddle over people?

And that is not the only painful criticism to which we find ourselves subjected. Other criticisms arise from the fact that the word "hell" sounds so horribly mythological to us. Some time ago, when a magazine asked, "Is fire burning in hell?" it was sure of eliciting mischievous grins from millions of readers. Even inferior intellects convinced themselves that they were infinitely above that sort of superstition. Where could this place of torment be located geographically, anyway? Geophysics has taught even the unlearned that no metaphysical secrets are to be drawn out of the center of the earth.

Those with a more profound knowledge, even convinced Christians, also have their misgivings. Doesn't it sound strange when Jesus, of all people, talks about hellfire (Matt. 5:22) and says that weeping and gnashing of teeth will someday seize the loveless and the unrighteous (Matt. 22:13)? And what about his speaking of a frightful time when we must render an account of our lives and answer for what we have done (Matt. 12:36; 25:19; etc.)?

Isn't the idea of a twofold result of history—and especially of an eternal damnation that is final and irrevocable—simply inconsistent with a God of love and with a Savior who sacrifices himself for the lost? Wouldn't a happy ending to all the fuss and confusion of our life be much more in keeping with the basic theme of a religion of love?

Question after question—not for those who simply turn up their noses and walk away, but for those who are determined to listen and take things seriously. Is it really supposed to be a binding article of faith, then, when the official confession of the church does a monstrous thing like permitting Jesus Christ and hell to occur together in *one* sentence, "He descended into hell"?

If we take that statement seriously, instead of rattling it off in a conventional way, we must think those questions through. No one can get off so cheaply that he can say merely, "You just have to 'believe' that." On the contrary, I would set up the opposite thesis. *You ought never to believe something that you dare not think over.* The "mystery" that we run into in this thinking comes soon enough. But we dare not allow this mystery to become an excuse for the lazy, the unreflecting, or those who are "pious" in a cheap sense.

We can quickly dispose of what we just termed the "mythological" side of the matter. It is obvious that we can speak about what lies beyond our world of experience only by means of imagery and analogies. And every intelligent person knows that all analogies break down. How much more, then, must earthly images of things that are *not* of this world lead to distorted perspectives! Thus, hell is represented as a sort of spatiotemporal condition, but this conception belongs to the realm of imagery and not to the thing itself. As far back as Luther the conception of hell as a geographical place drew sarcastic remarks: "I think very little of the idea that there is supposed to be a special place where the damned souls are now, as the painters portray it and the belly-servers preach it."

And to precisely the same extent that it is impossible to localize hell, it is also impossible to name the dates at which it begins for us. Hell is certainly not relegated solely to the time *after* death or *after* the last judgment. It can draw us into its demonic field of force here and now, as Luther liked to emphasize. For hell is separation from God in all its forms. It is ultimate forsakenness.

Anyone who loses his grip on life and no longer finds sense in it falls into the bottomless pit and knows what hell is. But the loss of the one dearest to me, the final torments of multiple sclerosis, the sight of a brutally murdered child—all this need not be hell as long as I hold on to the fatherly hand which reaches out to me in my darkness. But if in my pain I also find no sense in holding on to the hand of that One who *can* make sense out of things and whose "higher thoughts" I can trust, then the burden of outer and inner torment can reach the critical point where it becomes a hell. For the terrifying thing about hell is not the blisters one gets from the alleged fire there. The real terror comes from being completely cast off without hope and from being devoured by the pangs of a conscience that knows no forgiveness. When the murderous King Claudius in *Hamlet* tries in vain to pray, he cannot break the evil spell of his own burning conscience. So he cries out, "Pray can I not." In this line Shakespeare has described hell exactly, and, in general, he shows an uncommon understanding of this dimension of torment.

Thus the essential part of the article of faith concerning hell is not what happens after death. That is, at most, a *part* of the condition of being cast off, which is the *real* concern. If it is only a matter of a posthumous sequel to my unsuccessful life, then it is all fairly harmless and need not disturb me right now. Why worry about tomorrow? Why worry about a future so distant that, if grammarians talk about "perfect" and "pluperfect" for

the past, they would have to call that future a "plu-future."
Today is today, and, after all, I'm still alive and kicking. There
will still be time enough after the second stroke to make peace
with God and cheat the devil of his prey.

But it is quite remarkable—and this is also true of other doctrines—that the Bible never speaks of future things as though
they were *only* in the future. The future consistently encompasses the present moment of my life and irradiates it.

If Jesus really should come again someday "to judge the quick
and the dead," (just for the sake of argument) wouldn't everything I experience now literally look different to me? Perhaps at
the moment nothing seems more important to me than getting a
car or working out my love affair or pulling off the big deal I
keep dreaming about. But if Christ is coming again one day (just
for the sake of argument), then all such standards of value as
"important" and "unimportant" change. Whatever currently
feeds my burning passion like oxygen and sweeps me along with
it may then seem like a bubble to me. Then it may no longer
seem a goal, but precisely the thing that distracts me from my
goal. The coming glory that the message of the Bible proclaims
throws its shadow far back and touches me in *this* moment. It
does not take until Christmas Eve for a child who is waiting for
Christmas to be filled with joy. The waiting permeates him and
cheers him and gives him wings long before Christmas arrives.
He who is permitted to know that his redemption draws near lifts
up his head right away, and he can laugh without fear when
others run for cover.

When we talk about hell in its negative aspects, the same relationship holds true.

If there really were such a possibility of absolute failure and
rejection (only for the sake of argument), then I would get a
whiff of this terror here and now. It would become an actuality
that could change my life, and it wouldn't require anything as
sadistic as being grilled on an infernal rotisserie to do it. For me
the crucial thing is to realize that we face the possiblity of that
failure and the irrevocable loss of our life's purpose *now*. We

tread the edge of the deadly crater *now*. I want to attempt to make my meaning clear in a few logical steps.

First, however, an objection could be raised along the following lines: All conceptions of hell have two things in common. First, they imply that a person has *finally* forfeited his salvation, that he has been thrown out of the father's house *once and for all* and has been doomed to eternal exile. Second, they imply that this condition may be described as one of suffering and torment. But (this sort of objection might continue) *that* is just the point at which all conceptions of hell are vulnerable. For separation from God isn't torment at all; at least, it doesn't have to be.

In fact, there seem to be very impressive illustrations of this lack of torment. All told, very few people seek out the presence of God. By far the majority of mankind isn't the least bit interested in God. God's party members are a splinter group, and even those who gather in a large church on Sunday are only a fraction of those whom the church is to serve. But the people who go for a drive on Sunday morning without the slightest prayer don't feel that their separation from God is torment *at all!* On the contrary, they enjoy themselves immensely. And if they give any thought at all to divine things, it is at best a regret that there are people who are plagued by the fear of an imagined hell or lifted by longing for heaven, who huddle between gloomy walls on Sunday instead of letting the spring breezes waft about their ears.

Everyone who thinks that way certainly doesn't *suffer* because of his separation from God. This separation is no hell at all for him, nor is it any torment.

Isn't that really a very serious objection to the doctrine of hell? The concept of hell does conceive of torment and separation from God as one and the same condition, although it now develops that they don't necessarily belong together at all. Men can be supremely happy in their separation from God, and atheists even believe that they have found true life at last and have liberated themselves from the tormenting guilt complexes of those still bound by religion.

I have purposely developed this objection somewhat because when we think it through it can lead us to hell's deepest mystery.

In many respects, this objection is well taken. In the "springtime of our sins" we can actually be supremely happy in our separation from God (and, on the other hand, Christians who talk about God all the time can frequently be classed as sourpussed killjoys). That is because we can actually overlook God in our life without ever becoming clear about what we lose when we lose him. For at present God is making himself known in a word that we can ignore without being disturbed. At present he is speaking only to our faith, and we can refuse that. But one day the moment will come—as I have expressed it before—when we *may* see what we have believed, and when we *must* see what we have *not* believed. From this point of view, hell is simply the situation in which we must recognize God as God without being able to come to him. As long as I don't know that from which I have been cut off, the separation really causes me no anguish. What I don't know doesn't hurt me, and *whom* I don't know leaves me indifferent. But to have to look at the spring of life without being able to drink from it—that hurts! That is to suffer the torment of an exile from which there is no return.

No one has expressed this state of an unalterable past with more terror and depth than Christopher Marlowe, the creator of modern English tragedy. In Marlowe's *Doctor Faustus*, which Goethe admired so much, Faust asks his infernal companion, Mephistopheles, how he managed to get out of hell and work his mischief on earth, since Mephistopheles was to have been bound eternally in hell and imprisoned there. Mephistopheles answers Faust with a confession of his background:

> Why, this is hell, nor am I out of it.
> Think'st thou that I, who saw the face of God,
> And tasted the eternal joys of heaven,
> Am not tormented with ten thousand hells,
> In being depriv'd of everlasting bliss?[1]

Isn't this the same ironic rejection of the idea that hell is a place where people will be chained fast? Hell is not a place; Mephisto-

[1] *The Plays of Christopher Marlowe* (London: Oxford University Press, 1961), p. 160, ll. 316–20.

pheles takes it with him wherever he goes. He carries it within himself, even when he takes his excursions into earthly existence. He has the wretchedness of Lucifer, the fallen angel, who saw God himself and sipped from the heavenly cup of joy. Therefore he *knows* what he lost when he cut himself off from God. Hell means having to know what one has forfeited once and for all. It means not being able to dispel this knowledge by rubbing our eyes in the hope that it will go away. Hell is being sadder but wiser about a wrong decision that cannot be changed. It is being sadder but wiser about lost stakes after the game is over.

Now, that is actually an allusion to the *future* nature of hell, for it is really possible for me to escape hell "now" as long as I repress the question of my salvation. But the moment will come when repression is impossible and I must face up to what I have not believed.

In the same way, the parable of the rich man and the poor beggar Lazarus shows us how the question of "eternal blessedness" and "eternal rejection" leads from the distant Beyond into the midst of our present life. It is really astonishing how this parable merely sketches in the future situation with what we might call dotted lines or elusive images which neither can nor even should be seized upon. What is "Abraham's bosom," anyway? What is the "place of torment"? That is anything but a geography of the Beyond! The real point of the parable lies somewhere else. It lies in the fate of the five brothers who are so occupied with the activity and epicurean comforts of their life's unsuspecting joyride that they don't even notice they have reached a crossroads where they must choose. One way leads to eternal and blessed fellowship with God; the other ends in God's announcement, "I know you not, for you, on your part, have not known me when you met me, when I called to you in my word, when I gave my most precious possession for you and suffered on your account, and when I came to you in your imprisoned, hungry, and naked neighbor."

"But just you wait. Wait for the first quarter-of-an-hour's silence," writes Georges Bernanos in his novel, *Diary of a Country Priest*. "Then the Word will be heard of men—not the voice they rejected, which spoke so quietly: 'I am the Way, the Resurrection and the Life'—but the voice from the depths: 'I am the door forever locked, the road which leads nowhere, the lie, the everlasting dark.' "[2]

The five brothers face this decision. We all face this decision. We ought to know what freight the decisive hour of our life is carrying. We are neither on a random trip nor on a pleasurable stroll in the sunshine of a "loving God" where nothing can happen to us.

On the contrary, something *can* happen to us. We can miss the point of our life. One day it can all be lost. God is not to be mocked, and in no event can he be toyed with. His love is not a banal life insurance policy, but a miracle that snatches us away from the catastrophe into which we are about to stumble. It is the miracle of the everlasting arms into which we may let ourselves fall, to which we *must* entrust ourselves if the abyss is to have no power over us.

So then, hell is like an alarm which is to make clear the seriousness of the decision for us. The decision is something that can be missed, and that then effects a separation. We can gamble our life away. We can miss its point. We can live in vain. This is an open possibility.

Woe to those who make light of this seriousness and dare to talk about mythology and chimeras. Those who deny this possibility of darkness on the horizon of our life have not somehow liberated us from an illusion but have accomplished precisely the opposite. They have made our life itself into an illusion, a joyride without a goal. They would have us, like the "Titanic," travel across the ocean with eating and drinking, celebrating and merriment, never suspecting the iceberg that will mortally wound us and send us to the bottom.

If we recognize and take seriously the fact that faith is something other than a religious form of optimism—that it has dark and frightening edges and that it involves the question of winning or losing one's life—then really it is no longer so difficult to

[2] Trans. Pamela Morris (New York: Image Books, 1954), p. 16.

conceive that the figure of Jesus Christ has to be placed in some relation to that dark power we call hell. For the fact that I have a savior certainly cannot mean—as I have already indicated—that "now nothing can happen to me," that missing the point of my life is out of the question, and that the possibility of an eternal defeat is excluded. If that were the case, then the savior would become a trite and harmless symbol, a figure who would guarantee a happy ending. Cross, blood, and tears would then suit him no longer. He would become the figurehead on the gaily lighted ship of our life on which we could eat, drink, and be merry as it bore us safely to a distant goal—while, as the Högveld book paints it, beasts of prey might prowl along the banks.

Our life is not an innocent pleasure cruise like that. If it were, there would have been no need for the sacrifice on Golgotha by which the man of sorrows had to save us.

On the other hand, it is just when we think of Christ that it becomes almost unbearable that there should be such a dismal place of defeat and torment, a place which his saving arms cannot reach and from which lost souls call to him in vain.

So it is no wonder that the thoughts of faith come back again and again to this problem of "savior and hell." The image of Christ's descent into hell represents an attempt to express this mystery.

Some, especially Calvinists, intended to say in this way that Jesus even took upon himself the extreme humiliation of stooping to solidarity with the lost and becoming *their* brother, too. Didn't he cry out from the cross, "My God, my God, why hast thou forsaken me?" Here, in the last hour of his life, hadn't he already taken upon himself the uttermost darkness of the godforsaken? Didn't he expose himself to the despair of nothingness so that even on the bottommost level of soul torment he could be *with* us to hold us by the hand? We sense what it means to journey from Golgotha to hell, and we sense what love and self-forgetting sacrifice it bespeaks. The Heidelberg Catechism answers the question about why Christ went down to hell in this way: "That in my severest tribulations I may be assured that Christ my Lord has redeemed me from hellish anxieties and torment by the unspeakable anguish, pains, and terrors which he suffered in his soul both on the cross and before."[3]

Others, especially Lutherans, have interpreted the image of the descent into hell as picturing Jesus Christ bursting in upon even the darkest regions as victor and conqueror. As Luther said in his sermon at Torgau in 1533, he "went in and captured the colors like a conquering hero, flinging open the doors and rummaging around among the devils so that one fell out through a window and another through a hole in the wall." Here, with a touch of that Christian humor which is in itself an attitude of having overcome the world, we enjoy the drama as that One from whom neither death nor demonic powers can separate us takes control and dispels even the deepest darkness. And behind this scene the image of the Crucified appears, not as one who is humiliated and dishonored, but as Christ the king ruling from the cross.

These interpretations—and there are many, many others—do not contradict one another. They are more accurately described as complementing each other. They must be understood as a multicolored print; this is the only possible way to let the meaning shine out in all its fullness and brilliance.

Who could dare to say that all this is an unreal myth? Who would not have to confess (provided he understood a little of all this) that something we can build our life on happened here? Perhaps we might describe this event by saying that what has been expressed in pictures is so *different* from our "normal" reality that we simply cannot describe it by our earthly concepts. Yet it is so real that we cannot avoid trying to zero in on it with precisely those earthly images and similes.

By means of such suggestive, parabolic language, the New Testament goes on to point out one last idea which lies right at the limit of those things that can still be said at all. That is, it says that the gospel is proclaimed even to the inhabitants of the realm of the dead (I Pet. 4:6) and that Jesus himself pressed this far with his liberating word.

[3] *The Heidelberg Catechism* (Philadelphia: United Church Press, 1962), p. 46.

I said that this statement lay at the limits of possibility for saying anything at all, and I must briefly explain what I mean by that. For us men, the span of life between birth and death is the time in which we hear the call of God and must make up our minds. This time is the limited period within which everything that matters happens. It is the limited period in which we, like the five brothers in the parable, stand at the crossroads where we can win or lose everything. We dare not dawdle away the hours, for we have no assurance that this period can be prolonged, or that there is anything like a remedial course in the Beyond. The rich man knew what he was doing when he implored Abraham to tell his five brothers, "Your time is running out." The only way to reach God is to take him seriously when he calls. "Today (today!), when you hear my voice, harden not your hearts."

But perhaps God has still other ways of getting to *us*, ways that, as men, we do not have at our disposal. Perhaps *he* yet has ways, beyond death and beyond our limited period, to reach those who did not hear his call—those who lived before Christ (wasn't he a latecomer in history?) and those millions who even today live beyond the range of his word. We simply cannot understand that what is the word of life for *us* should be held back from others and should act as a judgment of damnation on those who did not hear it in their earthly lives. Is the Savior who said of himself, "No man comes to the father but by me" to mean exclusion, judgment, and a barred door to the millions in Russia and Asia who do not know him?

If our meditations on the love of Jesus and his immeasurable mercy are diverted into such agonizing and enervating thoughts, then this most enigmatic of all statements should ring out to us: "For *you* to whom the word of salvation has been spoken, it is true that death forms the final limit to your decision; and I will even take to heart the last sigh of the dying when he says, 'God be merciful to me, a sinner.' For me, however, the Lord over both the living and dead, no limit exists, so that my mercy may prevail. And I know how to find even the dead who call to me: all those who prayed to false gods because they didn't know me, and who now have been forsaken by their fetishes and idols; all those who were carried off in their childhood and died prematurely; and even the atheists who were withdrawn from my word or who heard only a distorted caricature of it. My mercy has no end. Even death cannot limit it. I cannot let the lost souls go. My suffering was great enough to make up for them, too."

Have I succeeded, despite this obscurest of all subjects, in making clear that even hell and Christ's descent into hell are no more than the dark reflector behind the burning light of joy and mercy and the message of salvation? No matter how distant the region we penetrate with our thoughts, no matter how oppressive the desert—even hell and the kingdom of death—we always encounter the glory of Jesus, welcoming us and offering us security. "If I ascend to heaven, thou art there! If I make my bed in Sheol, thou art there! (Ps. 139:8)." What looks like capture one minute —the fact that we aren't able to escape him—turns out to be an unspeakable comfort. For we are surrounded and encircled by a love which is anxious for us and will not let us go. It wants to gather us under its wings as a hen does her chicks.

Thus even the most difficult thoughts, thoughts that sometimes lead to the very borders of conceivability, end in the simplest and most straightforward pictures just like those in children's prayers.

> Children of the heavenly Father
> Safely in his bosom gather. . . .[4]

That is basically all we need to learn. In the shelter of those arms, we are no longer frightened of even the darkest mystery, for we see everything from the vantage of our place of refuge. From the harbor we look out to the tossing sea, and from our Father's house to the far country. The peace of God surpasses all understanding, even the *believing* understanding. A very well-known and prominent lady once told me a story about her eight-year-old son, who—as is sometimes the case with children—was very taken up with the question of heaven and hell. As he sat at table, he said to a diplomat whom he had embroiled in a dispute on this

---

[4] No. 572, *Service Book and Hymnal of the Lutheran Church in America* (1958). Hereafter cited as *SBH*. (Trans.)

point, "I don't believe that there is a hell, and Daddy and Mamma don't believe it either." Bringing the very prominent parents into the picture put the diplomat in a predicament, yet he didn't want to back down, so he took the childish tone of his little table companion as he replied, "But if there is no hell, where shall the bad people go?" Then the little prince said, "The bad people go to paradise too, but with sad hearts."

These matters really can be said just that simply. For the little man belonged to those children out of whose mouths God has brought himself praise. The sad heart that has seen God and can no longer come to him—that, and only that, is hell.

But we live in the acceptable time, in the hour of promise, and the door to the wedding feast is open. However, we would not take seriously its being a door if it didn't dawn on us that not we but someone else had charge of the keys, and that the door could be locked if we neglected to enter before closing time.

AN ADDITIONAL QUESTION: WHERE ARE THE DEAD?

> But our commonwealth is in heaven, and from it we await a Savior, the Lord Jesus Christ, who will change our lowly body to be like his glorious body, by the power which enables him even to subject all things to himself.   —*Philippians 3:20–21*

As we spoke about hell in the last section, we repeatedly ran into the question of death and of what happens to us beyond the grave. I would like to continue this discussion by talking about the nature of death and the question of survival after it occurs.

Isn't the rhythm of the seasons—the succession of spring, summer, autumn, and winter—a portrait of life itself? What dies in winter rises to new life in the spring, reaches the fullness of summer, and finally comes to fruition in the autumn. Then the round begins over again, and the rhythm of death and resurrection repeats itself in an eternal cycle. Isn't that also the law of our human life and its successive generations?

We know how obvious this parallel has always been. And yet we must ask if this is not where the big lie, our common self-deception, begins.

I read a characteristic experience in the diary of a young flyer who later lost his life in the First World War. He stood in fascination before a lilac bush in full bloom. As he separated the branches, he caught sight of the half-decayed body of a soldier. Why did he recoil in horror? He had long been accustomed to the sight of the dead; that could hardly have upset him. But in his decay that dead man formed an unbearable contrast to the blooming natural beauty which had just touched the young man. If he had found broken-off and wilted flowers lying thick beneath the lilac, he would not have been shocked. He wouldn't even have been surprised. For in fact they would only have signified two stages of the same life process. One was an indication of the upward rhythm, the other of the downward. But in this case a contradiction that didn't seem to fit any natural formula cried out to him. At any rate, that was his spontaneous impression. The dead man lay outside the natural framework.

Although the young flyer could not give the deeper reason for his reaction, it was nevertheless peculiarly close to what the New Testament knows about human death. The New Testament does not understand death simply as a "part of nature," a merely physical process of dissolution. Death appears there as the very personification of what is unnatural and as precisely what should *not* be. That is certainly one of the meanings of the narratives about Jesus raising the dead. They are a sort of protest against human death, against death as the "last" enemy. They are the portentous flashes of the promise that even this last enemy shall someday be conquered.

In this case, death is understood as nothing less than a foreign body in God's creation. In fact, God's plan for creation contained nothing about simply letting the robber called Death come in and rupture the bonds of love, nothing about requiring separation and the breaking off of relationships in which our hearts experienced the innermost fulfillment of love. And it contained nothing about allowing mass graves and violent defeats, nothing about the premature death of infants, and nothing about our being senselessly snatched away.

The puzzling presence of this stranger, Death, in the midst of creation can also be felt by men whose outlook is quite worldly. Thus the psychiatrist Alfred Hocke once wrote in his book *Annual Rings,* "It is a strange spectacle that man, who knows that the cessation of every life around him is an irrevocable law of perishability, finds it so difficult to resign his own person to it. He carries about within himself an intensely subjective world which lives only once in this form. It seems unbearable to him that this world is to be simply wiped out. It is unbearable simply to collapse beside the road while the others continue, chattering as though nothing had happened. The power of this feeling defies logic."

What Hocke here designates as an "unbearable feeling" points up the fact that in the death of a man something happens that is beyond nature and therefore cannot be explained naturally. Who has ever heard that a law of nature—even that of growth and decay—was unbearable and that it defied the grasp of its own logic? Then what *is* there in our dying that goes beyond nature and lies "outside" it?

Paul made the puzzling statement that death is the "wages of sin" (Rom. 6:23). This statement strikes us as surprising because a completely nonbiological concept, sin—separation from God—is utilized here to cast light on the mystery of death. One would like to ask if we aren't confusing two viewpoints which are simply incongruous and which in fact have nothing at all to do with one another. Then what does Paul intend to say when he relates sin and death to one another in this odd confusion of categories? Paul is alluding here to events which are familiar to us through the narrative of the Fall. When Adam and Eve take the forbidden fruit, that means that they have broken into God's sovereign territory. They have therefore exceeded their "human limitations"; they have wanted to be "super" men, grasping for an illegal equality with God. Since they thus exalt themselves to limitlessness—the old Promethean drive is at work here—and since they enter the forbidden territory of the eternal, they are pushed back behind the barrier of temporality, and once again, with underlined significance, they are linked to the perishable "dust" from which they were made. They are thus sent back behind the border of their finitude, and Death is set on this border as a watchman. Therefore, *amid* the cycle of the biological process, *amid* the dissolution of the organism and the disintegration of the cells, something shows itself to be quite different from a merely physical process; an event between God and man is signified there. In the infirmity of his dying, this man learns that he is *only* a man, that he is a frail creature, and that he still is separated from God's eternity by a gaping grave.

Thus in our death God has erected a sign that we are only *men* and not *gods*. The very Promethean man who flies through the cosmic void in a space capsule and is sometimes prompted to exult in his similarity to God—this man ends in a narrow grave, and the thousands who stood cheering along his triumphal route must remain behind when he faces the last gateway alone and empty-handed.

Modern man sees anything as technically possible. Isn't he precisely the one who needs this reminder of his true nature? I think how Justinus Kerner, the poet who wrote "The Prophetess of Prevorst," displayed a premonition of the technical age long before it dawned. He it was who stressed so strongly that death was the barrier of temporality made visible, behind which the eternal judge sent the modern Prometheus, who thought all things were possible and who greedily grasped them to himself.

> Rush on, Mankind, as fast as you can,
> From steamship to airship,
> Flying with eagle and lightning!
> You shall get no farther than the tomb.

There are still other important indications which prove the uniqueness of our human dying as compared with the natural "end" of animals. We men—and we alone!—actually *know* about our death. We know that a certain length of time is meted out to us and that our lifetime is limited. Thus Hoelderlin can write:

> The woodland birds breathe freer
> Though man's breast swells more grandly.
> And he who sees the future dim must also
> see death and fear only him.

Since that is so, and since we know about this limited time when we are still young, the concern about death is not just the terror of our "last hour" or the somewhat frightening question of what will happen in the death throes when we take leave of our life. Will we sink into nothingness or stand before our judge? If it were only the last hour that concerned us, then obviously only *old* people would be interested in death, and *they* would be interested only because they were getting very close to it and their imaginations would naturally be occupied by the hour of departure. Strictly speaking, these questions are not at all involved in what Hoelderlin says about our moving toward our death knowingly and with open eyes.

But in our modern poetry and philosophy, from Rilke to Heidegger, there runs a quite different type of knowledge about death. We know that we are finite and that our life resembles a one-way street which continually presses toward a destination without offering any chance to turn around. That we know for sure, and we take it into account, too, when we are still young and unconcerned, even if we don't indulge in any philosophical speculations on the matter. For example, when we rush to complete a task, we do it because time "flies." This idiom—"time flies"—is very revealing.[1] Or think of the anxiety of a young person who, in his desire to "get with" everything that youth has to offer, doesn't want to miss anything or let anything happen without him. The knowledge of death looms behind the knowledge of fleeting youth, as it also looms behind the common at-

---

[1] The parallel with death is even stronger in German, where "die Zeit vergeht" could be translated, "time passes away." (Trans.)

tempt to conserve youth forcibly by those who want to avoid aging at all costs. "Life's a fleeting shadow." One knows from the very beginning of a sentence that it rushes toward a final period.

And this brings up another intuition which we are certainly too prone to forget. Our life unfolds in a one-way span of time which is bounded by birth and death. For just this reason the image of the rhythm of the seasons that I mentioned at the beginning doesn't fit. That rhythm repeats itself over and over. It runs in a cycle, curving back on itself time and again.

But our life is quite different. Nothing that we have once experienced repeats itself. We ourselves do not repeat, once the end of the line has been reached. One might say that we walk down a long corridor with many doors that have no knobs on the other side. We cannot retrace our steps or revise what we have done or have failed to do. So we must go on, dragging our past along with us, holding our IOUs in our hands, and adding more notes to them as we proceed. That is also the reason that "coping with the past" becomes a problem—in fact, a problem that remains fundamentally unsolvable.

In this situation, then, Jesus Christ suddenly becomes relevant. For Jesus is not the conqueror of death simply because he helps us over death's border and then reveals eternal life to us in the fact that *he* will not depart from us when *we* must finally depart. No, Christ has already conquered death by loosing the fetters which bind us to our past. When he tells me, "Your sins are forgiven," he erases everything that I have not coped with in my life, in all that I have behind me. It no longer belongs to me. Then at once the moment arrives when I can say, "Now I may begin my journey anew, for the One over whom death has no power has made himself known to me. He who will change my lowly body to be like his glorious body has taken me by the hand." Now I can enjoy the present moment of my life in calmness and composure. I no longer have to feel burdened by what is past: the false starts I have made, the things which I owed and for which I became guilty, everything that I didn't carry through on, and everything that I still haven't mastered. There is One who waved it all away with a commanding sweep of his hand. He tells me, "Nothing can separate you from me. I have taken this burden of yours upon *my* shoulders. I have suffered *with* you and *for* you in this way, and for precisely this reason you are dear to me and I love you."

Just as he has taken the burden of my past, he also bears the burden of my future. Certainly there are still many times when I catch myself going virtually out of my mind with worry and alarm for my future. I ask myself what will become of me and my children. What lies ahead for my nation? Will it collapse because of inner weakness? Really, there are plenty of specters creeping out of the future toward me and reaching out for me. The last of these specters is death itself. But when He against whom death lost its power declares himself on my side, then I know that nothing that has not passed his censorship can reach me. The more anxieties torment me, the more I have to "cast on him" ("Cast all your anxieties on him" [I Pet. 5:7].) And by referring all this to him, I am bound more and more closely to him. Again and again he has the opportunity to reassert himself as conqueror and to become lord of my life.

Thus he transforms everything I entrust to his hands. Finally, he transforms even death. I no longer need to remain artificially young, holding tight to the past with stiffening fingers. Now I can grow old with confidence. Now I know that he holds his surprises and gifts ready at every moment of life, not merely for children, but for the elderly as well. Where death and finitude once seemed to be only painful departure, loss, and negation, they now have become victory and homecoming. For now I know *who* awaits me on the other side, calling me to eternal fellowship with him. Now I can say—and, heaven knows, it is no pious phrase—"From hence I go with gladness to Christ my Brother's side,/That I may soon be with Him and e'er with Him abide" [No. 529, *ELHB*].

Although that is all very comforting (at least for me, since I still travel on that part of the road that lies between birth and death) a difficult question still remains. This question overtakes us sometimes at a newly dug grave or even in a quiet hour when our gaze wanders over the pictures of our loved ones—sons, fathers, and husbands—whom we lost on the battlefield or in air raids, or who were taken from us by sickness or accident. Where shall we seek our dead? Where are they? The love that wistfully wants to follow in the footsteps of the dead is too strong to let this question drop. Perhaps, though, this question has actually been put in the wrong way. If so, no answer is possible. The puzzle cannot be solved. Then we shall have to see to it that we are delivered from the agony of this question. And in fact that is the case. Yet let it stand for a moment just as the childlike impulse of our hearts has posed it.

What, then, happens to the people we have loved when they close their eyes? What will one day happen to *us*? Will we sink into a black night until the last trumpet calls us forth from the tomb?

Luther said on occasion that we shouldn't let our thoughts dwell too much on such insoluble questions. Quite simply, the situation is like this: The dead are called out of this time scheme, while time continues to run for us who remain. Therefore we cannot conceive of the manner of their existence in death. It is like sleeping—dreams don't hold to the normal course of time, either. We may awake from a long sleep knowing nothing of the time which has elapsed. So it is with the sleep of the dead which ends at the last day. When we shall be awakened, this intervening period shall have disappeared in a moment; when the last trumpet shall someday burst open our tombs, we shall think that we have just fallen asleep. Only those who remain behind, imprisoned in the world of time, see the intervening period as a lengthy one.

Then it all seems to turn out to be amazingly simple. What happens after death is no longer a problem. Yet this solution doesn't satisfy us in the least. Despite everything, we would ask with the hymn if "the night of death be fraught still with many an anxious thought" [No. 220, *ELHB*]. It *does* make us wonder. Are our dead alone in this night, or are they in glory? When one of my dearest students was killed in the war, I heard his father pray, "If it is possible, greet him for me." I have never forgotten that prayer. In completely childlike inner faith, without any prying, the father was asking where to look for his son.

It is both noteworthy and thought-provoking that the Bible hardly mentions what happens after death. Certainly there must be a reason for that. As a rule, it mentions only what directly concerns us. We are forbidden to ask even the anxious question about "tomorrow," to say nothing of the day after tomorrow when we will wake from the sleep of death! Everything is focused on *today* as the acceptable time; everything centers on the present moment. "Today, when you hear my voice, harden not your hearts."

As the father of the great theologian Adolf Schlatter lay dying, pious friends stood around his bed seeking to comfort him with reassuring and edifying thoughts. "Soon you'll be in the golden halls of Zion, gazing across the crystal sea. Soon radiance from the throne of the Lamb will surround you." And so they talked, giving free rein to pious fantasies which they drew from the venerable images of the Bible. Then the dying man raised himself up and snapped, "Don't bother me with that piffle! I want only to embrace the Father." For him, the only image that mattered was that of the Father receiving the prodigal son.

Schlatter's dying father put his finger right on the essential point. He didn't want to know anything about a heavenly "milieu"—about the scenery in the great Beyond or about the streets of Zion. What mattered to him was that he was secure in the Father and that he would find the peaceful place his Lord and Savior had prepared for him.

That is precisely the sort of questioning and viewpoint for which the Bible wants to condition us. The only thing that matters is the certainty that the fellowship with Jesus Christ to which we have been admitted cannot be broken by anyone or anything—not even by death. One must recall the powerful language of the Bible, its words of great certainty: that neither death nor life may separate me from the love which has once and for all bound me to itself; that in life and death we are the Lord's; and that we have a habitation in heaven when the hut of our earthly life falls into ruin. "Could the Head rise and leave his members dead?" So runs a Christian's hymn of triumph over death. [No. 220, *ELHB.*]

This *one* comforting thought constantly recurs: the faithfulness of God, enfolding us and drawing us to him, never ends. There is not a moment, not even the moment of death, when that faithfulness can be interrupted.

Therefore our immortality does not lie with *us*. It does not consist in the indestructability of a soul-spark that decay and death cannot touch—that would be a dream by which we would try to push away the hard reality of death. Instead, our immortality and our immunity, our invulnerability against the last enemy consists *only in that faithfulness* that does not let us go. Luther could say, "Once God has begun to speak with a person, be it in anger or in mercy, that person is truly immortal." He remains a participant in that event forever; God speaks further with him in all eternity. This fellowship with God, which we already have received as a gift and have experienced, still remains our portion when death's dark night arrives. It remains true to us. His hand extends even into that abyss. Jesus Christ will stand between every dark danger and me.

Only in this way can the question about the long night of death become, in a sense, "unimportant." The question is no longer, "What will happen to me?" but rather, "Who remains with me and holds me fast as his own?"

There is a saying of Jesus in which this loftier indifference to the long night of death is expressed in a uniquely compact sentence. It is the word to the thief hanging on the neighboring cross who said to him, "Remember me when you come into your kingdom!" Jesus answered him, "Today you will be with me in Paradise."

"Today!" Then *is* there a direct passage from the last breath to the green pastures? But *what* this garden of Paradise is and *when* the thief will enter it are questions that fade far into the background. The whole emphasis of what the dying Lord said lies solely on the two words "with me." "You will be with me, for since you have confessed me I will also confess *you*. You will remain beside me and with me, starting now as our death struggle sets in and as the last agony breaks in upon us. Here my hand cannot reach you because it is nailed to this bloody beam, yet you are with me and in me. *Behold, this is paradise.* For now the crime that brought you to this gallows need torment you no longer. Now you are no longer alone and no night of death can close over you. And in the very moment when you give up your spirit you will be at my side in a new way. I wait for you on the other side. Then we shall meet again in the presence of him into whose hands we now commend our spirits. This 'today' when you are at my side will not end. Look, dear friend, this indeed is paradise. This indeed is the kingdom into which I now come: the kingdom consists in my having you beside me and in my not letting you go, from Golgotha to all eternity."

Paradise is not space and it is not time. There is no moment when it begins and no spot where one can look for it. When the felicity of faith is granted to us we are *already* in paradise. And when one day we see Him in whom we have believed, paradise will surround us in its fullness. The "today" in which our history with Jesus Christ begins is also the beginning of paradise. And at bottom it is never a "condition" but a "shape." It is the Savior himself in whose peace we are secure. It is the Father upon whose bosom we fall. This is what Kierkegaard expressed in his epitaph:

> Yet a little while and it is won.
> Then the whole battle dissolves and is done.
> Then I shall refresh myself at life's river
> And speak with Jesus forever and ever.

We are pointed to the One who is our only comfort in life and in death, and thereby our gaze is kept from any undisciplined wandering.

There is one final question that I don't want to dodge, simply because it is posed, perhaps with some hesitation, by those who have stayed with me thus far.

Will we see the dead again?

Perhaps this is, once again, a human, all too human question. And maybe we will have to learn to conquer it, too, instead of

answering it, just as we have already learned to do with the
question about "the long night of death." But we can't jump to
that conclusion so simply. We must think about it.

We can pose this question about seeing the dead again with
hypocrisy—as in the case of a person suddenly "getting religion"
upon the death of a loved one. This religious interest usually
stems from the hope that the "mediator" Jesus Christ can act as a
go-between in contacting our departed. But then we are not concerned about Christ himself. He is just a means to an end for us;
he is to be our contact-man.

A high school senior wrote an essay about the effects that the
deaths of his mother and grandfather had upon him. He noticed
"a stronger bent toward Christianity" and added, "Perhaps this
may be explained by the fact that one would like to see the loved
one again. An eternal separation is unthinkable. Christianity
promises one this reencounter."

Then we are like the five thousand people whom Jesus miraculously fed. He was merely the one they needed to pacify their
rumbling stomachs; they had no interest in him personally (John
6:26). But he secretly slips away from us (just as he slipped away
from that multitude) when we don't care about *him* as our one
and only concern. If we misuse him as a means to an end—even as
contact-man for those who have fallen asleep—he becomes a wall
of silence to us, and all our questions are unanswered.

We may renew our inquiry only if we remain self-critical and
modest. Then our questions may actually press on a bit further.
There are certain mystical conceptions that picture our human
life as a stream which empties into the infinite ocean of eternity. If
that were the case, and all our lifestreams did empty into the one,
then our individuality would end, and all the separately flowing
brooks would merge in that all-encompassing sea of eternity.
Then the question about a reencounter in eternity would also be
pointless, since this question is meaningful only if we presuppose
that individuals who can meet one another remain.

But what we experience with Jesus Christ cannot be fit into
this image of an ocean and its tributary streams. There is a decisive difference. As those whom he accepted, we naturally remain

secure in him. If his faithfulness endures, then those to whom he is faithful certainly will endure, too. Of course, we shall be changed! "What is sown is perishable, what is raised is imperishable. . . . It is sown a physical body, it is raised a spiritual body" (I Cor. 15:42, 44). And between these two forms of our ego lies the pause of death. Our identity however, remains preserved in both. The image of the streams that lose their identity in the ocean is replaced by another, far more comforting, image, the image of a father and his children. They *remain* his children simply because each of them lives in his heart. Whether they live or die, they are their father's, they remain his children.

But do they meet one another in eternity? Will they recognize each other? Will the mother find the young child she lost? Will the widow find her life's companion who has gone before? Will she be permitted to embrace him again?

Why do we recoil when we ask these questions? Isn't it just because we spoke about living on in eternity that we have the right to ask? If we are not streams that disappear in the sea of eternity, isn't it natural for the question of reencounter to arise?

I believe I know why we recoil. As we pose these questions, the thought of a joyful reunion threatens to *master* us, and God is left out. But our dead no longer belong to us; they are sheltered in His everlasting arms. We can seek them only insofar as we seek those arms. And we can be sure that if we are near those arms in which His own rest, then the ones to whom our hearts cry out are also quite near to us. *That must suffice for us.* To the extent that we let it suffice, we can be governed by the only two questions that really matter. The one question is whether we have found Him who gives this security. The other is whether we have clearly told those nearest to us, whom we may yet accompany a bit farther on our earthly way, where we one day hope to find them and to Whom we may entrust ourselves in life and in death. There is only *One* who solves all questions and who saves us from all false questions. There is only *one* subject upon which all depends, and there is *one* thing needful. Everything else that we also crave to know or for which we also long (such as clearing up the mystery of death and the long night that follows, or certainty about the fate of the dead and of the living)—all that will "open up" to us from this *one* point. But all questions that bypass this central theme end in illusions, superstitions, and occult nonsense.

Sometimes when we must part from a loved one because he is taking a long journey (as often happened during the war when a soldier had to go to the front) we agree that at a certain time in the evening we will both look at a certain star, so that our gaze will meet in infinity and we will remain linked to each other by that sparkling point of the universe. We have the same sort of link with the dead. We know the identity of the "star" to whom we may look when one of us sets out on his last journey from all things temporal. Therefore we also know at which star our lines of sight will cross. One sees it from *this* world and one from the *other*, for indeed this star shines upon both. Jesus Christ is the lord of this world and the next, keeping watch even over the "uttermost parts of the sea."

Apart from this link, there is *no* connection with those who have fallen asleep. Yet we are permitted to tell Him everything that is on our hearts, both our greetings and our anxious questions. He will not despise even our most foolish wishes. Even if our last murmur is too faint for any human ear, it will press upon *His* heart and he will receive it.

He is the star to whom we look; he is the bridge between time and eternity. In him have they lived, and in him have they died—patriarchs, prophets, and apostles. And so it will be down to the end of time. Thus the last word can only be one of praise: "Thou, O Lord, art all in all."

ROSE AGAIN FROM
THE DEAD

FIRST QUESTION: WHAT IS
SO UNUSUAL ABOUT THE EARTHLY JESUS?

> "All that the Father gives me will come to me; and him who
> comes to me I will not cast out."   —*John 6:37*

There seems to be a good deal in the Christian faith that we can accept without difficulty, even if it is our nature to be critical. For example, the gospel teaching about brotherly love goes down easily with us. We can include it neatly in the catalog of our virtues. Also, anyone who remains true to his task, as Jesus did, to the bloody and bitter end demands our respect. It provides us with a sort of prototype for uncompromising convictions, and we react sensitively when anyone insults this picture by ridicule or argument. The man on the cross is taboo even for those who otherwise chafe at the doctrinal side of Christianity.

Then there appears to be a fairly broad basis for a kind of Christian "consensus." There is only *one* point at which the heartiness and friendly head-nodding stop abruptly, namely, when the assertion is made that the corpse of this revered man came back to life and strolled out of the tomb. I put it coarsely on purpose in order to make clear that not only our reason, but also our imagination, feels the strain. When we hear the claim of a "resurrection," our inner man figuratively slams the door, and the image of the touched and touching Man suddenly seems to become a ghostly figure out of mythology, crowding out again that which for a moment began to stir us.

But we so-called Christians should subject ourselves to a little self-examination on this point, too. Of course we don't dismiss this phrase "risen from the dead" right off the bat—it belongs to the gold reserves of the Christian economy, so to speak, and we have grown somewhat accustomed to it through the Sunday-by-Sunday "confession of our Christian faith." It probably doesn't make any difference to us as we say it along with everyone else.

It "doesn't make any difference." This statement of the case is basically a worse and more radical rejection of belief in the resurrection than any atheistic agressiveness could ever produce. Either Christ *is* risen or he *isn't*. If he is, both my life and the world will take on totally new and different aspects. If he isn't, then everything stays the same. Does that "make no difference"? If I blithely rattle off my little Christian cliches while holding to the pious faith of my fathers, I really have no idea of what is at stake in this matter of the resurrection.

Dorothy Sayers, the great English detective-story writer, once put it this way. "The people who saw the risen Christ were at least convinced that life was worth living and that death is nothing—a very different attitude from that of the modern defeatists who are so convinced that life is a misfortune, and that death, somewhat illogically, is a still greater catastrophe." How could this decision between two basic possibilities so crucial in my life leave me cold or "not make any difference"?

It's easy to understand why secular man has stopped patronizing a store where the people who stand behind the counter seem to think so little of their wares. If I as a Christian—whether in innocence or in carelessness—assure someone that I still carry around this doctrine of "risen from the dead" in a side pocket of my intellectual baggage when this phrase means absolutely nothing in my life, what good does it do? If this phrase is true, then it would have to become the "Magna Charta" of my life. It would have to *precede* even my name on my driver's license—and in capital letters! It would have to become determinative in every area of my life, working its effect in my work, in my office, in my living room, and in my bedroom. *If* Jesus lives and rules, then I am—for example—no longer completely without hope. My cares are driven away. Then I know that my loved ones who have passed on have not passed *away* from me but have passed *on* to him. I do not have to take much of the disappointment in my life so terribly seriously any more. Doubtless even my car, my television set, and the hoped-for raise take on a somewhat different rank in my life's scale of values.

Who knows how many dogmas have been thus carried down through the centuries without having the least effect on our lives? This simple rote-religion of the Christian must be an abomination to God; it must be agony for him. We are like an odd and somewhat dim-witted man who is looking for a marvelous flower. Contact with it would be sure to change his life. He is convinced that this miracle-flower must be growing somewhere, but he fails to notice that he is already carrying around the seeds of this flower in his pocket (in that side pocket of his intellectual baggage). We are people who carry in our pockets all we need to fulfill our lives and to bring us to our goal. But we forget to sow it and cause it to become active. Thus it remains inert and bears no fruit.

But if that is the case, then it would be worthwhile to consider *why* the message of the Resurrection plays such a minor role for us, or even signifies no more than a shaky legend. We certainly get along much more easily with the Crucifixion. Just why is this?

Quite simply, I believe it is because we encounter our own life story in the *crucified* Jesus. We look for comfort to that brotherly one who is not a stranger to anything human and who himself has experienced what it is to be alone and forsaken, to see oneself surrounded by intrigues, to feel one's heart thrill to the enchantment of temptation, and to break out in the cold sweat of fear when death approaches. *We seek this human solidarity.* We seek someone who is like us. But a divine being who is removed from everything earthly leaves us cold. When we are nervous before an operation, disappointed in a colleague, or stuck in a financial mess, we find comfort and relief when someone tells us, "I know what you're going through. I've been in the same fix." Then they don't need to give us a "solution"; in fact, we can do without their good advice. It is enough for them to be there, listening to us, and giving us the feeling, "I stand on the same rug as you, and I know what it is like to have that rug pulled out from under me."

Apparently that is why people flock to church on Good Friday. They want to see the image of their own misery—someone who stands with them and who knows what it is to be a man. They want to see this image in order to cope with their own lot. The crucified One doesn't have to "solve" anything. He doesn't have to "dissolve" the bonds of death; he doesn't have to "rise." It's enough for him to be nailed fast there, powerless, his head bowed, just as we let him hang.

We are far too enmeshed in much that would enslave us and drive us to despair not to be deeply suspicious of neat solutions and pat answers. The idea that someone has been able to cope with death, that something other than the long dark night awaits us, and that we will be caught up by everlasting arms—that certainly is too good to be true. Thoroughgoing suspicion is the order of the day—not only enlightened suspicion of myths and legends, but moral suspicion concerning the coward within us who is too fainthearted to stand up to life and who therefore dreams up such happy endings. Isn't it the simple truth that even the greatest lives come to an end? Even Plato and Francis of Assisi, Michelangelo and Bach are dead. There is no star in the intellectual firmament that will not set, even though posterity may still catch some reflections of its brilliance. Why should it be any different with this *one?* Or, even more, why should it be any different with us? Is he really able to pull us through the vanity of life and the nothingness of death so that we need no longer "pass away" like cattle but may "pass on" to a fulfillment that surpasses all dreams and all understanding, to a peace that never ends?

If that is true, then this certainty cannot be easy to come by. Above all, we must be suspicious of ourselves and of any cowardly tendency toward wishful thinking. We must face our doubts squarely. As a doubter, I must abandon all Christian traditions and doctrines at the very outset. I must be ready to fall into the void, supported only by one last certainty: if there is a Christ, he will not *let* me fall but will catch me up. The decision depends on him and him alone. And if I should encounter him, as doubting Thomas encountered the risen Lord, and if I must say, "My Lord and my God," then I shall get back all the doctrine that I threw overboard in the wild venture of my doubt. I shall get them back again "incidentally," almost as a waiter gets a tip.

As I see it, there is *one* annoying problem, above all others, which I must face up to, if I want to be more than a hand-me-down Christian.

Everything connected with the Christian faith would seem to be smooth sailing if I could see Christ as a teacher of ultimate truth—someone who had valid things to say about love, about the "principle of hope," or about "death bringing life," and who knew how to demonstrate these things in his own life and death. In such a case my conscience would certainly react immediately and positively, and would be ready to place him in the pantheon of the great teachers of mankind. But that just won't do. The point of all the Gospel accounts is that something is *"told"* to me about him—what he said, did, and suffered. The account of his resurrection belongs in the same category. Thus I cannot say simply, "This speaks to me in propositions which convince me by their inner truth, as, for example, Plato convinces me when he speaks about justice or love, or Bertolt Brecht when he lashes out at middle-class morality." On the contrary, here something is really "told" about a man: that he faced the tempter and withstood his crafty diversionary tactics; that he performed mighty works that were astounding and thoroughly miraculous; and that his love included even the very men who sought his death. The news that he did not stay dead, but that God raised him, belongs to these same accounts. Obviously, everything depends on whether these quite human (and sometimes more than human) things are true and whether one can *rely* on them. *If* they were true it would be a shock that from then on would have the profoundest effect on the way I acted with regard to my future, to my fellowmen, and to my own death.

But isn't the real shocker the very fact that such questions about my future *depend on the credibility of historical accounts?* Under such circumstances, doesn't Gotthold Lessing's thoughtful comment seem appropriate—his exclamation that only universal truths of reason, such as mathematical theorems, attained the ultimate degree of certainty? "Contingent historical truths," however, accounts of things by historians and reporters, could never be more than "probable." But if such accounts always contain one last factor of uncertainty (because they rest on statements by witnesses who could err, or on conclusions by historians who may fall prey to shaky sources or wrong interpretations, how can my fate for time or eternity be based on such slippery ground? How can my eternal salvation depend on historical opinions or even fads?

Why does God make it so hard for us? Wouldn't it be better if he treated us to eternal truths, moral rules, or wise sayings at which no doubt could gnaw and to which we needed say only "Yea and Amen"? Why does God make it so hard for us? Why does he overtax our desire for honesty? Our doubting is certainly neither malice nor intellectual snobbery. Indeed, we *want* the truth; it is our very honesty that drives us to skepticism.

I believe that if you think about the message and person of Jesus, one day you will hit upon the solution to this deep and disturbing question. This solution involves the very heart of the gospel, the heart that tells of Jesus Christ (and of God himself in Jesus Christ) stepping in on our side, exposing himself to the pressures of history as we are exposed, and experiencing with us hunger and thirst, desire for life and fear of death, guilt and suffering. He doesn't want to be a distant God; he wants to be as near to us as a brother, so that we can believe that he loves us and cares about us (about you and me) with an infinite passion.

So then we are not dealing here with "Great Ideas" as they have been conceived and formulated by gifted minds through the ages; we are dealing with an act of the God who declares himself to us.

On my trip to America I crossed paths with a man (he was a well-known and quite highly respected attorney) who was profoundly disturbed by the demoralization and brutalization of humanity in the worst slum areas. Plans for slum clearance were and are available *en masse*. But this man knew (and he knew it precisely because he was a Christian) that social commissions which ventured into that area of vice and misery only under police protection could never gain the trust of its ostracized inhabitants. Such commissions would meet rejection and would not be able to rekindle the dead spark of humanity. The slum dwellers knew that they were only a sore on the body politic as far as the social reformers were concerned, and that society would gladly be free of them. But the fact that they were also "men" did not interest the reformers at all. The latter only wanted to wipe out a center of infection (in both the moral and hygienic sense).

These slum-dwellers remained animals even when one clothed (or disguised) them in civilized garments. But the lawyer knew that the human in these dehumanized beings could be awakened only through *love*. Since they did not trust a love that climbed down from the Olympus of its middle-class world now and then to pay them a welfare visit, he rented a shabby hole in the middle of that filthy and vermin-infested area. He lived there with them and let them know that he was serious about them—he wanted to be their brother, he loved them, and he was not merely a welfare worker who saw them as a "social problem."

Then those who met him actually began to *believe* his love. They received new hope from him, hope that it could signify something to be a man. Something in them which they had long since lost track of began to breathe and awaken. Perhaps he could have directed great projects from a desk in some skyscraper. But he wanted a deeper form of satisfaction. He wanted to arouse the sparks of "hope" and "faith." He wanted to be salt that combatted the decay from *within*. So he lowered himself into the depth of brotherly companionship and shared the fate of those whom he wanted to be near—authentically near. And if you had seen him, you would not have been able to distinguish him from the others, so completely did he identify with them, even outwardly.

In Jesus Christ, God has dealt similarly with us. He has come into the "depressed area" of human life seeking out not only poor Lazarus with his sores, but also the rich man in his glittering wretchedness. This is why we can believe in his love. If we rove afield into shady operations, if we succumb to the overwhelming force of our drives, if we are mean and jealous and full of hatred and greed, or if we slink away forsaken and stricken by fate, we need no longer tell ourselves in bitterness and cynicism, "You coward, a fine 'Image of God' you are! In this spot you'll have to do without the luxury of pious feelings, to say nothing of prayers, for there are no more gods and no more 'dear God.' You are still only a wriggling worm. You tremble with anxiety or are made miserable by boredom so that life becomes a worthless burden to you."

No, I now can know quite simply that he to whom all authority in heaven and earth has been given has laid aside his divine untouchability and has plunged into the abysmal darkness that surrounds me with its terror. If I want to locate him with my eyes, I should not look up to the stratosphere (movie scenes which show someone looking ecstatically upward when he prays are patently false). No, I must seek him in the depths, in a shabby stable with the animals, in the wilderness with its thirst and its satanic temptation, in the abandonment of the cross with its god-forsakenness and its fear of death—*maybe* even in the gaiety of the wedding party at Cana, where everything was so human and turned out so well.

He is there at every point of my life, whether I laugh or cry or sit in silence. For nothing human is foreign to him, and he wants to come to me right *here* where I am now.

However, this very nearness to me means that he can be *mistaken* for other human figures like that lawyer in the slums. Thus I can say, for example, that he is the "founder of a religion" as Muhammad was (and I can classify him in the general history of religion, thereby becoming a relativist about the whole matter). Or I can say, "This man of antiquity made a splash for a few years in a province of the Roman Empire. What is that supposed to mean for me?" Or I can take him for a religious man, a saint, a failure, or a visionary. *All that is possible.* I can say with a certain sadness (or even snobbery), "If God wanted to be so kind as to address me personally and familiarize me with eternal things, why has he disguised himself to the point that he is unrecognizable, meeting me on the historical level as one point among many others on the timeline? How then can I *recognize* him among all the others and convince myself that here (*here,* of all places!) I can learn more than from Socrates or even from Mr. X and his carpenter's trade?"

Do we now understand what lies behind this question and what it is getting at? Do we understand that we are on the trail of a unique mystery? God doesn't shout eternal truths at us from heaven, an act that our inspired reason would applaud; instead, he meets us in a bit of earthly history. God thus meets us in a completely *earthly* way so that the story must be retold from generation to generation—that is the mystery of his coming! Precisely this historicity is the reverse side of a love which appears in the midst of our human existence, sharing it and throwing aside all divine prerogatives. It was not because certain propositions from the preaching of Jesus were so full of insight or so persuasive that the men of the New Testament were overwhelmed and came to a new phase of their existence, to faith. Had that been the case, then undoubtedly the intellectuals and the smart people would have had the inside track in preference to the innocent and the unpretentious. Instead, the latter experienced a great transformation in their lives because they discovered the *Lord.* Suddenly they discovered, in him who looked like them and who was "found in human form," the Savior before whom they drew back afraid and finally had to stammer, "my Lord and my God." But then the new certainty gripped them deep within. It was no mere play of waves on the surface of their intellects; it was printed firmly in their hearts.

I heard an interesting story in South Africa. A group of primitive bushmen from the backwoods were taken to a great technical exhibition showing all the wonders of our civilized world. From the viewpoint of cultural history, these men stood about on the level of stone-age man. In order to make their encounter with the modern world as dramatic as possible, they were even taken up in an airplane. Obviously, the situation was made to order for the psychologists, who fell upon the poor savages immediately in order to elicit (naturally, not by using a questionnaire!) what had made the deepest impression on them. The scientists had already wagered among themselves that it would certainly be the flight at thirty-five thousand feet or perhaps an electronic brain that they had seen.

But the good people gave a different and very disconcerting answer to the question about what had made the greatest impression on them. They had been most fascinated by a quite ordinary kitchen faucet. How anyone could charm valuable water out of an ordinary wall was for them *the* shattering experience. The high-altitude jet and the electronic magic with numbers were, as far as they were concerned, events in a fairyland, the mysterious region of gods and demons where anything was possible. There certainly was no need to marvel at such things! And precisely for that reason it didn't strike home to them. But the faucet! That was something out of their everyday world. They knew what thirst was. They were acquainted with the troublesome search for water and with the terror of drought. Therefore the thing that mattered to them (today we would probably say, "What mattered 'existentially' to them"), the thing that was *the* miracle, was something both familiar and foreign *to the sphere of their life*, something which had to do with their thirst, their trouble, and their hope.

Our encounter with Jesus may also take place in this way. The sphere of eternity, out of which he comes and to which his elevation returns him, may be as strange and distant to us as the jet ride was to the bushmen. But something else may strike closer to home: the fact that he is with us in the room of our life, in this room where we watch with laughter as our children come tumbling in, where we delight to read a fine letter, where we sometimes stretch out fatigued on the couch, consume our scanty or sumptuous meal, and sometimes also pace back and forth in despair. He is with us in this room of our life and has experienced this same life's fear and desire. And right here, in this room of my existence, he causes living water to spring from the wall. *That* gets to me. For he did not and does not let eternal matters float in heavenly radiance above our heads. He puts them in the middle of our life. He blesses the children (they can be so irritating and nasty with their runny noses and torn clothes). He brings the blessing of God to the outcasts. And heavy, frozen hearts are suddenly melted by a ray from the Eternal. Amid the struggle with hostile contemporaries, the door of his heart never slammed shut (as is usually the case); instead, the miracle of love occurred right there, and a hand of blessing could be discerned amid anxiety and pain.

Thus here, in the worldly, all too worldly pettiness of daily life, the tap of living water is opened. We are not talking about otherworldly, heavenly dew that may be detected only in pious withdrawal. This is water that I can have in the room of my earthly life. He has shown me the faucet that turns it on. In him I see that the miracle of eternity has come into my own day and has changed everything.

Now life simply teems with indications that I am loved, and that messages are being sent to me and tasks set for me. Suddenly life doesn't roll along so automatically and monotonously; it becomes the scene of an exciting interchange that keeps me constantly on my toes. Every man I meet, every affliction I must bear, indeed every joy that is not denied me, carries a letter from the heavenly Father with personal greetings or with news that comforts me or calls for thanksgiving, that contains a test or even a great gift for me to enjoy. It is a permanent interchange with God, and it suddenly revises all the questions which life poses for me.

When I reach the point where I have discovered that living water in my room, it is inevitable that I should then begin to ask whence it comes and where the eternal fountain flows. Once I pursue this question, the figure of Jesus again becomes a mystery, but in a different way. I cannot avoid the fact that he is indeed with me in my little boat or in my room, but neither can I avoid asking why wind and wave obey him and how he can command the springs of living water in my desert. Then questions arise. In all his humanity, was he really *only* human as you and I are? Did *his* shining face, too, fall into the abyss of mortality? Did death have the last word in *his* case, too? Then the question becomes acute: Does he live and rule, and is he still present? Granted, he bowed his head and died. He is my brother even there, where it is all over for me. But how can I dare to say, "At the time of my departing, depart not thou from me"? Can I speak like that to a dead man, or only to one who is *alive*, one who will receive me on the other side and lead me to eternal habitations?

Thus we confront the question of Easter, the miracle of the third day. Like the disciples at Emmaus, we must travel far before our hearts begin to burn within us and we are forced to ask whence this fire comes.

In this chapter, we have traversed a long road. We started with a doubt, with the problem of why God poses the decisive question of our life in historical and very human terms instead of using eternal truths. We have simply thought this doubt through to its end. Has it really been a "bitter" end, or have we come upon precisely the unique element that can free us? Didn't we suddenly find ourselves on the road to Emmaus, where the risen One drew near to us? Even doubt is an envelope in which messages from God are concealed. Therefore we should not refuse delivery of this dreaded envelope; we should open it.

Before his death, one of the greatest philosophers of our time, one of the last great idealists, was stricken by the most terrible doubt. He doubted himself, his point of view, and even that which he understood to be the Christian faith (which he did not want to abandon completely). Shortly before, he had lived through his wife's terrible death from cancer. He felt that our human individuality was also destroyed by death and that there was nothing that could be pulled through the final decay of the organism. He asked me (actually with the look of a wounded animal), "What awaits me, anyway? Does anything at all remain?" Then I spoke to him about the poor in spirit (who include even the intellectually gifted) and about the empty hands that alone can be blessed. I told him that we humans *cannot* see what awaits us and what of us endures. Our human frame may dissolve and disappear into nothingness. We are kept only by him who remembers us and leads us through that night of death which our sight can no longer pierce. We all share the life of him whom God awakened from the dead. If that is not so, then it's all over for us.

But He is *not* a dream. We shall "become like those who dream" when the flashes of glory in his human life brighten into the eternal light that shines upon us. Even now, our doubting hearts and empty hands receive the touch of blessing which awakens us to new life and grants us the certainty of new shores and a new day.

I recall how this great and honored man who saw everything slip from his grasp and who went as the "poor in spirit" to meet the Savior who awaited him in death's dark night.

SECOND QUESTION: IS THE RESURRECTION OF CHRIST LEGEND OR REALITY?

And when the sabbath was past, Mary Magdalene, and Mary the mother of James, and Salome, bought spices, so that they might go and anoint him. And very early on the first day of the week they went to the tomb when the sun had risen. And they were saying to one another, "Who will roll away the stone for us from the door of the tomb?" And looking up, they saw that the stone was rolled back; for it was very large. And entering the tomb, they saw a young man sitting on the right side, dressed in a white robe; and they were amazed. And he said to them, "Do not be amazed; you seek Jesus of Nazareth, who was crucified. He has risen, he is not here; see the place where they laid him. But go, tell his disciples and Peter that he is going before you to Galilee; there you will see him, as he told you." And they went out and fled from the tomb; for trembling and astonishment had come upon them; and they said nothing to any one, for they were afraid.

—Mark 16:1–8

That very day two of them were going to a village named Emmaus, about seven miles from Jerusalem, and talking with each other about all these things that had happened. While they were talking and discussing together, Jesus himself drew near and went with them. But their eyes were kept from recognizing him. And he said to them, "What is this conversation which you are holding with each other as you walk?" And they stood still, looking sad. Then one of them, named

Cleopas, answered him, "Are you the only visitor to Jerusalem who does not know the things that have happened there in these days?" And he said to them, "What things?" And they said to him, "Concerning Jesus of Nazareth, who was a prophet mighty in deed and word before God and all the people, and how our chief priests and rulers delivered him up to be condemned to death, and crucified him. But we had hoped that he was the one to redeem Israel. Yes, and besides all this, it is now the third day since this happened. Moreover, some women of our company amazed us. They were at the tomb early in the morning and did not find his body; and they came back saying that they had even seen a vision of angels, who said that he was alive. Some of those who were with us went to the tomb, and found it just as the women had said; but him they did not see." And he said to them, "O foolish men, and slow of heart to believe all that the prophets have spoken! Was it not necessary that the Christ should suffer these things and enter into his glory?" And beginning with Moses and all the prophets, he interpreted to them in all the scriptures the things concerning himself.

So they drew near to the village to which they were going. He appeared to be going further, but they constrained him, saying, "Stay with us, for it is toward evening and the day is now far spent." So he went in to stay with them. When he was at table with them, he took the bread and blessed, and broke it, and gave it to them. And their eyes were opened and they recognized him; and he vanished out of their sight. They said to each other, "Did not our hearts burn within us while he talked to us on the road, while he opened to us the scriptures?" And they rose that same hour and returned to Jerusalem; and they found the eleven gathered together and those who were with them, who said, "The Lord has risen indeed, and has appeared to Simon!" Then they told what had happened on the road, and how he was known to them in the breaking of the bread. —*Luke 24:13–35*

In the previous chapter we were concerned with the basic question whether or not we can base the structure of our existence, the very meaning of our life, on historical accounts like the Gospels. We also asked if we *ought* to take such a step, and why God comes to us making such unreasonable demands. If I am to "believe in" something, then it must be absolutely certain. But it is precisely historical accounts that are laden with many elements of uncertainty! Who will guarantee me that the witnesses are reliable and that no error has crept into the tradition? And then, when it comes to miracles (as in Jesus' resurrection from the dead), basically rational grounds require me to ask questions from the outset.

Everything we have discussed has been only an approach to the main point, which is to concern us now. Now we shall speak of the mysterious things that happened on the third day after Jesus' crucifixion.

Rudolf Alexander Schroeder tells how, when his best friend died suddenly in the prime of life, the discouraged family would huddle together with him in the evenings. Time and again the conversation would revolve around the incomprehensibility of what had happened. Then he said to himself that mere whimpering and empty palaver was not helping anyone. After all, a death was serious enough to call for meditation on essentials. And so he simply reached for the New Testament and read aloud the four Evangelists' accounts of Jesus' resurrection, one after the other (that is, virtually the same thing four times without a word of interpretation). The texts themselves spoke in their monumental simplicity. It was striking to see how a breathless silence ensued, how numbed spirits gradually began to melt and the theme of the conversation changed at once. It actually got down to the essentials as thoughts turned, calmly and collectedly, toward the last things. This turn of events appeared to Schroeder as a creative intervention, a miracle.

If a person lets the Resurrection accounts have their effect on him without getting his guard up (and, for the moment, without intellectual skepticism), at first he is bound to be struck by something in their *style* of expression. They are, in fact, an example of the Bible's use of a veiled and, one might say, discreet language in pointing to events that no words could adequately describe. Thus the way of speaking must be indirect and even cryptic. Naturally, one cannot talk about the Resurrection the way one reports a traffic accident or an historical event. A newspaper account of the Resurrection would be absurd. Everything that happens around the tomb is bathed in a mysterious, indirect light. We hear no details of what went on; no sensationalism or miracle-mongering rips asunder the veil drawn over this mystery. We see only the reactions and effects which an event, itself invisible, produces among the disciples and the women. Therefore it is hardly surprising that the accounts differ from one another. It is natural that the subjectivity of the narrators would play a role, and that their imagination and their efforts to interpret the events would also be involved. Thus we end up with anything but four objective chronicles which may simply be summed up into one account. Involvement in the Incomprehensible is so intense that each witness speaks of it "in other tongues." Each must figuratively ransack his supply of words, concepts, and ideas in order to give utterance to the Unspeakable by every means at his disposal.

Therefore, as far as I am concerned, precisely those contradictions are indicative. They seem to be "relevant," as it were.

I should like to try to eludicate my meaning by an example. In the first half of the last century there lived a physiologist named Johannes Mueller who was famous for his doctrine of "specific sensory energy." By this he meant that our sensory organs (our eyes and ears) reacted to all outward stimuli in special ways peculiar *to them*. For example, if someone gets punched in the nose, his ears buzz and he sees stars. In other words, he has optical and acoustical impressions even though what happened to him had nothing at all to do with optics or acoustics, with seeing or hearing. Nevertheless, that blow registered in terms of "sense impressions." Eyes and ears, seeing and hearing are, so to speak, drawn into sympathetic partnership. They are involved and they act in accordance with their peculiar characteristics, the eye through color impressions and the ear through a vibrating buzz. Our sense organs thus react to outward stimuli, but they react in completely different ways. They must figuratively convert that blow on the head, which was nonvisible and nonhearable, into their own peculiar means of reaction. Naturally the ear translates the event differently than the eye, and the difference is even greater among various individuals. One man hears humming, another hears bells; one man sees dancing stars, another sees a rainbow.

While a blow on the head may not be exactly the prettiest example to illustrate the background of the Resurrection, the main point of the analogy is still important. Those who experienced the mystery of that Resurrection morning were suddenly confronted by a reality that simply exceeded the capacities of their eyes, their ears, their reason, and even their imagination. Their normal functions were overtaxed. This wasn't the view of trees to which the eye had become accustomed, nor was it the clatter of donkey's hoofs or a girl's laughter as the ear usually registered it. This was the incursion of the totally other, of the nonhearable and nonvisible. The human perceptive faculties reacted in their usual ways: eyes and ears had their impressions, imagination conceived images of the occurrences, and reason put it all together and made connections. Thus an account of what had happened arose, although everyone's story sounded somewhat different.

Naturally, it would have been possible to reconcile these accounts with one another and to harmonize them a bit, just as some eyewitnesses settle on a completely consistent statement in order to make their testimony more credible. But that doesn't happen here; the "dancing stars" and the "rainbow" are left standing beside one another, unresolved. The witnesses certainly knew that what they wanted to report just couldn't be "reported" in the strict sense; it burst the usual relationships of earthly events. They could say, "Whoever takes offense at these differences has simply not yet grasped what is going on here: something incomprehensible is breaking in upon us, and our concepts begin to waver when we try to grasp it. Indeed, this event *engages* everything we are and have: our eyes, our ears, our imagination, and even our faculties for expression. We can do nothing else than speak about it. But on the other hand it is too powerful for us to be 'objective' about it. So we cannot describe the event *itself;* we can only speak about the reactions which it has evoked from us. Thus we cannot manage without the forms of statement peculiar to legends."

Now, what can we *learn* from these effects? How can we recognize the impact of the Incomprehensible from the shape of its crater?

It is not without significance that the women are the first to arrive at Jesus' tomb. The men are sunk in consuming sorrow and bitterness. They have crept into the corner like hurt animals. We know, too, why they are hurt. The so-called "Christian world view" has completely collapsed for them. On Golgotha they clapped their hands to their heads like people who had suddenly seen the light and muttered to themselves, "How could you have been so brainless as to imagine that this man was different from the rest of us, that he stood outside the framework of a normal man's biography, which admittedly and without exception ends in *death. How could you?*"

Certainly it is no disgrace for a man to die. That is nothing against him; indeed, we all have to die. And it is even an honor if someone dies for an idea, as Socrates did. But if this One dies, that is a catastrophe. For of course he was not just someone who brought a new teaching, a teaching that God is love, that there are thoughts higher than ours, and that the goal of history is the Kingdom of God. If the Nazarene had only brought a "teaching" like that, his death need not have mattered. At any rate, it would not have been a catastrophe. For it would have been conceivable that this teaching of his could survive, just as the Pythagorean theorem outlived its discoverer.

But in Jesus' case things are entirely different. He obviously did not merely bring a "teaching" that God and man had been reconciled and brought into fellowship with one another. Instead, he claimed that he himself was the one who could fill the gap between God and us "with power." He (and no one else) could restore a world thrown out of joint and torn by sorrow and injustice; he could challenge the awful majesty of death.

But if that is so, then it is indeed a catastrophe when this One is himself overpowered by death or when the hands of sinful men are able to get a stranglehold on this God-begotten (or *supposedly* God-begotten) life and drag it down into the grave.

It certainly seems likely that this was why the men were swept aside and the women came alone to the tomb. But even the women do not come with the idea, say, that someone has broken through the barrier of death; it is exactly the reverse. They intend to offer a dead man their melancholy memorials. They come in the same frame of mind that motivates so many people to attend church on Good Friday: they feel, "This was a noble man. Of course, he failed, but we do not want to forget that, for a while, he brought comfort and light to our lives, and that for a short time (perhaps for an innocent childhood) he gave us the dream of a Father in heaven and a Savior in whom our life is secure."

Not one of all these people thought that he could rise from the dead. On the contrary, the only thought they had was, "Who will roll the stone away for us?" They were, in fact, seeking only the dead among the dead. Then, when they found out that he had entered a new, inconceivable life, they were so poorly prepared psychologically for this event that it was a tremendous shock for them. The text tells us again and again how a shudder, in fact, a panicky terror, overcame them. They immediately went for cover; they took flight, and their mouths seemed sealed, so that no word of what they had seen escaped them.

We know neither what happened nor how it happened. The event itself lies in an area of silence, shrouded by a veil of mystery. How (this question has already arisen) could something our categories do not cover be stated in the form of an historical account or of a newspaper report? Our mental equipment is obviously adequate only for the occurrences of our objective world. Within the human sphere, for example, it is tuned to the *historical*—the range of those things that appear and disappear, but in any case end in death. But in the Resurrection accounts the understanding tries in a stammering way to testify to something that breaks through the tried and true forms of all historical processes. This "something" confuses our perceptive equipment and our faculties of expression, just as too great an earthquake can throw off a delicate seismograph so that it can no longer register precisely. We see neither the event itself nor the thing *per se.* We notice only the "before and after," the "before" where the disciples remain hopeless and depressed, and the "after" where they are gripped by a completely new faith. In a moment of absolute, objective hopelessness, in an inferno of the most terrible despair, we see arise, suddenly and without any psychological preparation, a new church against which the gates of hell cannot prevail. This church hands on the message of that event from generation to generation like a baton, daring to tell us that we all draw our life from that *one* decisive hour.

Let him who can understand it; I can't. On the other hand, it isn't possible to escape the overpowering nature of this event by saying to oneself, "This is a myth that is told hundreds of places in the ancient world." Although men were gripped in their totality (and that includes their imagination) by this event, and although they added legendary elements, praising God not only with words, but also with images and symbolic figures, this is *not* a myth. A myth is always the result of clothing an idea (for example, the cycle of nature) in the robes of history, so that it need no longer be expressed in purely abstract form but can be recounted as "history" with an easily guessed meaning. Then children can enjoy it as an exciting tale about gods or heroes; only the mature and grown-up have the feeling that there is still more hidden in the story to give it added meaning. For this reason too, mythical figures are always gods or heroes of *antiquity* who neither can nor should be taken as historical figures.

But the news, "He is risen; he is risen indeed," was not proclaimed about a nebulous dream-figure. It was spoken about a man whom they had all known and with whom they had all spoken.

The man of antiquity could certainly participate in the cult of the resurrected Dionysius without compromising himself as a rational being. He could even cultivate deep thoughts in connection with this myth. But no rational man would dare to say, "Do you remember the man you saw day before yesterday on the Via Dolorosa, the one who looked up to the balcony of the corner house and whose mother—you know her, the woman from X Street—followed about half a block behind him, crying and leaning on the arm of Mrs. Magdalena? Well, he has come back to life!" Even in those days one couldn't be that madly reckless. And the people of Jerusalem would have repudiated this maddest of all messages just as firmly as we would, if—*if* they hadn't been bowled over by the upsetting facts.

But of course a new question arises immediately. *Today*, how can we arrive at this certainty (this still very odd-appearing certainty)? How can we be sure that we may deal with Jesus as a living man, that is, as someone who commands the waves of our destiny and who hears us when we speak to him, even today? Once again I recall Lessing's resigned comment, "It is one thing to have been there yourself, and another merely to hear about it." Put more pointedly, "How do we find the Easter certainty?" When it comes to the question of what our only comfort in life and in death can be, then we need to have something *different* and something *more* offered than an old story that says something completely unheard-of happened once, even if this story should be ever so well attested. Is that any reason why it should determine *my* destiny? Is that any reason for it to upset us? Why should that give *us* a new being and a new lease on life?

The first generation of Christians could have asked precisely the same question. The alleged resurrection of Jesus from the dead could never have brought the disciples to faith if they had not believed his word. For in that case there would have been plenty of other explanations handy—for example, that Jesus' body had been stolen or carried away. No one has yet been brought to faith by a miracle. At any rate, I have to confess for myself that a plain miracle story would never be enough to bowl me over. A miracle can always be explained away.

Even the empty tomb did not bring the disciples to faith. (That is important!) In fact, something quite different happened. Seeing the empty tomb and hearing the angel's words made the scales fall from their eyes. In the Easter light of the third day they saw at once that all Jesus' words and deeds had become like geometrical points spelling out the truth that death could not hold him.

When Jesus said, "Your sins are forgiven," and the cripple really got up and went away a new, literally unburdened man— that could be said only by someone who stood on an Archimedean point, inaccessible to us, from which he could move our world. "You shall find rest for your souls in me"—that could be said only by one who lived in such peace and communion with the Father that nothing, not even death, could rupture or interrupt it. The words, "Come unto me, all you who are weary and heavy laden, and I will give you rest" could be said only by someone who really understood weariness and oppression. He must have shared this weight with us as a brother would, yet his life was fed from other sources. From him flowed unfailing streams of living water.

All this suddenly dawned on the disciples in the light of that third day. A new perspective encompassed the whole life of the wandering Savior who walked this earth healing, helping, forgiving, and offering new beginnings. It was just as though the key to his secret had suddenly been pressed into their hands. They simply had not recognized him during the everyday fellowship of their life with him. To be sure, their hearts had burned within them and they had felt the shadow of a vague suspicion that something unheard-of was in the offing. But now, for the first time, it occurred to them *who* it was who had walked with them. Now, suddenly, light flashed through his enigmatic words. Heaven opened above them. He whom they had held to be one of their own (even if the greatest) now proved to be "totally other," coming from the eternity of the Father to share their life as master and friend.

This revolutionary certainty did not come to them because, for example, they believed in the resurrection (we can't "believe in the resurrection" either; one simply can't believe *in* a thing or an event). The newness came into their lives because they learned to believe in the risen One, and because his manner of self-testimony literally overpowered them. The Emmaus story shows us, with as much precision as we could wish, just how that happened.

The conversation carried on by those men as they walked along was apparently a disconsolate one. They kept coming back to the question of what could have happened to the Nazarene. The affair had only become more puzzling. They too had heard what people said had happened on Easter morning. For example, they had heard that the tomb was empty and that some people had seen a vision of angels. But it had done them as little good as such reports do for us when we hear them today. It never even occurred to them to put all the reports together and to draw the conclusion, "He must be. risen." Thus their confusion mounted, and their heads spun even more rapidly.

Only when the living Lord joined them, at first mysterious and unrecognized, only when he interpreted the great lines from scripture that intersect in him and point to him, only then did their hearts begin to burn. And only later did they notice the source of this burning and realize who had spoken with them.

It was not the news of the Resurrection that convinced them (for in that case they would have been just as highly skeptical as we moderns are, although in a different way). No, it was not the news of the Resurrection that convinced them; it was the figure of the risen One himself and his word that overpowered them and put them on a new track.

So it is no longer surprising that only those who had traveled with Jesus and had lived in fellowship with him became witnesses to the "Easter miracle." It was only among these that an effective connection could be made between, on the one side, what they had done and experienced with him, and, on the other, that unheard-of new thing that they experienced on Easter morning. Only among these could that effective connection be made which would ignite the sudden spark of faith, whose inconceivable testimony would leap like lightning from the living Christ, kindling generation after generation into a torch of God among the dark valleys of our earthly pilgrimage. *The resurrection is a fact that takes place only for believers.* It is a deep and very indicative element of the Easter story that, despite the empty tomb, the disciples were not permitted to "see" the Easter mystery (one could say that it was not "demonstrated" to them); they had to "believe" the word—the *word*—of their risen Lord.

Only because they did believe and did satisfy themselves with "Moses and the Prophets," so to speak, was the mystery of Jesus' new life revealed to them. They learned that he "was in the midst of them" when two or three gathered in his name, and that he would remain with them until the end of the world.

Therefore it is somehow sheltering and unspeakably comforting to entrust ourselves to him and, finally, holding to his hand, *our-*

selves step through that night of death which one day will engulf us all.

How much more cheering that is than believing in something as empty as a so-called immortality of the soul! In this regard I can understand the Bolsheviks and other aggrieved parties who don't hold such ideas and who find total disintegration of the organism more congenial. "There's no great Beyond, no re-union," they say. And I can understand why they announce that without a trace of sadness, but with a certain bright equanimity. For is it really pleasant never to come to an end but to have to live on and on? Whoever takes the common belief in immortality seriously will soon discover for himself that he is caught by a somewhat depressing conviction.

Once again I quote Christopher Marlowe, the sixteenth-century writer of *Dr. Faustus*, who speaks about this horror of immortality. After twenty-four years in league with the devil, Faust has a dread of immortality. He implores the mountains to fall on him, the earth to swallow him, and the universe to dissolve him away. *Pure horror is to live forever without the grace of God.*

But on Easter we are told *whose* hand it is that grips us when the night of death breaks in upon us. We are told that we need not wander alone over an empty and endless plain. The one who today offers us a new life, who makes our conscience sing, who takes upon himself our burdens, and who gives wings of confidence to our heart, *He* will receive us at last and enfold us with his presence. The faithfulness that we experience here and now can never end. And as he once came to us in the front lines of our human existence, in order to suffer our fate with us and for us, so one day we shall become partners in his glory.

> He bursts through death
> Through world, through sin and need.
> He bursts through hell.
> I am his constant fellow through it all.

The acceptable time has not yet run out. We may still venture to entrust ourselves to him in the great experiment of faith. His arms are still open to us. The master still looks for workmen.

Perhaps God will demand my soul tonight. Who knows? Therefore everything depends on my entrusting that soul to his hands *today*. For his hands can calm the waves, rend the tomb, heal our wounds, and forgive our sins. Then the cemeteries will really become what they once were for a deep-delving mind: "God's acres," where we lie dormant, as kernels of that eternal seed which (as Klopstock once said) God has sown to ripen for the day of harvest. Then we can speak the paradoxical and superbly triumphant Easter confession of Kohlbruegge: "Therefore, when I die (but I shall no longer die) and someone finds my skull, that skull will yet preach to him like this:

> I have no eyes
> and yet I see him;
> I have no brain nor understanding,
> and yet I comprehend him;
> I have no lips,
> and yet I kiss him;
> I have no tongue,
> and yet I praise him with ye all
> who call upon his name;
> I am a hard skull,
> and yet I melt and soften
> in his love;
> I lie out here in God's acre,
> and yet I am in Paradise.
> All suffering is forgotten.
> His great love has, for our sakes,
> made him bear the cross
> and climb the way to Golgotha.

THIRD QUESTION: HOW CAN I BE SURE OF THE RISEN CHRIST?

Now Thomas, one of the twelve, called the Twin, was not with them when Jesus came. So the other disciples told him, "We have seen the Lord." But he said to them, "Unless I see in his hands the print of the nails, and place my finger in the mark of the nails, and place my hand in his side, I will not believe."

Eight days later, his disciples were again in the house, and Thomas was with them. The doors were shut, but Jesus came and stood among them, and said, "Peace be with you." Then he said to Thomas, "Put your finger here, and see my hands; and put out your hand, and place it in my side; do not be faithless, but believing." Thomas answered him, "My Lord and my God!" Jesus said to him, "Have you believed because you have seen me? Blessed are those who have not seen and yet believe."   —*John 20:24–29*

There is a small thirteenth-century miniature from Cologne that depicts the decisive encounter of Jesus with doubting Thomas.[1] Christ, followed by his disciples, steps through the church door while Thomas stands outside, ready to test Jesus by placing his hand in the nail prints. There are some significant details in this scene. Jesus stretches his arms over Thomas like a cross. It is as though the unhappy seeker already stood under the cross without realizing it. While he yet doubts, he is already touched by that gesture of Jesus' blessing. The lines in the figure of Thomas have about them a tense excitement. It seems as though Thomas is saying, "Everything depends on what happens in the next few moments. Nothing less than my identity is at stake. Am I saved, or have I fallen prey to a gigantic illusion that will leave me spiritually bankrupt?" But one final intimation of the painter is the most astounding of all. Although he stands outside in a state of unmastered doubt, Thomas is encircled by a halo, the aura of a saint. He is already enveloped by rays of glory that Jesus' other followers still lack, even though they appear secure in their discipleship.

What kind of figure is this, surrounded by doubt and hope at the same time? In a few strokes I would like to try to sketch a portrait of this man for you.

Here we are confronted by one of the New Testament stories that don't lend themselves to theology or formula. What sort of

[1] It is in the Gospel-book from Great St. Martin's in Cologne, which dates from 1250. (Bibliotheque Royale, Brussels.)

theological doctrine would be distilled from this story? Could one, for instance, formulate from this story the thesis that faith requires confirmation by experience? That is, that one cannot hold something to be true unless one has established it by all means of verification (beginning with eyesight and sense of touch)? Obviously, our story resists being pressed into such a mold. Indeed, Jesus expressly rejects the idea that faith is based on proof from experience. "Blessed are those who have not seen and yet believe."

Perhaps one could formulate just the *opposite* thesis on the basis of Jesus' words and say that faith is not really true faith if it wants to "see" and "experience." True faith, rather, is blind. Without any reassurance, faith must take the risk of falling blindly, so to speak, at the Lord's feet. But even this thesis doesn't work, for Jesus *lets* Thomas see and feel! That may be illogical; it may be theologically "questionable"; but that's what Jesus did. So Jesus foils our attempts at theologizing.

It is a good thing to encounter a story that cannot be neatly pigeonholed. It quite definitely trains one in openness of mind, in hearing and accepting surprises. In addition (and this too is good!), a story that is so illogical and that resists all doctrinaire formulations reminds us that Holy Scripture is always greater than our minds, even greater than our theology, and that an explosive power lurks within it. No matter how industriously and cleverly we dig our intellectual canals, they cannot contain or channel the wealth of scripture; it floods over us in its surge and its fullness, drowning in its waters the old theological know-it-all called Adam.

Now let us begin by looking at the figures who appear in our text. The fact that Thomas, the doubter, comes to believe is due in no small measure to the miracle of the fellowship. We must first devote our attention to this group.

Certainly we cannot say that Thomas was a so-called "leading member" of the congregation, or even that he was a "model Christian." By current standards, he would be classified as "on the fringe" or perhaps even as an "intellectual radical." At crucial moments in the life of the fellowship, he had not exactly demonstrated staying power. To be sure, he had not separated himself from the fellowship of the disciples, but he wasn't exactly a pillar, either. He was not a man endowed with rousing, consoling, and encouraging words.

Nevertheless, in a certain sense he *was* faithful. He was even ready to die with Jesus. In spite of that, there was a crippling hopelessness about him. Time and again he came out with things that the others hardly dared think about in their most anxious moments. "What are we fighting and preaching for?" was the burden of his questioning. "We don't know what will come of this whole venture, and yet we have invested our lives in it." "We do not know where you are going; how can we know the way?"—those were his actual words as he talked aloud to himself (John 14:5).

Of course the others were just as much in the dark about whether or not they were serving a lost cause, but Thomas said openly that he didn't know. And once this is spoken, the door is open to the specter of fear. We know how it goes when people speak out in that way. Suppose you have heard a good sermon—not as good and not as authoritative as Jesus would have preached, but still a good, rousing sermon. Right afterward someone says to you (and his words fall heavy on your ear), "Granted it was a good sermon, but outside the masses pour from factory doors without having heard it. What will happen to us if the masses remain without a shepherd and if secularism stifles all searching for God? What use is one good sermon when we need a revival throughout the country? Aren't we heading for collectivism, robots, and cities like anthills? Where is Jesus going? Isn't it all fruitless in the end, and isn't the night coming, when no man can work?"

Even if we have silently thought the same thing ourselves a hundred times, something like that is paralyzing. And that was certainly Thomas' constant effect.

Finally, he absented himself *completely* from the gatherings of the disciples. He no longer put up the "opposition" but, like a wounded animal, crept into his burrow. If the disciples, the fellowship, had then said, "Thank heaven we're free of that fault-finding wet blanket," we would understand perfectly. But that is just what they did *not* say; they remained faithful to Thomas. They kept him posted on their experience with Jesus. And they obviously told him in such a way that he felt himself buoyed up by their brotherliness, so that he brought himself to return to their fellowship at the decisive moment.

At any rate, this fellowship is no society of the ninety-nine righteous ones, eager to get together in order to form an association for undisturbed mutual edification. They endured the uncomfortable presence of a man who could disturb them acutely and who constantly teetered on the brink of heresy. In other words, it was not a closed group or party intent on homogeneous exclusiveness, nor was it a chemically pure denomination, permitting no one to step out of line. Notice: they endured a man who doubted the *resurrection*, the basic teaching of Christianity. If he held office in any self-respecting church today, he would certainly be saddled with a heresy trial. And if the members didn't go that far, it would not usually be because they were willing to "bear with" the annoyance; it would likely be because they didn't take the church too seriously. They would tell themselves, "In the general church game a few 'extreme' or 'liberal' elements don't matter. The rest of us, after all, are pretty good plants, and we can endure the weeds until things can be sorted out on Judgment Day. Then finally—finally!—we at God's right hand can once again be by ourselves, undisturbed."

That is, of course, the reason why no revivals and no awakenings break out among us; that is why we have so few Thomas miracles. Where we have nominal members on one side and friendly tolerance on the other, no sparks are likely to fly. No one catches fire. Thomas must have noticed that it pained the disciples' fellowship not to be permitted his *complete* presence, and that it hurt them that he had excluded himself from the blessing which they shared. He bore deep wounds in his heart, but precisely for that reason he must have been moved to see that his brothers suffered pain on *his* account. In the Kingdom of God the prescription runs, "Wounds heal wounds." Which of us feels a twinge in his heart when he uses the popular phrase, "those on the outside," or, "the fringe members of the church"? Haven't nearly all of us classified our environment into Christian and heathen, believing and doubting, active and indifferent? But he who wants to save men's souls, concerning himself with doubters and secular mankind, must suffer pain. Otherwise he doesn't "bear with" the other person, he merely "bears" him. When he bears him, then the other *lets* himself be borne, that is, he remains neutral and is assuredly *not* on hand when Jesus' appearance behind locked doors is in the offing. I fear, however, that in such a case Jesus never comes at all. Behind the unblessed, hermetically sealed doors, people *without* Thomas go on whining for an awakening or a new power of the Spirit that will rouse the valley of dead bones. They forge "strategies," carry on "public relations," organize great conferences, and resort to all sorts of gimmicks. But nothing happens. The miracle of Pentecost fails to occur. How could it be otherwise?

Then there is Thomas himself. Thomas—we all are like him, of course, or at least *one* voice in us is. Let's see precisely *how* he doubts, for there is one way of doubting that contains a promise and another that does not.

We hear of Thomas' doubt in the story of the raising of Lazarus (John 11:16). It happens like this: In Jerusalem there has been a growing consolidation of powers hostile to Jesus. Thomas, like everyone else, has assumed Jesus will bring in the theocracy and set up a reign of peace. Then is it possible (and this is the question of doubt) for this assumption to be correct when the force of the Messiah, instead of making headway and in fact winning, only creates a *counterforce?* And then what happens when, in a dark and depressing hour, the feeling arises that the counterforce is actually growing stronger and that one's own chances for the long-awaited "Christianization" are proportionately dimmer? What sort of dismal prophecies are these that clutch at the heart? *If* they prove accurate, then isn't the assumption that Jesus is victor over the world false? The introspective Thomas grapples with tormenting thoughts like these. He becomes depressed.

Then comes a last drop which brings this cup of gloom to

overflowing: Lazarus dies. So, in other words, there is something that is stronger than Jesus, namely, death. If death can drag off the friend of Jesus as booty, that means he can seize even Jesus himself.

Perhaps this experience contributed to the fact that, later, Thomas was not able to believe the resurrection of Jesus either. Golgotha proved the case; there death carried things to a conclusion and took the friend of Lazarus too. If a man has to give in to death, then he cannot be the Savior of the world. Thus Thomas argued and calculated, and therefore he doubted.

Yet it was a *special* sort of doubt that agitated Thomas. The peculiar feature was that he didn't turn, say, to the Pharisees, or to philosophy, or to some other world view for security. All of us want something certain to hang on to. So did Thomas. But still he didn't leave; he said, "Let us also go, that we may die with him." That is certainly the most disconsolate statement in the Bible. It is the speech of a man with empty hands, bereft of hope.

But if Jesus calls the poor "blessed," shouldn't that also imply a promise for those who are poor in *faith*, who are downcast and hopeless? That must have been the case with Thomas. His hopelessness did not seduce him into seeking other hopes. He was ready to die in his hopelessness and perish in faithfulness.

Now we must try to understand that the divine promise is already active in this sort of hopelessness. But first we must examine Thomas' hopelessness still more closely, for what we have said so far does not yet fathom the deepest secret of that hopelessness. Thomas didn't want just to die. He didn't want something merely negative. He wanted to bind the hopelessly lost cause of his life with the lost cause of the Nazarene. He was ready not merely to die, but to die *with* the very man in whom he had placed all his hope. If I am ready to die with another, then I surrender myself to him absolutely; I wager my entire existence on him. And that is exactly what Thomas did. Therefore, clouds of blessing floated above his hopelessness. He did not bind his fate to Jesus because he hoped that by so doing he would become rich, happy, or comparatively free, or perhaps would even be able to expect a cabinet post in the messianic kingdom. He did not give himself to Jesus in order to obtain something else.

If Thomas lived today he would certainly not give himself to Jesus in order to save the Christian West or to have some sort of counter-ideology against the East. All of those things for which he *also* might hope (the salvation of his people by the religious leader Jesus, peace among men, the propagation of a world-transforming view of love) had vanished like a dream, like a beautiful dream. Thomas certainly had had such dreams. There isn't a Christian who hasn't dreamed them at some time or other.

But Thomas was *completely* without hope. So he did not hold to Jesus in the hope of getting something. He held to him because he loved him, because he was faithful to him, and because he wanted to die with him. It was precisely his complete hopelessness that forced him to the primary, central thing, the person of the Savior himself.

I only wish that we, too, had a dose of this divine hopelessness within us, so that we didn't yet know what clouds of blessing floated above us and had no intimation of whose hands held us.

However, let us (as comrades of doubting Thomas) allow our hidden hopelessness to stand for once: the concern, for example, that *no* awakening will again sweep across our land, that secularism and indifference will continue to grow, that the trend toward a mass society will increase, that the facts will more and more disprove the lordship of Jesus, and that only a few old people will still huddle around the altars. With one brave, heroic, despairing blow, let us free ourselves from all dreams of re-Christianizing culture and even from optimistic church statistics. Let's be clear for once that we Christians may become very lonely people, and that the last old woman who still listens to us (even in this "promised land") will one day die, and that then the onetime preacher can peddle door to door. For once let's not console ourselves by saying that this is the "tribulation" that Jesus predicted. Let us rather expect the cold, chilling, furtive thoughts that will come then; let us entertain the possibility that all this could be a *refutation* of Jesus Christ and, therefore, that he had left us, as Jean Paul once expressed it, as waifs without a father, and that he himself was a poor orphan lad. This would mean that we had been taken in by a terrible deception.

Let us not cease doubting too soon! Repressed doubts are bad; they smoulder on. And our faith should certainly not be the product of repression! Let us maintain this extreme hopelessness as Thomas did. For, as Luther said, "Testing teaches us to heed the Word." But *if* we doubt in that way, we won't want to run away or die or put a bullet through our head. Then our final word will be, "All right, then, I'll just die with him. Was *he* wrong? All right, then I will be wrong too. I'll profess his error, then; I'll not disdain him but rather fall into the abyss *with* him."

If I say that, then I have cast myself on Jesus in a way that no one who secretly lives on other hopes can do. Then I am his disciple totally and to the end. I am his disciple *only* and not a secret devotee of a Christian civilization (some sort of effective Christian counterslogan against the East, which would not really obligate me to anything). In that case my complete hopelessness (precisely *that*, of all things) has driven me to him.

Therefore, even the poor in hope are blessed. For they alone have tied their fate to Jesus, even if in despair. And Jesus does not let us down. *Our* hopes deceive everybody. Our life, you know, is full of disappointment. Our plans don't work out; we have to conquer long dry stretches in our lives; and many people whom we trust fail to keep their promises. But Jesus does not let us down.

We should serenely (or despairingly, as far as I am concerned) lay the responsibility of proof upon him. We may say to him, "Show me what you've got, and if there's nothing to you, then nothing else matters, either." And Jesus shows what he has. I am tempted to recount the story of my doubting-Thomas-nature in which this experiment with Jesus was tried, but I won't. One thing, however, is sure: the hopeless doubters have *one* decisive chance. All the props are knocked out from under them; now they are thrown on Jesus himself without knowing whether or not this foundation will hold. But in testing this last support they are dealing with Jesus alone, and that is the greatest opportunity for our faith.

Now Jesus, and he alone, has the floor, and he says, "Blessed are the poor; blessed are the poor in hope; blessed are the doubting who are willing to die with me, for with such I am willing to *live*." That may be consoling sometime, when we are at our wits' end, with all human possibilities shattered and all exits blocked. Then can come the moment when we say, "This is it. Now God is my only defense. Now I can only let myself fall into the dark like a child."

Have we understood, therefore, that Thomas' doubt is of a quite special kind? In any case, it is not to be equated with that blase doubt that fairly bursts with self-assurance, and even less with that false snobbish doubt that wants only to argue without getting involved. Involvement is Thomas' salient characteristic. He throws himself and all he has into the balance. He is prepared to die for his doubt. He is not ready to spare his old life by avoiding Jesus' questioning eyes. His longing doubt hungers for the truth. Therefore, not only the promise, "Blessed are the poor," but also "Blessed are they that hunger and thirst" are valid for him.

We have to take a look at the background of our text; then we can understand it rightly. It is, as we have seen, the last act in the drama of doubt. It portrays the moment in which doubt reaches its climax and in which all the promises come to fulfillment.

Thomas is once again in the fellowship. He has been, so to speak, "loved into it." The disciples told him, "We have seen the Lord. He came through locked doors." Of course, this report cannot satisfy the doubter's deep honesty. That, too, is characteristic of him.

"You say he came through locked doors?" asks Thomas. And he adds to himself, "It could have been a spirit. And spirits that people think they see are usually products of their own imagination."

So this report does not satisfy Thomas. He is willing to believe only if the presence of the risen One is *real*. He is not interested in "ideas" or "spirits" which are reasonable facsimiles of the genuine article.

While Thomas is thus doubting, Jesus again comes through the locked doors, and says, "Peace be with you." He doesn't say,

"Peace be with you—except Thomas, because he has no peace—he is quarreling with me." He includes the dear doubter in his salutation of peace. And not only that—he even addresses him immediately, commanding him to place his hands in the prints of the wounds.

That is a grand and comforting thing. Jesus' attitude to this poor doubter—to *us* poor doubters—becomes clear.

We must begin by discovering that Jesus is not angry with Thomas about his questioning. Instead, Jesus lets him know that he understands. That is the last thing we can hold to when doubt comes over us: Jesus knows about us, but he does not doubt us in return. He is far from doubting *us* when we doubt *him*. (He has even taken our doubt upon himself. Didn't he go through that fearful agony when he cried out from the cross, "My God, my God, why hast thou forsaken me?" He has borne our doubt in exactly the same way that he bore out guilt and our death.)

Next, Jesus does not wait until Thomas asks him; he is suddenly there, unasked, with his answer—and in a way that Thomas had never dreamed of. This is another illustration of Paul Gerhardt's words, "He will act in a way that will amaze you."

Finally, Jesus does not come to him with a "theory" about faith. He doesn't say something like, "Your request is not quite legitimate, theologically speaking. In reference to me, the appropriate posture is not seeing, feeling, or experience; it is blind faith."

That's the way we theologians always speak in our discussions. And that's why so few people believe us. It would certainly have been *true* if Jesus had said that. For faith is actually independent of verification by sight and touch. But in that moment, such a truth would have been an excessive demand to place on Thomas. He simply wasn't far enough along to have been able to bear that truth. Were he alive today, then there would be plenty of answers from philosophers like Kant and Jaspers; and in a twinkling a furious debate would arise, ending (as most debates do) in smoke.

Jesus, however, does something quite different. He does the completely unexpected. He lowers himself to this poor doubter.

"Seeing is really not important," Jesus may be thinking, "but Thomas is still a poor beginner, an amateur at faith. He still has no idea of what's really essential." Yet that does not hinder Jesus from yielding to this poor beginner in faith. Jesus didn't act properly, one might say. He didn't act in conformity with the prescriptions laid down in dogmatic textbooks under the heading, "Christology." He would certainly have lost points in a theological examination! Notice, please, that Thomas' request, innocent though it may be, places a *condition* on the Lord. He says, in effect, "Do thus and so, otherwise I will not believe in you." May one speak this way? No, one may not so speak; it is not proper. But Jesus does the improper. He does what the phrase of Paul's, "by faith alone," seems to contradict directly. Jesus *shows* himself to Thomas; he lets him see and touch a little. The Son of man is not only lord of the sabbath (Mark 2:28); he is also lord over dogmas, and, even more, over the methods of handling those dogmas.

The fact that Jesus became man means that he wants to bring man back from the depths of his life. Jesus' activity is always downward in its motion. Thus, in this encounter he lowers himself yet another time, going just a little bit deeper—not only to the level of the human heart, but right down to the fingertips.

This may also be instructive for us who are witnesses of Jesus. Perhaps we know someone who hasn't the slightest inkling of the correctness of orthodox belief and who therefore is so much the more depressed by uneasiness and anxiety. Should we give him a lecture about the Holy Trinity or the mysteries of predestination? Or should we do as Kierkegaard did and start out by simply "describing" to him what it is like when Jesus comes into our life: namely, that one finds something like peace; that that is a very fine thing; and that one then sees the whole world with new eyes? Of course, that could smack of emotionalism and subjective experience. Such ways of putting the matter certainly do *not* contain the ultimate mysteries of the faith, either.

But if we spoke in that way, we would show that we did not consider ourselves somehow or other above bending to such a person's poor amateurish faith. Perhaps he would understand us.

Then an occasion might arise for us to say, "You know, faith doesn't depend on subjective emotion, or on seeing and feeling. The case is, rather: Blessed are those who do not feel and yet believe." It is at the end, however, that Jesus says this, and not at the beginning. It is very like the progression from milk to solid food. We should learn a little from Jesus in this matter of how to speak to our neighbor.

And now we look on and are amazed; Thomas is conquered by faith. He exclaims, "My Lord and my God."

What, precisely, brought him to his knees? Was it really the unique opportunity he had to touch Jesus? Was it that he was permitted an experiential proof of the risen One's reality? That would be a bad break for us. *We* don't have that chance anymore, and for us Thomas can be no more than the subject of an historical incident.

Or could it possibly have been something entirely different, perhaps the fact that Jesus lowered himself as he did, that conquered him? Was he simply overpowered by the fact that someone did not scorn his poor doubt, that is, that someone stepped to his side and did not place himself and his resurrection glory *above* Thomas? Was it that he thus discovered the infinite love which sought him and followed after him? Did he see how Jesus left the faithful community of disciples standing there and sought him, him alone, although he had nothing to offer?

I'm sure that we would have no difficulty answering the question as to which of these two actions conquered Thomas. If it had been the experiential touching and seeing, then he would have come up with something like a medical diagnosis: "Yes, it all fits. The nail prints are discernible and they are genuine. He is the one. He is actually risen and alive." Thus Thomas would have had to speak of Jesus in the third person. "He" is alive; "it" fits. But that is precisely what he did *not* do; he said "you" to him. He said, "My Lord and my God."

Immediately, the matter of touching, feeling, and experiencing became inconsequential. We are never told whether Thomas acted on Jesus' offer at all, that is, whether he *really* placed his hands in the woundprints. All of that immediately fades into the background and becomes unimportant. It either never even happened or it no longer needed to be mentioned at all.

Then does Thomas' belief really rest simply on seeing and touching Jesus? Would his heart have remained spiritually dead without the aid of his fingertips? And are we poor souls of the twentieth century lost for sure, since we obviously can no longer perform the fingertip test?

No, Thomas' belief does not rest on seeing and touching. When he says, "My Lord and my God," he is expressing infinitely more than he could have seen and felt. He says, "*My* Lord." Mere seeing and touching can never produce anything like that.

To cite a parallel situation, think of an historian investigating the Resurrection. Even if he should come to the scientific conclusion that the historical documentation for the resurrection of Jesus was without loopholes of any kind and beyond all doubt, would he experience anything more than a great shock or bewildered astonishment in the presence of an historical anomaly? This line of procedure would never bring him to confess, "My Lord and my God." The fact that Thomas did not simply say "it fits," but rather "my Lord" shows that he recognized the Lord by his love and not by physical characteristics, just as Mary had probably done on Easter morning.

The fact of Jesus' presenting himself to sight and touch is thus placed back in its proper perspective. It was a sort of icebreaker, a loving concession to a blocked-in faith, but it was not the cause of the faith. There is a similar clearing-up operation in our proclamation, too. It has not yet come to the point where faith is born; it merely sweeps up and prepares the cradle.

For instance, I think of Mr. X. He has met some Christians in his life who were just plain lemons and who bitterly disappointed him. How many others have been hurt by a pastor whose egotism or whose life contradicted his preaching, so that Christianity in general became untrustworthy in their eyes? Naturally, even that is not a valid objection to the faith, for faith depends on the Lord himself and not upon imperfect men. But this perfectly true comment is as much help to Mr. X as it would have been for someone to have told Thomas (with absolute propriety) that faith was not dependent upon experience. Then, in prison, or among his colleagues, or somewhere on vacation, Mr. X meets a Christian who doesn't say much at all, but who is so thoroughly genuine that his discipleship seems to shine through. One can tell by the way he acts with simple people, by his loyalty, by his selflessness, and by other things of a moral or less definite nature. Mr. X says, "With Mr. Y one feels that his faith gives power to his life," and Mr. X is at once ready to revise his skepticism. He is also ready to listen, should this man take him along some evening to a group where a section of the Bible is studied, perhaps, or where faith and nihilism are discussed.

Let us suppose for a moment that Mr. X goes along to these meetings fairly frequently out of personal attachment for Mr. Y, and by no means out of a thirst for faith or a need for salvation. Let us suppose he tells himself, "My Christian friend may be a dreamer, but at least he is a dreamer with breadth and determination. He rings true. That illusion which he calls his 'faith' can't be too bad, even for me. It may be nonsense—O.K., then I'll go down with him." Let us suppose that he comes to take the first steps of faith in some such roundabout way, and that he touches the robe of Jesus for the very first time. Then he matures bit by bit, from that point on, because Jesus himself has now entered the picture. Who would believe that his friend would take Mr. X aside one day and tell him, "Look here, it was wrong of you to let those no-good Christians you met take your faith away from you, and it is just as wrong if you believe just because you find, or think you find, a bit of Jesus' glory mirrored in me. Blessed are they who never 'see' such men (maybe they crouch in a modern police-state prison and come in contact only with robots). Blessed are they who do not see and yet believe."

Maybe that's what happened to Thomas. Jesus' showing himself to Thomas was an icebreaker, a touching concession to an undeserving skeptic. Jesus did not want to argue with him; he wanted to take him by the hand. And then at the end of this encounter (but really at the *end*, after love and leading had done their work), then Jesus untied the water wings of support that seeing and touching had provided. Then Thomas must swim for himself. And, as we said before, maybe Thomas never even grasped for the water wings; he may have taken the first strokes of faith boldly, as soon as he saw who was watching over his efforts to stay afloat.

It would be a fine thing if we, as Thomas' companions in misfortune, could likewise come to the point where we could say, "My Lord and my God" after having doubted so long or having spoken half-blindly about "Christendom" or the "Christian West."

It would be a fine thing if, in our moments of direst inner turmoil, we ourselves could hold fast to the one thought that, even then, Jesus understands us and keeps us from falling. Blessed are the poor in hope, for they are the ones who may say, "My Lord and my God." But if we learn to know this about him and become his disciples, may we be given the grace not to exalt ourselves above the doubting Thomases around us. We will no longer want to argue with them, but we will try to show them a little of the glory of Jesus as we understand it, perhaps even without words, letting the simple deed speak for itself. We should not worry about whether that word is letter-perfect and chemically pure in its orthodoxy. The person to whom we are speaking at the time is not going to endorse any "dogma"! He is simply invited to meet the Master and to receive his peace.

We shall never tire of asking that the Lord come to us and to the other doubters, saying in his immeasurable goodness (as he pronounced at the death of Lazarus), " 'This illness is not unto death; it is for the glory of God' (John 11:4). And precisely those who are at the end and have lost all their chances shall be the bearers of the promise. They shall be showered with wonders beyond their wildest dreams. And as they stand baffled, looking for a way of escape, I have entered through a different door and already stand beside them."

ASCENDED INTO HEAVEN, AND SITTETH AT THE RIGHT HAND OF GOD

Then he led them out as far as Bethany, and lifting up his hands he blessed them. While he blessed them, he parted from them (and was carried up into heaven). And they returned to Jerusalem with great joy, and were continually in the temple blessing God.   —*Luke 24:50–53*

If then you have been raised with Christ, seek the things that are above, where Christ is, seated at the right hand of God. Set your minds on things that are above, not on things that are on earth. For you have died, and your life is hid with Christ in God. When Christ who is our life appears, then you also will appear with him in glory.

And whatever you do, in word or deed, do everything in the name of the Lord Jesus, giving thanks to God the Father through him.   —*Colossians 3:1–4, 17*

Once at home, when our children were still small, we had retold the story of Christ's ascension when our youngest noted, "When the Lord Jesus finally got to heaven the Father told him, 'Better stay up here, otherwise something will happen to you again.' "

The young man, in all innocence, had made a statement which accurately describes one of the two great misunderstandings which threaten to block our access to what the Bible means when it talks about "heaven." That is, he conceived of this "heaven" (understandably enough for a child) as a safe place, withdrawn from all the catastrophes and breakdowns of our long-suffering world. The philosophers—all those before the great Plato—could express it much more spiritually than my little son, but basically they remained bound to that same level of thinking. Thus, for them heaven was the embodiment of a far-off region, timeless and alone, the dwelling place of the eternal ideas, arching in pure and untarnished radiance above the cycle of growth and decay, and withdrawn from the vanity of this transitory world. "The soul's true home is in light above"—this hymn smuggles that same heathen contraband across the border into Christian territory.

The heaven of the Bible, on the other hand, looks entirely different. When the Bible speaks of the "God of heaven and earth," it always means the *active* God whom heaven and earth must serve. This heaven is never a "timeless beyond"; it also belongs to the realm of created things and is therefore delivered up to transitoriness too. Only *one* shall stand when the world's vast grave opens and when (as those mighty visions describe the great finale of the world) the stars fall and the powers of heaven are shaken (Matt. 24:29). Heaven and earth will pass away, the "world . . . and the lust of it" will come to an end, but "my words will not pass away." Finally, only *one* figure remains —and will remain—standing at what Teilhard de Chardin has called the "Omega Point." That figure is even greater than heaven. It is as though heaven's last function were merely to reflect the afterglow of the dying world. Thus it too, in the biblical view, is drawn into the finite created realm of growth and decay.

This "relative" nature of heaven is expressed even more re-motely by the fact that occasionally heaven even appears as the home of threatening or demonic and destructive powers. In the letters to the Ephesians and Colossians the heavens symbolize the environment of sinister powers which encompass our world and which would break in upon us if the protecting hand of God did not hold them in check (Gen. 1:6 ff.). Thus heaven is presented as a region that must be conquered and deprived of its power; at least, it is never portrayed as a fabulous dreamland in the eternal great Beyond. It almost seems as though these mythical pictures were meant to assert that God the Lord is the only one before whose sovereignty everything in heaven and on earth and under the earth must bow. He is the one and only; in contrast to him everything is a mere creation which is just allowed to exist and which is certain to perish. Heaven can indeed be called the "throne" of God, but of course even the throne is less than the sovereign himself. Heaven must be content with the rank of a very inferior piece of furniture—a footstool and a few square inches of floor.

If heaven is not simply the position to which Jesus was "elevated" (and for this reason the phrase "ascended into heaven" is a dubious one and somewhat misses the point, despite its venerable age) then we must be clear what majesty is ascribed to Jesus by our calling heaven his *kingdom*. He takes possession and subdues it (Acts 3:21); together with the earth it forms the "body" whose cosmic head is Christ (Eph. 1:10; Col. 1:16, 20). Now let us draw the inevitable conclusion from this analogy. Just as every body turns to dust, so this universe will one day disintegrate; the sea will be no more, the flowers will turn to dust, the songs of birds will be stilled, and Mozart's *Kleine Nachtmusik* will die away. But Christ's word shall endure forever, regally calling a new heaven and a new earth into being.

Maybe we could put it this way. Heaven can be an impressive symbol of God's lordship when we compare it to what we are as *men:* we humans with our fear of tomorrow, our bickering, our illusions, and our vulnerability to death. Jesus refers to this superiority of heaven over the world when he teaches us the prayer, "Thy will be done by us on earth as it is already being done in heaven."

However, this same heaven can also be demoted to insignificance and seem like a wretched footstool when we compare it to the eternal majesty of *God.* Thus it is out of the question to regard heaven simply as a timeless great Beyond or as the otherworldly sphere of the so-called divine, as philosophers do and as my small son also did, in his own way.

In dealing with this first point, I have already brought up a *second* misunderstanding which blocks our access to the true nature of heaven. I am speaking of the *spatial* misunderstanding.

It goes without saying that men in earlier centuries visualized heaven (and consequently the ascension of Christ) within the framework of their world view. They saw the earth as a disk with the crystal sphere of the firmament arching above it. As yet, obviously, they knew nothing of light-years, space, or the planetary nature of our earth. Today no one could come up with the idea that, all modern astronomy to the contrary, we should maintain this ancient world view simply because it is the world view of the Bible. But the more obvious it is that at this point we have gone far beyond the Bible to the position of Copernicus and his successors, the less obvious the possibility of answering *another* question seems to become. This question is inevitably connected with that change in world views, and it goes like this: Doesn't the *content* perish along with the obsolete world view which embodied it? Can the phrase "Christ ascended into heaven" still be repeated without reservation in the age of modern astronomy and space travel? Doesn't it, perhaps, become a mythical ghost which even half-educated (and quarter-educated) people deride with an air of superiority? Isn't it theological sophistry and insincere trickery, then, when the church comes along and flavors this mythological soup with a few modern existential spices in order to make it palatable to contemporary man? We must be very honest at this point, but we must also use our heads.

Certainly the first point to establish would be this: the gospel wants to approach every period of history in that period's own language and every people in *their* own language; therefore the gospel undergoes one new incarnation after another. And just as nations preach the eternal word and hear it in their languages —German and English, Japanese and Hindustani—so the various centuries express it with the help of their current world views. They utilize the Babylonian signs of the zodiac or Einstein's theory of relativity in order to find ever-new ways of using their languages to express the mighty acts of God and to differentiate between the permanent and the perishable. For us, the change has been in the very conception of space itself. We realize that the message about heaven and the ascension of Christ is clothed in the conceptions of an outmoded view of space. The message itself, however, is much *more* than that conception. It therefore remains for us to fit the message into a new frame; the problem is merely with the frame. That is roughly what some contemporary theologians mean when they say that we modern men can no longer seek God "up there," in spatial terms, but only in the "depth of being," which is an entirely nonspatial dimension. That is perfectly true, but it is also almost trite, since it is just a matter of terminology and conceptual means rather than a matter of the thing itself. This problem has been vastly overemphasized.

Some time ago it was reported that American astronaut John Glenn met his Soviet counterpart, Titov. The Russian, who had apparently had a thorough ideological indoctrination, asked the American with a somewhat disdainful smile, "Did you by any chance encounter God on your space flight?" To which Glenn replied, "The God in whom I believe is not the sort you could see from the window of a space capsule." I wonder if that answer stimulated the Russian to do a little thinking. I wonder if Titov's statement, "I didn't see a man with a long beard in space," perhaps didn't come to seem as silly to him as the observation of the pathologist, Rudolf Virchow, appears to us moderns: "I have dissected countless cadavers but have never found a soul."

Aren't completely different dimensions of existence being confused with one another when people talk so wildly? The English language lends itself to careful and precise differentiation in this matter. It has two completely different terms: "heaven" and "sky." When we talk about the atmosphere which the meteorologists describe on their weather maps and which we can see as we look up to the star-strewn firmament at night or as we lie tanning ourselves on the sand, we speak of the "sky." But then we have another word, "heaven," which refers to the throne of God and therefore describes a spiritual, rather than spatial, dimension. Heaven is not simply "above," so that we have to lift our eyes to see it; it surrounds us on all sides. It is that "depth of being" that I mentioned earlier. The old Gothic and Byzantine painters had that same insight when they painted heaven gold instead of blue and selected it as a background for the human face.

That style, it seems to me, shows a radical change in the times. Today when someone paints a portrait he tries to bring out the characteristics of his subject with nearly photographic detail, taking pains to over-accent his subject's "individuality." A clever photographer, too, employs lighting effects that can turn even a Milquetoast into a character study. Things are quite different with those painters of the golden heaven. The individuality of faces is hardly brought out at all, and the drapery is stylized. But that makes no difference. The painters are trying to tell us that the essential thing about man is not his unique individuality but the fact that he stands before the background of heaven. That is, man is referred to the glory of God, reflecting something of that glory in his own countenance. Heaven is not a space overhead to which we lift our eyes; it is the background of our existence, the all-encompassing lordship of God within which we stand.

Once we have grasped this idea, it becomes clear that presenting heaven in spatial terms is merely a visual device that is not at all identical with the truth it intends to convey. To be sure, this is not the only place in life where we constantly must distinguish between *what* we mean and the *way* we visualize it. A child, of course, can actually visualize God only as an old man with a long beard. And why not? But when a person grows older he soon realizes that that was only a childish picture which helped him to "visualize" the wisdom, goodness, security, and wonder of a fatherly heart. As we learn to overcome the image of the Father-figure (without, however, abandoning the wonder of the fatherly heart along with it), we must also grow up enough to give up heaven as simply "space," as an imaginary "somewhere over the rainbow," and to seek God in the depths of being rather than in the heights.

This is not at all intended to start a rearguard battle with pious people who give way only grudgingly and with grumbling to certain results of astronomy. Human nature being what it is, such a turn of events would not be unlikely! However, it may be a comfort to know that even Luther saw the Ascension in exactly the same way, even though he did think Copernicus was a pretty weird fellow. That's understandable enough. After all, it obviously must have been a terrible shock to medieval men when the earth, which had borne the Lord's cross and on which Abraham, Isaac, and Jacob had had their dealings with God, suddenly lost its central place in the cosmos and dwindled to an out-of-the-way corner on the edge of the universe. Whoever smiles at this shock today shows only that he is a snob with little or no sympathetic imagination. But precisely because Luther's conceptual world was undoubtedly still captive to ancient cosmology, one cannot but be impressed by the fact that, despite this limitation, he could see more in the ascension than just a spatial ascent to some cosmic sphere. In his well-known graphic way he could recall people who had such an awfully naive conception of the Ascension that "they don't know what it means to say that Christ ascended to heaven and sits at the right hand of God. For it didn't happen the way you climb up a ladder in your house. It means that he is *above* all creation and *in* all creation and *outside* of all creation." Here again, he did not climb into the blue sky; he entered the icon's golden background for the world.

At this point I must call your attention to a very remarkable precedent. The first attack against this spatial misunderstanding about heaven is launched from the lips of those mysterious heavenly messengers to whom the Book of Acts refers as "two men in white robes" (Acts 1:10 f.). These men mingle with the apostles at Christ's ascension and comment to them upon his transfiguration, his new mode of existence. In effect, they tell the disciples, "Why do you stand there looking up at the sky? Why do you gaze after him, gawking up in the air? You have no time for idle nostalgia or grief at parting." They point out to the disciples that he will come again and that they must use the limited time until that happens. Now, between his departure and his return, is the hour for loins to be girded and lamps to burn (Luke 12:35). Now they are put to work. For he who has gone to the great Beyond is not "up there" out of our sight; he is the lord of our world, the ruler of peoples and nations; he embraces Orient and Occident; he encompasses both capitalism and communism. He is even the hidden driving force behind the atomic age in which we are called *today* to proclaim his lordship.

We humans, of course, begin by seeing only the negative side of the ascension. That is, Christ has vanished and we seem to be left alone. Apparently our world has become autonomous; life seems to roll along according to its own laws. Now might makes right; the unremitting battle for supremacy rages in business and in world politics, and when we think about unrest among newly independent nations, about racial conflict, and about dangerous tension between the great ideological systems, we see power struggles and takeovers that occur pretty much according to their own laws, while God, apparently, plays no role at all. Meanwhile Christ sits in the great Beyond, or maybe even deep in our hearts, where we piously worship him. Unfortunately, though, we don't notice a single trace of any worldly sovereignty issuing from him.

Granted, there may be people who pray to him, but doesn't that remain confined to the ghetto of spiritual life? Where can we discern mountains being moved by this faith? Where has it shoved the rigid power blocs of East and West even one inch from their positions? And where is it possible to recognize the least indication that faith in him who died for black and white humanity intervened creatively and changed anything in the racial conflicts here and in South Africa? Aren't economic and social results achieved exclusively through ice-cold political calculations? And if, in some parliament or senate, the name of Christ were to be proclaimed as the plumb line for political life, wouldn't it stick out like a sore thumb and promptly be passed over in favor of the regular agenda? Where, then, is that plan of God which the course of world history follows or which we should learn about in order to know what we are to do, how we are to govern, or what socio-political decisions we are to make? Isn't Christ all too terribly absent and uninvolved? And isn't the whole business of the ascension just a very optimistic way of speaking about his actual nonexistence or his hopeless irrelevance? Isn't the German custom of holding stag parties on Ascension Day a kind of gigantic satire, commenting on this absence or nonexistence of Christ with appropriate hilarity?

Yet the message of the ascension makes the secret of this withdrawal from the world clear to us. Granted, we don't see him. We are not privy to God's thoughts about our feverish world and about the shadowy ways our lives are led. "For as the heavens are higher than the earth, so are my thoughts higher than your thoughts." *Yet there are thoughts.* We can't think God's thoughts after him, but we can trust the One who thinks them.

This is the only way we have access to those thoughts. And we gain this access only by knowing Him who walked our earth, blessing children, comforting downcast and anxious hearts, giving new meaning in life to despairing seekers, and cradling the head of the dying. The Body from which streams of living water flowed is now enthroned over the world, and that Heart full of mercy has the lordship of our earth. We don't know what's going on around us or what's going to happen to us. We really don't know. But we do know that it comes from that Heart; everything that happens finds its underlying meaning in a love that streams from that Heart, a love for which that Heart suffered death.

It is therefore essential that the message of Ascension Day include His coming again to reveal publicly what is thus far happening secretly. An intimation of this activity came in a dream to the prophet Zechariah long ago: God's lordship is already active and powerful in heaven (remember, not the stratosphere, but the golden heaven of the icons) while on earth politicians and captains of industry, policymakers and those who pull the strings of history imperturbably carry on their business without suspecting anything as yet. It is immaterial whether their plans provide for atheism or for religion. Without suspecting it, they themselves have a place in God's plan; unknowingly they must play their part, led where they do not want to go. They are only commas and periods in a text written by God. While man proposes, God disposes. He builds his kingdom somewhat the way a monument is built—hidden from sight by high scaffolding. Sometimes we hear banging and hammering, but we see neither the workman nor what he is working on until the construction fences fall away and the sign and token of God's majesty rises among us. Meanwhile, we have kept our eyes on our *own* path.

Thus, the ascension does not mean that Jesus Christ *leaves* us; on the contrary, it means that he comes terribly near us. The boundary between this world and the Beyond, which has been passed on Christmas night, is just being crossed once again, and in a new way. For to say that he is exalted to the right hand of God means that now he is over all and that he is, in Luther's words, "above" all creation, and "in" all creation, and "outside" all creation. Before, when he walked the earth, he was close to only a few—only the little group of disciples; his presence was limited by time and space. Only a few heard his word in those days; today it spans the world. Then, only a handful of his friends could plead, "Stay with us, for it is toward evening"; today millions of hands fold in prayer, and where two or three are gathered—at family prayer in Chicago, in a Siberian peasant's cottage or in a little group of faithful prisoners of war—he will be there among them. He passes through the doors of our homes, through the walls of prisons, and through the barbed wire of the "isms."

Thus, the ascension is the festival of Jesus' lordship. But a better way of formulating it would be to apply it to ourselves; it is the festival of my sonship, of my life's journey beneath an open heaven. *It is the festival of this present world*, a world tied in knots and yet living under the proclamation of a secret lordship, guided by higher thoughts. And I may know Him who thinks those thoughts! I don't know what is going on (I do not conceal the fact that the riddle of these occurrences concerns me, and that I am bothered by the question of why an airplane full of tourists crashes, why miners are crushed in a cave-in, or why a child is run over); I really don't know *what* is happening. But I do know about the theme in the *name* of which it happens. I know the heart of Him who holds the drama of history and my life together within that theme, steadily carrying it through to its last act.

Now we have reached a point where we can begin to sketch the consequences which can be drawn from our investigation.

First, if it is true that God directs the drama of history, then all contrary powers are destined to serve him. Then Nebuchadnezzar and Hitler and present-day dictators are given the task of preparing the way for goals which Another has set for them. Then even the most perplexing mishap in my life, which otherwise might infuriate me and give me wrong ideas about God, forms merely one small stone in a mosaic that fits into a picture from "heaven's" point of view. I don't have the slightest inkling of the whole design, but if I could see it in its entirety I would be ashamed of my unbelief. God is weaving a tapestry which I now see only from the wrong side; if I lose sight of the hands that are weaving it, the meaninglessness will make my blood run cold. But whoever has known Christ has seen not only the hands that do the weaving but also the heart that devises the woven design. And my now seeing the tapestry of life only from the *wrong* side kindles the deepest passion, as Kierkegaard once put it, to be close to that heart, drawing comfort from it and resting in it.

Next, if it is true that Jesus Christ is at the right hand of God, "in" all creation and "above" all creation, then the word must be spread. "Mission" becomes necessary to carry this message into the world of gods, idols, and ideologies. It must not be done as though we were spreading a little bit of propaganda for the sake of expanding Christian conviction and a particular nation's way of life. It must be done because Christ is the Lord and the very theme of the world. If that is our motivation, then we are not merely Christian activists, drumming up business by grabbing the arm of our Lord and stretching it across the world through proven advertising techniques and all sorts of tactical refinements. The situation is precisely the opposite. If we have rightly understood the message of the ascension we know that his arm is indeed already stretched above the world and all we have to do is to follow this outstretched hand. Our task is not to figure out how to master the public; we are only to be earnest about making the Master public.

In that case, many of our current prejudices will have to collapse. For example, there is the absurd assumption that today's world falls into two hemispheres: there is the so-called "Christian" world (the West, naturally) where the members of God's party are situated; and then there is the other world, dominated by Buddhists, Muhammadans, fetishists, atheists, secularists, and the indifferent, in which the Lord has no say and no concern. Now, we know that the situation is quite different. Even the atheists dwell in the shadow of Golgotha and its cross, for they are all dearly bought. They all live their lives before that golden background where a secret throne stands. They are all gripped and sought out by Him who is "in" all creation and "above" all creation and who weaves the threads of their lives into his design. When we call for them to "be reconciled to God," we are seeking their souls because they belong to Him and because He has paid dearly for them. His sadness at their lost condition and at their going to a far country then becomes our sadness too.

Finally, if it is true that Jesus Christ is at the right hand of God, then he is the first, last, and only one. Stated in less beautiful technical language, this attribute is called his "absoluteness." Who else would there be to look forward to? Could anyone top him? Could someone else come and tell us something other than that we have tribulation in this world, that it is a far country with barren plains, broken cisterns, and deceptive mirages where life seems to go on without a Father's presence and where the trumpets of nothingness sound on the horizon? Once we have heard the voice of Jesus Christ, could we ever again fall prey to those siren songs that would like to have us believe that there will be paradise on earth, that there will be progress and development, and that there will be a more highly cultured mankind without thieves, murderers, and adulterers? Hasn't Jesus of Nazareth made us immune to false prophets and their utopian dreams? That all seems insipid, once one has heard the voice of the Nazarene.

Or could someone come who would be able to give us something greater than the certainty that we are not forsaken in the midst of this wilderness, but that we are beloved and sought out, that we have been followed all the way to the cross? Could there be a greater message than that of a love which surrendered itself to the deepest humiliation but which also was enthroned at the right hand of God, where it now holds sway over the earth, secure in the promise of victory? What more could any message bring us than the news that power and love are united in this one hand, and that what we know only in shocking contradictions is therefore reconciled in the world's golden background. The loving people in our world have, indeed, been powerless, and often enough history has rolled right over them. Francis of Assisi, Friedrich von Bodelschwingh, and Albert Schweitzer could only flash out weak signals to intimate what God really wanted with us and from us. And the mighty of this world—well, could they have won their power if they had been loving or less unscrupulous or less autocratic? But in the ascension the loving one is enthroned, and the man of sorrows becomes the conqueror.

Thus we know our place of refuge. Thus we know that he not only remembers us with love when the waves of history break into the ship of our life, but that he also has power over wind, wave, and the elements, so that they must "lie down" at once when he tells them to.

We can look calmly into the future. That new savior, Mr. Z, will never come. We await no greater one. We rather wait for him who *has* come and who has sown himself as the seed of promise in our earth. We await him not only as the one who will come where two or three are gathered in his name, but also as him who will come again as victor, raising his banner at the end of time. We live in the name of a fulfillment, already prepared in heaven, but only *being* prepared among us here on earth.

Whoever knows this promise, therefore, can never completely despair. If catastrophes come, if I hit a stretch of bad luck, if I am forsaken, or if age robs me of one loved one after another, anxiety can no longer bid me take cover, for that is when the royal promise tells me to lift up my head because my redemption is drawing near. Whoever has rejoiced in this triumph and this comfort just once, as he wandered through a dark valley hemmed in by the specters of melancholy and bondage, that person knows that it is precisely in the depths that the ascended One surrounds us with his nearness. It is there that we learn to comprehend what a song of praise can be.

FROM THENCE HE SHALL COME
TO JUDGE THE QUICK AND THE DEAD

"But of that day and hour no one knows, not even the angels of heaven, nor the Son, but the Father only. As were the days of Noah, so will be the coming of the Son of man. For as in those days before the flood they were eating and drinking, marrying and giving in marriage, until the day when Noah entered the ark, and they did not know until the flood came and swept them all away, so will be the coming of the Son of man. Then two men will be in the field; one is taken and one is left. Two women will be grinding at the mill; one is taken and one is left. Watch therefore, for you do not know on what day your Lord is coming. But know this, that if the householder had known in what part of the night the thief was coming, he would have watched and would not have let his house be broken into. Therefore you also must be ready; for the Son of man is coming at an hour you do not expect."

—Matthew 24:36–44

These mythological-sounding pictures of the end of the world are so curious! Not that we are completely unable to understand that everything will one day end. Physicists have developed theories about the world's dying of heat or cold. But that doesn't bother us very much, since it won't happen for a few million years. The couple who marry today can still look forward to their silver anniversary in comparative peace without having to fear that their family will turn into ice cubes or evaporate in steam.

This thought about the end concerns us more directly when we think about the thermonuclear self-annihilation that hangs over our heads. It is possible that one day all the fuses may blow and we, like sorcerer's apprentices who have kindled an atomic fire, will be swept into its crackling flames. We know that it could all come upon us like a thief in the night. And, as fantastic as it seems to us, we must reckon with it realistically.

But how about that other "thief in the night" of which the Gospel speaks? Isn't the voice of the world's Judge, commanding imperiously out of the clouds, "Everything stop!"—isn't that quite *unrealistic?* Isn't it the product of an over-imaginative anxiety about the future? Hasn't every century, our own included, seen scripture experts and serious Bible students working with their slide rules to calculate the end of the world and the return of Christ? And haven't these calculations all been discredited and disproved when the sun, despite their predictions, rose as usual the next morning and the marrying and giving in marriage went on just as though nothing had happened?

Every thoughtful person, however, must be struck by the very fact that the continued revolution of the cosmic wheel has *not* driven people to resignation or confused them about the return of Christ. For even when the calculations were carried to ridiculous lengths, the anticipation of the end and the hope of the returning Lord arose (again, just as if nothing had happened) in a completely ingenuous way. Therefore, that hope must certainly spring from the deeper levels of our existence. Is there any other explanation for the way that all rational objections and momentary setbacks shrink to insignificant hurdles which faith in the Lord's final victory repeatedly vaults without seeming to break stride?

Any understanding at all of this process and of the source of this apparently insane hope depends on our penetrating to that deep level of existence. That would enable us to make an astounding discovery which a self-assured, superior-feeling snob could never make: the fact that what was important yesterday is still important today, and that what one could live on yesterday still has the power to carry and fulfill a life today. One must only have understood it.

Joseph Wittig once said that a man's biography cannot be written from his birth on, but only from his death back. One might say it must be told backwards. His meaning is clear. In order to say something about the totality of a life, it is necessary to have that totality before one. It must, therefore, be "finished." And in that case death itself belongs to a biography.

To me Wittig's statement has always seemed to be a parallel to the way the Bible speaks about the history of mankind. A "world history" of that sort is actually, of course, just like a comprehensive biography of the world. The biblical authors do, in fact, proceed along the same lines that govern every true biography. They write it in the certainty that God is the lord of history and that the final victory belongs to him. Seen from the perspective of the end, all chaos and confusion, all temporary triumphs of atheism, all catastrophes (no matter how senseless they may appear), all terrors of dictatorships, and all defeats for God's cause arrange themselves into clear architectonic lines. These lines show the startled observer that God has been building his kingdom in the surging chaos of history, and that all its waves break on the shore of his eternity.

This discovery has both a theoretical and a practical effect. The theoretical effect is that, seen from the perspective of the end, something like a "line of history" develops, "historical continuity" emerges, and history ceases to be a mishmash of unrelated occurrences and anecdotal details. Therefore, there is still good reason today for regarding the prophets of the Old Testament as the fathers of Western historiography.

The practical effect of viewing history from the end is the growth of an imperturbable faith. What does the triumph of godlessness or secularism matter, what does it matter to me if a deadly cancer eats its way into my body or if I am boxed in by a tyrannical "ism," what does all that matter to me *if* I can only be sure that even Nebuchadnezzar and Stalin appear in God's great plan and that they are therefore taken into consideration. Then suffering merely presents me with the question of confidence and teaches me the art of saying "Nevertheless I am continually with thee!" What do the billows of historical catastrophes matter to me and what can the storms of fate accomplish in my little life if I know that the Lord is sleeping in the boat and that we float upon a great tide toward his final victory?

He who can really believe that the end will bring the triumph of God can live a different life. He who has once tried to take that seriously knows what new, life-giving breath fills his lungs, what an overturning of all values follows, and how many things that he used to despise now seem important; likewise, many other things over which he formerly went to pieces now seem unimportant and laughable.

There are, if I'm not mistaken, really only three kinds of people and states of mind that right off the bat exclude this question about the fulfillment of history and the return of Christ. One might say that they have no mental pigeonhole for this question. The *first* group consists of people who agree with Friedrich Schiller's remark that world history itself is world judgment. Or these same people may overemphasize Otto von Bismark's statement that the scrutiny of history is more exact and relentless than that of the Prussian Auditing Office. In other words, in the course of history, guilt and injustice reap their own rewards. "Chickens come home to roost." "Murder will out." And "Honesty is the best policy." If a person is of the opinion that life always leads to a happy ending quite of itself—one might say, "automatically"—and equally automatically works out equitable solutions to all problems, then that person certainly doesn't need to anticipate a Judgment Day. Of course, it may be a long and losing wait until the moral order in the world performs as he expects it to.

The *second* group which have no antennae for the fulfillment of history are those people who, like Faust, think that life's meaning is not in a goal to be reached, but in the act of constant striving.

> How dull it is to pause, to make an end,
> To rust unburnished, not to shine in use.
> (Tennyson, "Ulysses," ll. 22–23.)

Thus, it is possible to let life stand there unfulfilled, with its guilt, its meaninglessness, and its suffering, *if* that simply gives us the raw material with which to come to grips courageously. The attack, not the victory, is the goal. Put succinctly, the act of Faustian striving *needs* the negative just as a hammer needs the anvil. The dubious side of life is not only tolerated, it is essential. But doesn't this sort of life lead mankind into a dreary, vicious cycle around itself? Didn't Mephistopheles speak the honest truth to the dying Faust when he spoke of their cycle's empty meaninglessness?

> "What good for us this endlessly creating?—
> What is created then annihilating? . . .
> I'd rather choose, instead, the Void forever."[1]

The life of Faustian striving, although it is filled with longing and restlessness, is a life with nothing to wait for. It is sustained by the dangerous illusion that the action-packed moment is all there is.

There is yet a *third* group of people whose senses seem to be dead to what the Bible means by the second advent: the coming again of the Lord and the end of the world. This third group consists of those who are addicted to the illusory belief in progress. Technology, especially, moving forward without ambiguity or relapse, suggests to many people that the world will become ever more perfect. From there it is a small step to the utopian idea that mankind itself is becoming increasingly ennobled and that ultimately it will be possible to bring in a classless society or a kingdom of peace that will embrace all people. Goethe discovered the Achilles' heel of this dream long ago when he wrote that *humanity* marches ever forward (that it does— who today can overlook the steady decrease in drudgery, the rising standard of living, and the perfection of society in the coming welfare state!) but *man* always stays the same, with his longings and his anxiety, his rage for life and his vulnerability to death. Even Albert Einstein poured cold water on such dreams of progress when he made the profound diagnosis, "We live in a time of perfect means and confused ends." Obviously, he meant that we smooth our way through the world, and life becomes increasingly easier. Technology relieves us of heavy labor and we become increasingly concerned about social needs. No one has to die of hunger, and no one has to lose out any more because he

---

[1] Johann Wolfgang von Goethe, *Faust*, trans. Bayard Taylor (New York: Modern Library, 1950), Pt. II, Bks. V & VI, p. 242. (Trans.)

cannot pay the doctor. Yes indeed, the means by which we manage life are really becoming more and more perfect.

But for *what*, exactly, are we living? What is the meaning and the theme and the goal of our life's journey? Don't we sometimes detect a dreadful, depressing emptiness? Why this general uneasiness instead of the anticipated happiness? Is it because living and idling threaten to become nearly identical? The perfection of our outward life can become a torment if we no longer know *why* we live and *for what* we are here. Our pace becomes faster and faster, and we like to persuade ourselves that the intensity of our life is thereby deepened. In reality, however, we are marking time or running in circles. The speed of our gigantic carousel creates the deceptive illusion that we are getting somewhere. Naturally, anyone who runs in circles like that soon forgets to ask about the end of history. The return of Christ on a carousel—that is really too much for a man to conceive of.

By contrast, how much more realistic is the view of the historical process which the Bible imparts! Nowhere is there talk about progress to an earthly paradise, a Christianizing of the world which ultimately would make all men brothers. Instead, the Bible says that in this age of the world there will be no end to wars and rumors of wars; that, in fact, the battle between God and Satan will grow increasingly intense so that the final battle lines will become even more entrenched. The last book of the Bible speaks in a way that causes one instinctively to think of modern dictatorships. It speaks of the "beast from the bottomless pit" that will ascend in the later stages of history and call forth demonic horrors.

Therefore there is no thought that things will get better and better, becoming more like paradise on earth. The opposite is true: the sun in God's heaven will become still darker; the depths from which we call upon the Lord will yawn below us in yet more gloomy abysses. The tensile strength of faith will be subjected to yet more severe tests, and, horrible to relate, even the love of the faithful will grow cold (Matt. 24:12).

The Kingdom of God which the returning Christ brings, therefore, is not an historical situation that ultimately could emerge from the level of history itself, something one could term the result of a "development." Then it becomes clear why the end of the world seems to be an act of *God*, confronting us as something from the other side which catches us unprepared, surprising us just like a "thief in the night." The bridegroom approaches while the foolish maidens sleep.

It is characteristic of the "style" of God's acts (if I may use that expression) that we humans cannot work them out; they don't lie on the plane of our philosophical principles. For that reason Jesus, in speaking of these events, consciously connected them with the situation before the flood when there was eating and drinking, marrying and giving in marriage, and when men devoted themselves to "business as usual" without any premonition that the great judgment was brewing in the background.

Count Lehndorff, in his *East Prussian Diary*, tells how the housewives still did their housework and their Easter baking and how the theaters continued to show movies while the Soviet army, near but as yet undetected, launched its deadly pincers movement. We go to work in the morning and sit in front of our TV sets in the evening. But in history's other rooms the table is already being set for the royal wedding feast, and the trumpets of the final judgment are slowly being raised.

Now, of course all that could be mystical, apocalyptic fantasy. If we as Christians intend to speak seriously about the future of our Lord, we cannot do it merely by "quoting" the Bible's statements about the end of history. Who knows how often such quotation can make us fall prey to long-outdated concepts? And how much real damage is done by resorting to such a biblically embellished eleventh-hour panic! To what sectarian nonsense has this alarmism and shock therapy, with the help of the last judgment, led! No, if we intend to speak seriously about the Lord's return, we can do it only by posing the question: What does the heart of our faith, as we *now* experience it and act upon it, indicate about these events of the End? If the encounter with Jesus Christ presents us with the gift of a new life, if we experience the forgiveness of sins from him, and if he imparts hope and confidence to us, then his return is entirely certain for us, so certain that we can live on it and die with it. It then *really* belongs to what I have just called the "heart of our faith."

We may therefore rephrase the question as follows: Does this central and most certain region of our faith perhaps contain hints of that event at the end of history, that demolition of the world? It will be worthwhile for us to follow these projected lines to see where they lead.

I would like to characterize hints of this sort in the following way: everything that we *now* experience in the encounter with Christ, and therefore by faith, has the character of *prophecy*. At the end of everything there is a mysterious punctuation mark—a colon—indicating that another sentence is yet to come and that we are standing in the momentary stillness of a great pause. This pause prompts us to anticipate a final word which still remains unspoken.

For example, we indeed know that we have been brought from death into life and that we stand under the protection of the peace of God. That is a reality for us. We know, we really know, that everything in us which is still incomplete and uncontrolled can no longer separate us from God, and that he remains true to us no matter how unreliable and rebellious we may be. We feel, however, that the spiritual gifts which God has thus far given us are only a "guarantee," a "down payment," and that the really decisive amount is still outstanding (II Cor. 1:22; 5:5; Eph. 1:14). Despite all redemption, for example, don't we feel the pain of "*un*redeemed areas" in our life? Perhaps Christ has really won our heart, but does this heart send the blood surging to all our members, including the extremities of our life, or do many of these outlying areas of our egos remain cold and clammy? How are things, say, with those legs of ours on which we stand in our business and professional life? Can we detect there anything of him to whom we have committed our life, or does everything continue in the old cut-and-dried way?

Perhaps we hear a sermon on loving our neighbor and are even gripped by it. Yet no sooner do we get outside than we merrily continue the quarrel with our neighbor, with our colleague, or with our competitor as if that quarrel hadn't a thing in the world to do with the message we had just heard. Our heart is like a cabinet with drawers that are strictly separated from one another. In one drawer lie our business activities; in a second are family affairs; a third has leisure activities; and a fourth contains inner matters such as our faith and the pious impulses which occasionally come over us when we hear organ music. All of them, however, are neatly divided from one another and remain without mutual contact and exchange. We can push this separation of the spheres of our existence all the way to a formally split personality.

The other people, then, who watch us Christians closely, are not without justification when they talk about hypocrisy and point out with glee that Mr. X, who is a zealous churchgoer, doesn't allow his Christianity to show at home or in his business.

That's what I mean by the "unredeemed areas" in our life. That's what I mean by the image of the heart which supposedly belongs to Christ but which does not pump its blood to its members.

Thus we look forward to the time when the battlefield that surrounds us here and now with contesting powers will become empty. Then God will be all in all and nothing more will stand between him and us. Then there will be an end to the meaninglessness in our life so that we no longer have to believe *in spite* of these things nor say any longer "Nevertheless I am continually with thee"; then we may see him as he is, and all the impenetrable confusion of chance and fate which plagued us in our life lines up in a straight path.

For this reason there is in every believer a pulling and hauling that moves him forward and causes him to anticipate the fulfillment of what is as yet prophecy and down payment but which points beyond the present moment. *Someday* the hidden Christ, who as yet works covertly and in lowliness, will drop the mask of his anonymity. *Someday* he will appear as he really is, as the one whom "the circuit of the whole world did not contain," as the king with sickle and crown. *Sometime* (in fact, in the last time), the judgment of God will become clear, too, when this king returns to judge the living and the dead. For what we know of earthly judgments, their ambiguity and inconclusiveness, points beyond them to a judgment day which will bring the hidden things to light.

Let me give a literary example. The song about the destruction of Napoleon's army in Russia runs,

> The Lord has smitten them indeed
> By striking man and cart and steed.

This means that history has decreed a mighty judgment upon the pride of a power-mad world conqueror. But was that judgment really so unambiguous? Might not a Frenchman raise the justifiable objection that *Europe* (and *not* Napoleon) was the power smitten by God, since it passed up a history-making chance in losing the Napoleonic principle of organization? Heaven knows, history's administration of justice is anything but unambiguous, and "one man's meat is another man's poison."

There is still more to be said, however. God's judgments are also *hidden*. While we imagine ourselves secure, judgment is often passed without our having the slightest premonition. The letter to the Romans contains a haunting passage which says that sometimes God passes judgment upon us by simply letting us do what we please and "giving us up" to the consequences of our action (Rom. 1:18 ff.).

This became clear to me once as I listened to the most impressive sermon I ever heard. After a terrible air attack we had gathered, a scattered little band, in a church where the smoke of the frightful devastation seeped in through shattered windows and took our breath away. Then the preacher touched us to the heart with a few startling sentences. He pointed out how Nazi Germany had succeeded in everything it undertook: first the unity of the German states, then military power, then the annexation of Austria, the march into Prague, the overpowering of Poland and France, and so on. And no one was ever able to interfere. The great Fuehrer outfoxed them all. He moved forward upon his dizzying course with the certainty of a sleepwalker. Finally, even sober, sensible people began to say that such triumphs were possible only through the blessing of the "Almighty." And "Providence" seemed to confirm the notion that it had given its approval. We Christians, however, said the preacher, had long since felt that it was not a blessing, but a judgment and a curse that was secretly brewing above us. The brilliant successes were merely the means used by the eternal judge to lull into a false security those who did not seek him. This judgment, however, was *hidden* in apparent approval, holding its breath so that the trumpet blast of catastrophic judgment would resound all the more appallingly. But now, when fire and brimstone rained from heaven; when we sat in that church, far from home, our eyes burning from the smoke; now, when the charred bodies lay in the street; now, finally, the judgment had fallen; the Lord appeared in the whirlwind. Despite all the horror, it was an indescribable relief, like a thunderstorm after oppressive sultriness. Now we finally knew where we stood. Now the Lord in heaven had begun to laugh at his abusers. He had given a sign that he was still in control and that the proud waves would have to subside.

That was a sermon which one probably hears only once in a lifetime. I know it almost by heart.

Everything the Bible says about the end of the world and the last judgment always points in the same direction. It says that whatever leads to false security here because it is hidden will one day be revealed and proclaimed from the housetops. To repeat a sentence used earlier, then faith will be permitted to see what it has believed; unbelief, however, will have to see what it has not believed.

In saying that, though, I must be on my guard against that wishful thinking for which I have criticized many others, the believers in progress, for example. Therefore I would like to raise an objection at this point, posing it to myself in the form of a question. Haven't I somehow pulled an insincere trick in my thinking? At first I said that our faith is not yet the last word, but that it leaves unredeemed areas. Then I indicated that there is no justice on earth. And it almost seems that from these two ideas I have deduced an arrogant demand: it must follow that there is an end for history, and even that there is a great Beyond in which everything is brought to fulfillment, contradictions are resolved, and absurdities are explained.

Anyone acquainted with the history of thought knows how many people have in fact argued this way. Has something similar happened to me in this chapter? If that were so, then I would not have been proclaiming the gospel; I would have been spinning a web of impracticable dreams around my hearers. Certainly no one can dare simply to demand that, since this world is a vale of tears, there *must* be a paradise out yonder where things are set right. And to maintain that there must be a last judgment simply because this world constantly fails to give us justice is to lay oneself open to the charge that one is apparently too cowardly to endure the roughness and the absurdity of our existence and therefore one gives oneself over to tranquilizing dreams of the great Beyond. At this point, the justifiable contention of the Marxists that religion can be misused as an opiate for the people can certainly serve as a warning to us.

When I spoke of the lines that point toward the last judgment and the royal lordship of Christ, I didn't project them on the basis of that sort of wishful thinking. They resulted instead from one single point of view: that in faith we know of a lord of history who will perfect his work. I certainly couldn't say, "My sins are forgiven" or, "I know that my Redeemer lives" or, "Nothing can happen to me that he has not seen and sent to me as a blessing"—I couldn't say any of that (and yet I *must* say it because it has mastered me and I draw my life from it) if I didn't say to myself at the same time, "This lord who found his way into your heart and laid out a completely new perspective on life for you is also lord over space and time, over America and over Red China. And as he spoke his creative words, 'Let there be . . .' in the beginning, so at the end of time he will have the heavenly host sing the great closing chorale and show himself as the all in all, under whose footstool all demonic forces lie bound."

Of course, I do not believe at all in the so-called "Return of Christ" nor in the so-called "Last Judgment." How could I? I *do* believe, however, in Jesus Christ who will be revealed in judgment and in truth and who will show himself to be the first and the last, the living One. I believe it because his hand has already reached into my little life and will never again let me go, neither in time nor in eternity, for now I can already detect the first-fruits of his lordship. That and nothing else is the basis for my certainty that *he will come again to judge the quick and the dead.*

Don't think, though, that these dreams of future fulfillment for the world have nothing to say to me here and now, as I plan to have a picnic in the woods tomorrow and then, the following day, to welcome my colleagues back to work with a cheery "good morning." My knowledge of that end of all things will profoundly affect today and tomorrow. I will be less upset by painful occurrences because I know that these grievous moments are but stages on that road which one day will end in victory for God. They too are accounted for in purposes of God's "higher thoughts." I need no longer to be bent on goals with a frenzied fanaticism, for the knowledge that all shall one day pass away provides me with a certain perspective, a whiff of that "having, as though I did not have" which Paul described so remarkably.

This attitude, though, has nothing in common with limp resignation or congenital pessimism. I take hold of the present moment in my life. I take its joys and its sorrows from the same Hand that will one day lead me across the last boundary to His eternal Heart. Whoever has this certainty can give himself completely to the present, no matter what hour strikes. He can win out.

That, too, became clear to me during the air raids. Sometimes I went through my beloved library and stroked the backs of the books. "Who knows whether you may become dust and ashes and charred paper this very night," I said. "You beautiful edition of *Faust;* you, my beloved Wilhelm Raabe, and you, Theodore Fontane, who helped me in critical times! But for the moment you are all still given to me." We have never loved with such intensity as when the very next night could bring the end of all things.

Whoever lives with God, filled with the certainty that everything passes away—the Uffizi Gallery in Florence, the Statue of Liberty, and my beloved garden—and that in the midst of this passing His lordship shines forth, that person lives completely in the present. The burden of our past and all the untamed areas in our life are taken from us and laid on another. The future, too, ceases to be filled with worry and specters of anxiety. It is true that I don't know *what* is coming, but I know *Who* is coming. Therefore I can drain the moment in which I live, laughing and weeping, almost (but not entirely) exultant to the skies, almost (but not entirely) troubled to death, and in either case with the face of God shining upon me. For "the world passes away and the lust of it"—its lust and its anxiety, the illusion of its progress and its desire for annihilation—the world and its lust passes away, "but he who does the will of God abides forever." And we can catch a fleeting glimpse of the magnitude of the future by the down payment we have already received.

The New Life and the Waiting
On The World To Come

I BELIEVE IN THE
HOLY GHOST

When the day of Pentecost had come, they were all together in one place. And suddenly a sound came from heaven like the rush of a mighty wind, and it filled all the house where they were sitting. And there appeared to them tongues as of fire, distributed and resting on each one of them. And they were all filled with the Holy Spirit and began to speak in other tongues, as the Spirit gave them utterance.

Now there were dwelling in Jerusalem Jews, devout men from every nation under heaven. And at this sound the multitude came together, and they were bewildered, because each one heard them speaking in his own language. And they were amazed and wondered, saying, "Are not all these who are speaking Galileans? And how is it that we hear, each of us in his own native language? Parthians and Medes and Elamites and residents of Mesopotamia, Judea and Cappadocia, Pontus and Asia, Phrygia and Pamphylia, Egypt and the parts of Libya belonging to Cyrene, and visitors from Rome, both Jews and proselytes, Cretans and Arabians, we hear them telling in our own tongues the mighty works of God." And all were amazed and perplexed, saying to one another, "What does this mean?" But others mocking said, "They are filled with new wine." —*Acts 2:1–13*

The pouring out of the Spirit on Pentecost is presented to us as an event of elemental and revolutionary force. Flames appear in the air and a storm both shakes and shocks everyone present at the time of the miracle. The words of the Lord, laid away like dead letters in the drawers of memory, suddenly begin to flicker and burn. All at once they become "dynamic" and rouse everyone there out of his lethargy. What has happened?

Today it may be somewhat astonishing for many people to learn that Christianity can become so exciting, so fiery and stormy, that it can catapult people out of the previous course of their life. For in our case (honestly, now) the situation often seems to be exactly the reverse. The words we hear from the pulpit or the old liturgies seem to be venerable, of course, but they are often dead as well. People can hardly imagine that those words too were once fire and storm. But that really must have been the case, for men are certainly not thrown to the lions or bound to the stake for dead letters and venerable concepts, nor are they ostracized from society and driven from house and home. However, that happened thousands of times. Flames, therefore, must have flickered once, and contagious life must have touched human hearts. But here we are, laboring under the sound of pious phrases, and wondering with amazement how the burned-out cinders and petrified lava we continue to hold in our hands could once have been molten.

Yet most of us have also experienced how the apparently extinct fire in a biblical passage which we have read or in a phrase from a sermon which we have heard has suddenly flickered to life again as though fanned by some mysterious bellows. How often have we heard those words from the psalm about "the valley of the shadow of death" and about the "good shepherd" who is with us through darkness and loneliness! But they meant nothing more to us than a little bit of pious poetry. They made no impression upon us and were laid aside in the storehouse of our old and yellowed philosophy. Then suddenly we were actually *in* the valley of the shadow of death with the stars above us snuffed out. There was no man to whom we could turn with confidence. We saw no opening, no exit; there was nothing but the black wall, rising ominous and threatening before us. And look, suddenly that presumably dead phrase about the good shepherd began to burst with life. We could literally feel the rod and the staff in our hand. We saw bridges thrown over the abyss, and escape routes of which we had had no previous notion were pointed out to us. And although our outward situation was just as desperate as ever, we saw that we were wrapped in a security which gave us peace and tranquillity. While our own breath was still gone, we received a new breath of life. All at once the old words, "I am with you always, to the close of the age," began to speak; they found sight and voice. The dead lava in our hands began to glow again. Anyone who has experienced that has obtained some idea of what the miracle of Pentecost is all about: a word can come alive, can "reach" me, and can become a creative, transforming power in my life.

Let me illustrate my meaning. Many churches have stained glass windows. These windows recount the mighty acts of God by means of pictures. The venerable figures of the prophets and apostles look down on us, and perhaps there are also scenes from the life of Jesus or symbols of the Holy Trinity. These windows are not intended—at least not primarily—to provide an ornamental border for the place of worship, nor to generate a meditative atmosphere. They are meant to deliver a message. They are the word "illustrated," and they want to "preach" through pictures the same way the organ "preaches" through music. Now if I see a church from the outside, if I just walk around it, these windows appear as a lifeless gray-on-gray. They are mute and have nothing to say. As soon as I go inside, however, all the colors blaze out, filled with light, the pictures come alive and actually begin to "speak." Everything they had to tell me had been pictured there before, too, as I prowled heedlessly around outside the church, but it was not yet for *me*. First I had to enter the sanctuary; then the message could reach me.

In plain words, that means that the miracle of the Spirit takes place in this way: the word which I have believed to be dead and which I have carried about, apparently useless, in my memory since my confirmation suddenly comes to life. When weighted down by guilt I suddenly hear, "Your sins are forgiven," and the heaviness oppressing my mind is whisked away. When terribly helpless, awaiting the next wave of terror as though I were paralyzed, I hear the words, "Nothing can happen to you that He has not seen and made a blessing for you," and they suddenly sound very different. Things *are* different. It's just as though you have burst out of a soundproof room into the open air. Then I may ask myself in surprise, "How was it that you knew all that and yet didn't know it? Just how could it happen that Isaiah, of whom you thought (when you thought of him at all) as a somewhat unusual prophet with an immense patriarchal beard and a solemnly obscure way of prophesying, of whom the pastor, for some strange reason, seemed to think highly, how could it happen that he has now—since the change—become a *comforter* for you, one to whom you can cling?"

The pentecostal miracle, which the ancient witnesses experienced as the "blowing of the Spirit," is precisely that joyful-fearful event when the word suddenly "reaches" me, when it jolts me and sweeps me off my feet, when it "clicks." Then this word quickly shows that it is a dynamic thing, and that the symbols of movement and elemental force, suggested so naturally by the images of fire and storm, simply point up its power as it bursts into my life. Viewed from the outside, this event is just as opaque as the windows of Chartres Cathedral when seen from the outside. People on the outside have no idea of the message that streams down from those windows, nor can they understand the mark of deeper meditation on the faces of those who come out through the church doors. In exactly the same way, the spectators of that event on Pentecost observed enthusiasm and ecstasy without being able to establish a reason for them. That leaves them stranded, so they make the commonplace diagnosis, "Those people, there, who have gone so completely out of their heads, have simply had too much to drink." Or they decide that they are fanatics, dreamers, and enthusiasts who have lost contact with reality.

From the outside it is simply impossible for anyone to see what happens as far as faith is concerned. One must be involved, one must be "inside," one must be touched by the living breath of the Spirit in order to know what it means to say that God speaks and that his word is cataclysmic.

Thus, when I speak of the miracle of the Holy Spirit I am confessing that something has "come to me" which I didn't comprehend before. Suddenly, something that had previously left me cold and had meant no involvement at all "gets through to me."

To understand that, one has to read Peter's great sermon on Pentecost, recorded in the Book of Acts. Peter really just retells the ancient sacred history from the patriarchs to Good Friday and Easter. A somewhat malicious reader could say, "Ho-hum, the same old shopworn traditions. Nothing new in Jerusalem!"

There is, however, a new *tone* in the old history. Peter now sees the tried and true narrative from a different perspective, and thus it has a new light and vibrancy. Peter reports nothing that was not already known, but he says it differently. He reports it as one who has himself become involved, as one whose life has been shaped by the mighty acts of God. He speaks as one who is involved to his fingertips and is excited about it. And this is why his message kindles his hearers, too. Fire spreads, leaving no room for the boredom of arid lectures on doctrine.

It would, however, be false to assume that the miracle of the Spirit aroused in men an enthusiasm that robbed them of their sanity. There have, of course, always been strange saints of that sort. I myself have seen such ecstasy in some American congregations. But enthusiasm can be a pitiful fire of straw. The flames soon burn out, and the darkness that follows is blacker than before. The old law of the night before and the morning after applies here. Besides, people can become enthusiastic about the silliest things, like LSD or the Beatles' haircuts. There is no insanity under the sun which has not at some time prompted screaming ecstatics to roll their eyes in sheer rapture.

Therefore we have to be careful in dealing with all kinds of enthusiasm, even pious enthusiasm. It should be noted how the New Testament repeatedly warns us to be sober, how it calls the subjective experience (the merely "religious" experience) to order and directs our attention to the real point at issue. It is sometimes like a cold shower to people whose nerves are still tingling from the great experience of renewal that gladdens everyone who can say, "Now I believe" for the first time. In the middle of this exuberance John pours the water of warning: "Do not believe every spirit, but test the spirits to see whether they are of God; for many false prophets have gone out into the world" (I John 4:1).

In fact, there have been many enthusiasts and ecstatics, from the iconoclastic radicals of the Reformation to the Jehovah's Witnesses. Even Communists and Nazis have been enthusiastic. That is why we have to distinguish between spirits, for not all spirits are holy; some are demonic.

Even satanic power is full of spirit; it virtually radiates spiritual fascination and loves intellectual discussion. One need only think about the "classical" moments of temptation to see that clearly. The serpent's question to Eve, "Did God really say that you were *not* to eat of the tree of the knowledge of good and evil?" is an eminently philosophical question, to be sure, and one cannot, in all honesty, deny its spiritual nature. Suppose the seductive serpent had come out with overly direct and brutal demands. Suppose he had said something like this: "Now then, my dear Eve, my task is to seduce you; I am the representative of Paradise's atheistic underground movement." Eve would immediately have been on her guard against the seducer's wiles. She would have battened down the hatches of her heart without delay, and the seducer's words would have found no opening. No one, not even Eve, *wants* to be led astray or to fall prey to a false spirit. Even when a sailor, bursting with vitality after a long trip, heads for the local bars, he certainly isn't going there to be "led astray," but to "experience" something and to leap at fascinating bait.

The serpent, therefore, does not proceed directly to a frontal attack; it camouflages its purposes and constantly takes pains to keep its mask from slipping off. It bases its position on reverence for God and involves Eve in a conversation on the question whether it really is consistent with the Creator's inner nature for him to reserve certain areas of this creation (for example, the above-mentioned tree) for himself and then post "No Trespassing" signs.[1]

With this question the serpent makes the first move in a very brilliantly arranged chess game. It proceeds in a Socratic fashion, bringing Eve to the point where her ideas come in conflict with one another. The serpent thus draws an exact demonic parallel to what the Holy Spirit also does. That is, it lets an idea get under Eve's skin, and this idea works itself deeper and deeper inside until it finally gives rise to a kind of cancer in the soul.

Satanic power, therefore, is actually rich in "spiritual" values. It can be highly intellectual in that it can subtly slip subversive

[1] Cf. the chapter on the narrative of the Fall in *How the World Began* (Philadelphia: Fortress Press, 1961), pp. 121–135.

thoughts into its intended victims, using these thoughts to out-flank the conscience and conquer it from the rear. Ultimately, it is Eve who seduces herself in this way, while the Tempter can withdraw and let nature take its course. In the end, Eve herself draws this conclusion: "If God has made me this way, planting desires, drives, and curiosity within me, then it certainly cannot be against his will for me to give way to them cheerfully!"

Thus Eve lives with the illusion that she has not said No to God at all. On the contrary, she has constructed a complete theology for herself, based on a consistently pious world view. Eve's theology gives the impression that God always sanctions and wants precisely what Eve wants. And that is especially devil-ish.

It is easy to understand why it is so devilish. Suppose someone says, "I hate Mr. X. He is blocking my career. He always makes the grade, and I don't even get off the ground. However, I have discovered a weak spot in his private life. There's something going on with his secretary. I'll just stage a little intrigue here and undermine his reputation with a clever whispering campaign. That way I'll finally get my finger on the trigger. Of course, I know it's a vile thing to do, and it's hard to reconcile with my being a member of St. Michael's and taking communion last Maundy Thursday. But that doesn't make any difference to me now—I'll just go ahead and do it."

It's awful, to be sure, when someone reasons that way, and God will sorrow deeply over him. But presumably such a man has not yet been morally ruined. As long as he at least *knows* that he is vile and that his life is tearing all the Commandments to shreds, he can still be helped. So far, he has not drugged his conscience; it still has the freedom to protest. Thus the possibility of a conversion is still there; he hasn't burned that bridge behind him.

But what happens when he argues like this: "Why *shouldn't* I push ahead with a minimum of scruples? Life is not pretty, and the urge for self-preservation and self-assertion is the strongest driving force there is. That's what keeps life going." And, nomi-nal Christian that he is, maybe he adds, "*I* haven't made this hard law called the struggle for existence. It's the fault of a Creator who built such structures into life. Therefore, I can, even as a religious man, justify my lovely little plot. It runs entirely along the lines of life as it must be lived, and therefore also along the lines of Him who *made* life that way."

Whoever speaks that way is a victim of the serpent and has fallen victim to its spiritual chess game. The serpent is a top intellectual. It has the spirit of discussion that lets *us* find the necessary arguments and philosophical positions to help us justify ourselves. But in the last analysis, the self-justified man, despite his certainty and nonchalance, is the poorest man of all, for there is no longer any place that God can use as a leverage point from which to awaken the longing for renewal.

That is also the reason why it is always the men with empty hands, the hungry and thirsty, and the confused who are called blessed in the New Testament. After all, it is usually only empty hands that are outstretched. And outstretched hands are the only ones God can clasp.

So we see that the opponent of the Holy Spirit is not something unspiritual, such as materialism or gross sensuality. That is a completely unchristian belief. The real opponent is spirit. It is a demonic intellect which works through convincing arguments and logical inferences. That is the reason why the Lord's last battlefronts can be described as places where spirit opposes spirit.

It is against this background that we note the demand to prove, to try, and to discern the spirits. Don't let the flames of enthusiasm or even logically worked-out convictions and cultural twaddle stampede you into thinking that you have found a true fire or the storm of the Holy Spirit. Instead, inquire what *source* fuels that fire and in whose *name* and *authority* that spirit is exercised.

Spirit, no matter in what form it occurs,[2] thus seems to concern more than fire and wind; it also seems to be a somewhat "windy" thing, vague and full of ambiguity. That applies even to human understanding. It too shimmers with the most unlike shades of meaning. Taken literally, "understanding" can be that

[2] In the original Greek, "spirit" is *pneuma,* the equivalent of "breath," "wind," etc.

faculty with which I "stand under" the tutelage of the eternal word. On the other hand, it can assume the ideological alias "reason" and enlist in the service of power, becoming, as Lenin said, the "spiritual instrument of power." In that role it provides the arguments to justify any specified goals. Even Mao Tse-tung calls on reason when he wants to turn men into ants. This is the background for Luther's hard words to the effect that reason is a "whore" who may be bought and who places herself at everyone's disposal. Goethe, too, understood the misuse of reason when he said that often enough it helps man only "to be more beastly than any beast."

If spirit is so windy and vague, though, why all this talk about the "Holy Spirit"? Why is the word of God dragged into this twilight zone at all? Why shouldn't the word alone suffice? Why do we have to bother the Holy Spirit with making the word understandable? Is the word itself so lacking in persuasiveness that we require some additional enlightenment?

Why, then, can God be known only through the Holy Spirit? Or why is it only the Spirit that, as Paul would say, "searches . . . the depths of God" (I Cor. 2:10)? When we ponder that question, we encounter a mystery that baffled Paul himself.

To be precise, we face the fact that we cannot know God "by our own reason or strength," as Luther says. That is a very remarkable assertion which one would do well not to brush off lightly. Yet the whole world talks about God—even the atheists do—and everyone believes he knows something positive or negative about him. How dare I repeat the phrase that we cannot know God?

But wait a minute. Are we *really* dealing with God when we use the word "God?" Or are we dealing with certain pious ideals or impious delusions? As a rule, it is a sentimental and somewhat insincere flourish when we utter the word "God"! Even at weddings, baptisms, and funerals—let's not kid ourselves—we use God over and over as a means of lending a note of solemnity and meaningfulness to the important occasion. Too often at these times his name is really only sound and fury, or even an opiate for the people that puts them to sleep—religiously. However, the harm goes still deeper. *Every* world view, of course, talks about God or at least about some ultimate reality. And most use the word "God" to cover everything they have knocked together for themselves to form their life goals and truths to live by.

I once spoke with a thief who, in a very subtle way, first surreptitiously gained people's confidence and even availed himself of their hospitality; then he relieved them of jewelry and silver. Even though he could tell all this in a very amusing way, and I shouldn't really have laughed about it (which, I'm ashamed to say, I did), I did work up to the point of asking him, "Didn't you think it pretty mean to abuse the confidence of those people like that?" Then he answered with a laugh, "Why? After all, they were only people with fat bank accounts, and I have just tried to do my bit for social equality." That man, too, had a special world view, and perhaps he even had built a certain idea of God into it. His world view, characteristically, was so constructed that thievery never occurred in it. It had become "social equality," a completely honorable affair.

World views like that don't put anyone on the spot; the God we fix up for ourselves in that way usually doesn't step on our toes. He is patterned upon our desires. He is made to order and doesn't pinch us anywhere. Most of us have the God we want for ourselves. One should treat the word "God" very carefully and use it sparingly, recalling the wise warning of Solomon: "Be not rash with your mouth, nor let your heart be hasty to utter a word before [German "of"] God, for God is in heaven, and you upon earth; therefore let your words be few" (Eccles. 5:2). We do not know the real God.

Why not? That is the decisive question.

Paul reflected profoundly upon this problem of why we cannot know God (I Cor. 2:11). The sense of his thinking is that like can be known only by like. We, however, are unlike God. Therefore we do not know him. The need for a certain likeness or equality as a prerequisite for understanding something becomes clear when a person talks with his dog. Even if I love my dog and we are pals, a wall of unintelligibility remains between us. If I get stuck when I am working on a sermon and ask him, "What shall I do?" he wags his tail, if pleased by this address, in order to show me that he likes me. Right at that moment, though, I'm not interested in whether he likes me; I want advice from him. But he cannot give me that; he has no inkling of my mental needs. He doesn't understand me. But on *his* part, the dog is probably thinking, "My dear master doesn't understand a thing about the wonderful scents which rise from the feet of his visitor and which transport me into such raptures. But he is a poor noseless being who misses the best in my lovely canine life."

Thus, in the decisive matters we just don't understand each other. Only the spirit of man, says Paul, knows what is in man; the canine spirit doesn't know. It is too "unlike."

When we apply this basically quite commonplace observation to God, it becomes very upsetting. For then we must logically say that God alone knows what is in God, since he alone is like himself. I, as man, do not know God. There are two reasons for this. First, no finite spirit can comprehend an infinite spirit, so it stands helpless, without understanding, before the latter's higher thoughts and counsels. Second, and more significant, we men have severed ourselves from God and have gone our own ways. God thus becomes the big problem. If we were to take him seriously, he would effect a revolution in our life. *And that we don't want.* We are in hot pursuit of our own desires. We have our own plans for life and we don't want anyone to call us to task or to carry us where we don't want to go. We don't understand God's thoughts; therefore we don't *will* them. This sentence can also be inverted to say that we don't want God, and therefore we can't understand him.

That is the basis for Paul's thesis that God alone knows what is in God. We thus may arrive at this somewhat astonishing observation: the only knowledge of God is his self-knowledge. Only his own Spirit knows the depths of his divinity. When we men speak about him, it is usually a matter of our ideals which we project on heaven. Maybe that is how the childish idea of an old man with a long beard arose. To many people it seems fitting that such a doddering old man, whose helplessness causes one to smile, should dispense simpleminded admonitions. But the facts are disturbingly and delightfully different. As Luther says, Jesus Christ is the mirror of his Father's heart. In him is God as he sees himself.

Has this discussion brought us a bit closer to the meaning of "Holy Spirit"? Haven't many things that previously were Greek to us become a little more understandable now? I think, for example, of the word "revelation," which, for many of us, has a strange spiritualistic flavor. It doesn't fit into the objective clarity of the rest of our way of life. If we interpret it on the basis of what we have just thought through, however, "revelation" means simply that God will give us his own Spirit so that we can thus participate in his self-knowledge.

Many other questions, with which I cannot deal here, crop up. My only concern is that the decisive point becomes clear: that is, that God gives us his Spirit so that we may have fellowship with him and may have a look into his heart. In that way we are rescued from the awful enchantment of our egos and are no longer imprisoned by the airy specters of our wishful thinking.

In this light we also begin to understand another thing. All to whom the joy and the miracle of faith are granted are no longer able to see the Bible as a book in which every conceivable type of person, from simple to sophisticated, favors us with his views about God. Instead they are to acknowledge the high claim that God himself speaks his word in the Bible. In that case, of course, the proclamation of God's witnesses can no longer be understood as religious instruction "about" God; it must be understood—halting and wretched as these pulpit tones may be—as a message which God *himself* wants to deliver, a message which calls men into its service, requiring them to say, "We cannot but speak of what we have seen and heard" (Acts 4:20). So powerful have these things become that the witnesses are surrounded by the signs of storm and flame.

All believers have testified to the mystery of the Holy Spirit in this way. They have done it soberly and coolly, or filled with a fire that consumed them. Sometimes they were geniuses who had a fine command of language and the full power of thought at their disposal. Sometimes they were simple people who, like the Salvation Army soldiers, played their guitars and sang of the light that had risen upon them, bringing a new luster to their hearts. From a human point of view, the choir of witnesses has been composed of very different spirits. Social differences, too, have been apparent. But these lesser and greater spirits of witness have always been somewhat like prisms which catch the same eternal light and then refract it in new and unending combinations of rays. Each individual "shines" with his own particular color. For the Holy Spirit creates originals. Copies are unknown to him.

Yet something unites all those who compose this many-voiced choir. They all confess together, "The new fullness which has broken into our life, the new joy, the new hope, the new image of man—none of it stems from us. *We* couldn't break through the wall of illusions, specters, and nightmares that surrounds us. Our old life that lies behind us now seems like an imprisonment in a deep dungeon from which we would never have been able to escape. But outside there was hammering and pounding, and we heard the scrape of shovels. There was One who dug through to us. There was One who gave us new confidence. We couldn't even give ourselves the confidence that he was our rescuer. Even *that* had to be provided for us."

We mean all of these things when we speak of the Holy Spirit. We mean him who enlightens us, so that what was dark before is now radiant. We mean him who leads us inside the sanctuary, where the windows begin to brighten, recounting to us the mighty acts of God. We mean him who, speaking out of the burning bush, makes the burned-out cinders of dead Christian doctrines glow again like lava.

We don't come to any of these discoveries if they are not given to us. Such grace does not allow itself to overpower us. But whoever has empty hands and a great longing that they may be filled, whoever suffers under a holy dissatisfaction with himself and says to his Lord, "Nothing in my hands I bring. Thou, O Lord, art everything"—he falls heir to the promise that he will not fail, but that he will be accepted. And whoever knocks on these doors, no matter how timidly, will quickly hear steps approaching from the other side.

I BELIEVE . . . THE HOLY CHRISTIAN CHURCH, THE COMMUNION OF SAINTS; THE FORGIVENESS OF SINS

"Behold, I send you out as sheep in the midst of wolves; so be wise as serpents and innocent as doves. Beware of men; for they will deliver you up to councils, and flog you in their synagogues, and you will be dragged before governors and kings for my sake, to bear testimony before them and the Gentiles. When they deliver you up, do not be anxious how you are to speak or what you are to say; for what you are to say will be given to you in that hour; for it is not you who speak, but the Spirit of your Father speaking through you. . . .

"A disciple is not above his teacher, nor a servant above his master; it is enough for the disciple to be like his teacher, and the servant like his master. If they have called the master of the house Beelzebul, how much more will they malign those of his household.

"So have no fear of them; for nothing is covered that will not be revealed, or hidden that will not be known. What I tell you in the dark, utter in the light; and what you hear whispered, proclaim upon the housetops."

—Matthew 10:16–20, 24–27

There are two mighty passages in the Bible which, like the foci of an ellipse, define the essence of the church.

One of the texts is the story of the building of the tower of Babel (Gen. 11:1 ff.). It forms the "dark side of the picture" against which the light of the church burns more brightly. In Promethean defiance, mankind has cut itself loose from God and has built a this-worldly shelter in which men hope to be left to themselves without any further disturbance from heavenly authority. But the lovely harmony of undisturbed humanity doesn't last long. It is as though a powerful fist has slammed down on the table. Men and nations are scattered in all directions, the lovely plan for a "collective humanity" falls apart, languages are confused to the point of complete misunderstanding, and the battle of all against everyone breaks out. In short, we hear the starting gun of world history. The textbooks, and our own lives too, confide to us that history is actually like that: a continuously surging battle for security and power, or for a place in the sun; a constant shifting between expansion and containment, terror and anxiety—and above the battlefield of these events hangs the Gorgon's head of distrust.

What is the meaning of this remarkable story which, in the language of myth, says that the chaos and confusion of history begin at this point?

As long as men are under God, they can trust one another; as long as there is trust, there can also be unity and fellowship. But in the moment men want to remove God and cut themselves loose, they also lose the freedom and autonomy that they seek.

Instead, a quite different and completely unanticipated law asserts itself. When man no longer wants God as his Lord, he turns at once to *other* lords, very cruel and tryannical ones, who oppress him. For example, he is lashed by his drive for power. Opportunism begins to master him. But if you know that someone else is driven by a will to power and reacts out of pure opportunism, you will succumb to apprehension. For now you know that he would walk all over you if it seemed convenient or if it served his purpose. The reverse is also true: if you know that a person obeys the commandments of God, he is "predictable." We know what to expect of him. On the other hand, if he obeys only the dictates of his own instincts, he becomes unpredictable. We don't know what will come over him while he is under their invisible tyranny. Where this sort of anxiety holds sway, confidence ends. And where there is no longer any confidence, all fellowship, from marriage and friendship all the way to the state and the commonwealth of nations, dissolves. That centrifugal tendency toward scattering in all directions arises, just as it is described in the story of the Tower of Babel. Then the age of isolation and loneliness begins.

The New Testament account of Pentecost, the founding of the church, stands like a contrapuntal analogy to that earlier judgment. They are all assembled there: Parthians, Medes and Elamites, Jews and Greeks, intellectuals and simple souls. They have little or nothing in common. The barriers of nationality, language, and, certainly, interest and temperament stand between them. Yet when the wind of God's Spirit sweeps over them, the Babylonian estrangement between them seems suddenly blown away. The superiority of the one common Lord acts as a binding force of fellowship around them all, and at once understanding reappears amid all their differences. The fire of a common bond inflames them. And joy at the unheard-of discovery that they are brothers and members of one Body sets their lives on a new course.

Once, kneeling in the prairie sand of South-West Africa, I celebrated the Lord's Supper with some Herero tribesmen. They had never heard of our city, and I had known nothing of that remote bush country, "where the deer and the antelope play." Neither of us understood a single word of the other's language. But when I made the sign of the cross with my hand and pronounced the name "Jesus" their dark faces lit up. We ate the same bread and drank from the same chalice, despite apartheid, and they couldn't do enough to show me their love. They held out their children to me and took me into their poor huts. We had never seen each other before. We were separated by social, geographical, and cultural barriers. And yet we were enclosed by arms that were not of this world.

Then the scales fell from my eyes; I began to understand the story of Pentecost. I understood the miracle of the church.

Have I overstated the case? Doesn't what may seem like a "miracle" there in the African bush look much more prosaic and even more wretched on the streets of New York, Hamburg, or Berlin? If I may be so bold, is the tax-supported church as we have it in Germany really anything like a pentecostal miracle? Or is it just a "legally constituted corporation," as the lawbooks put it?

Some years ago, when I wanted to give a book the title *Church and Public*, my publisher objected. "The church," he said, "doesn't catch the public eye. Please choose another title. I'd rather not publish a flop." Of course, I didn't change the title. But I asked myself why a title mentioning the church "didn't attract the public." Why doesn't it seem to "get across"?

If we were in a discussion group now, instead of being author and reader, I'm sure many hands would be raised to get the floor, for such a question offers an enticing opportunity to get something off one's chest. The enraged citizen whose tax money goes to support the church would probably lead the attack. Then cannon would be aimed and fired at boring sermons, wreaking great havoc. Some salvos would also be fired at the bigots, hypocrites, and philistines. A few especially self-righteous intellectuals would consider themselves almost too good to say anything at all; they would rate their mental capital too highly to finance a polemic with it, especially a polemic against an institutional has-been.

Now it's not my intention to play defender of the church on all these fronts. I would rather turn to the deeper objections which plague the *serious*-minded. I don't wish to hide my own problems with the church. The more one loves her, of course, the more one suffers on her account.

Several decades ago, when the ship of the church seemed to be sailing gaily along before a fresh breeze, and the Third Reich had not yet arisen, the great theologian Hans Iwand (who was later removed and expelled by the Nazis because of his love for the church) wrote these despairing sentences: "The alienation of the church from real life is growing greater and greater. [You see how he doesn't say that secularism or alienation *from* the church is increasing? He says the alienation *of* the church is increasing!] To live by her own vitality is artificial, breeding all sorts of clubbiness appropriate to such artificiality. The gospel that the world needs today becomes overfamiliar and is taken for granted. People want to use it as a motor to get everything possible moving. I must confess that this tendency often dismays me completely. And what good is it if a few other efforts are made here and there? They are only exceptions to the rule. . . . What we have is a state subsidy of a few million for the church authorities.

I don't believe that this fragile relationship will last much longer . . . and who knows whether this extremity might not become a terrible judgment. Nothing is more difficult than really to live in faith—that is, to gain the courage to live and work in the face of nothingness—for the future, after all, is in God's hand."

This is the voice of *pain* for the church, spoken by one who loves her and is involved (and not a mere spectator in the bleachers). If she were just a club like other clubs, he could say, "I'll leave." However, he cannot forget that this silly institution contains the place whence the springs of life flow. And at the same time he sees the thirst of his fellowmen. He sees them wasting away in nihilism, facing a yawning emptiness, looking around, bored and disconsolate, for something that could give their life meaning and fullness. Look! The church could provide them with the water of life. But obviously the springs are blocked up. A moribund institution appears to offer only brackish pond water which many spit out as undrinkable or else shun completely.

No pennypinching taxpayer could ever suffer as deeply and intensely over the church as do these members who see her problems and face them squarely.

There is, I believe, still a deeper reason for the general avoidance of the "church" theme. My thesis is as follows: *The church is never an end in itself.* To express it very tritely, we are not Christians so that there can be a church; there is a church so that we can be Christians, thereby gaining our salvation and finding our way to our eternal destination. To that extent, the church has a purely serving function. It is suspicious when anyone talks too much about the church. It may be that the institution means more to him than does the Lord whom the institution serves.

I know that it is necessary to say this today, because many people seem completely absorbed in elaborating the liturgical ceremonies of the church, studying the form of the worship service, and reforming it. I don't want to say anything against these honorable men. However, they must allow us to ask them if it is really God's will that we celebrate a pompous ritual (all too frequently, as an end in itself). Or is a worship service supposed to supply us with provisions and emergency rations for our needs in the world—outside the worship service—when we sit at our desks or stand at our workbenches or dictate our letters? The purpose of worship is obviously to send us out into daily life in a new and strengthened way; it is to provide us with the word of the Lord so that we may live on it while we are traveling.

That is why at the close of a service we sing, "Lord, dismiss us with thy blessing." We are asking that what we have just heard will regulate our very worldly doings, hovering over us as clouds of blessing.

Even the Lord's Supper is not a cultic act, some sort of "high point of the worship service" or communion of the "nucleus of the congregation" (what is that anyway?). It should still be today what it was originally, namely, a strengthening for our departure, when we must go out again to the battle and the work and the testing, when we shall be sent as sheep among the wolves. That is no cultic celebration; it is the assurance that the Lord remains with us when the worship *comes to an end* and when the world of the deadline, the telephone, and the motor surrounds us with its curtains of noise. It is to give us the certainty that he rules this world, too; that he gives us tasks of love in waiting rooms, in laboratories, and in our own homes, and that he has a greeting ready for us along every road, assuring us that he remembers us.

That is the church—*serving* us and giving us something to take along, letting us know she stands behind us. That is why Jesus sent his disciples out into the streets and marketplaces, the hedges and hinterlands of society to proclaim the invitation and bring men back. He didn't say, "Go and celebrate a ritual. Praise me through stylistically pure liturgical chants." (Nor did he by any means forbid liturgy, as long as it served the sending out of the faithful and was not merely intended as an edifying end in itself or simply as a pious refuge to which we might withdraw from the evil world!) The church is a mighty fortress from which we should launch sorties into a world where there are competitions in professional life, educational needs for our children, anxiety about tomorrow, wild adventure, and joyful moments. There we do battle using the weapons given us from the armory of the

Word, encouraged by the shouts that filter down to us from the walls of Jerusalem. But this fortress from which we sally forth is no cozy corner which shelters us from the cold wind, giving us over to withdrawal from the world through holy music and ritual.

When the persecutions under the Third Reich broke over the church, there were people who staged liturgical movements with Gregorian chants and elaborate vestments. For many of them (certainly not for all and perhaps not even for most of them) that activity may have been something of a cozy corner in a situation that would have demanded of them an open confession instead of that holy charade. For the fur began to fly wherever the church preached her hard, unvarnished truth in the face of the anti-Christians. Then the lambs of God were very quickly encircled by the wolves. All the Hitlerites reacted negatively because they felt they were being criticized. Where merely pious ritual was celebrated, however, people could remain undisturbed; nobody wanted to shear those sheep. Dietrich Bonhoeffer vented his scorn on this pious business by saying, "Only those who pray publicly for the Jews may sing Gregorian."

I am shocked and distressed when I see how widely the church has once again occupied herself exclusively with housekeeping within the mighty fortress and how people content themselves with the familiar home smells of what is presumed to be holy. "The church lives from her function as herald, she is God's company," said Karl Barth. "Where the church is alive, she must face the question of whether she serves this function or whether she is an end in herself. If the latter is the case, the church usually begins to taste 'sacral,' to act pious, to become priestly, and to turn sour. Anyone with a sensitive nose will smell that and find it dreadful."

It is quite remarkable and thought-provoking that we can observe the *opposite* tendency in, of all places, the Russian Orthodox Church. Not only do the holy, centuries-old chants resound and the icons speak their silent language, but it has come to the point where the proclamation occurs through living words. The powers that be have taken note of that immediately. They feel themselves under attack. The "wolves" begin to scent their prey. That is the way it is when the church is entrusted with a dangerous and endangering word. And if I am not completely mistaken, a prophecy uttered by August Winnig in the middle thirties is in the process of ⁎fulfillment. He said that one day Holy Russia would find its way out of the silence of its worship services, and that the word would be given to it so that it would begin to speak.

The Apostles' Creed, by a very significant linguistic shading, states that the church is merely the means to an end. It does *not* say (as it did in the first two articles), "I believe 'in' one holy universal Christian church"; it says only, "I believe this church; I confess the certainty that she gives." We may add that we don't confess her to be a branch of the heavenly Jerusalem in our pluralistic society simply because we have been convinced by the state church, the ecclesiastical authorities, or the management of the congregations and their organizations. They don't convince us that something more than or different from a club with religious interests is at work there. We believe the church for a far different reason! Anyone who views the church merely from the outside really perceives only one club among others and it may irritate him that this club is endowed with special legal and financial privileges. He sees how it acts like other men and plays the priest, but how precious little it evinces of the heavenly Jerusalem.

No, I believe the church for a far different reason. It is because the word of the Lord grips me there and leads me to the source of life, and because at a stroke two things now become clear to me. The first is that I have heard this creative and transforming word only *there*, and only there can I hear that this word may be heard only in the fellowship of Christians, that is, where two or three are gathered in his name. And a second thing also becomes clear: his people are found wherever this word is spoken. There the Lord will be "in the midst of them"; there the miracle of the church will take place.

This observation brings up the subject of the "holy" church. She is certainly not holy because the people of which she is composed are such perfect examples or just because she is especially attractive. (I may not care particularly for many officeholders in the church, nor do I have the impression that the Lord could display *me* in his show window.) We can talk about the "holy" church only because she lives from the words of her Lord and because she is the weak and often wretched body which belongs to that high and holy Head.

Jesus' words to his disciples as he sent them out tell us about this side of his church. It was as though he wanted them to understand even then that the public image of the church was actually unimpressive. Sheep sent among wolves are, after all, not exactly zoological showpieces. They don't lend themselves to heraldic symbolism. Lions are certainly more respectable on coats of arms. But Jesus wants to suggest something quite specific through this image of lambs among wolves. He points out that the church must be *defenseless*. Her strength cannot consist in stabilizing her social position through concordats and treaties. She cannot defend herself from heavy criticism by putting God's name in the Constitution or by enjoying the protection of a public taboo on blasphemy. The more she lives under human protection and secures herself by the possession of power, the weaker, more insignificant, and more ineffectual she actually becomes. That is a paradox, but it is so. Her strength consists only in confidence in her Shepherd and in belief in Him who sends her on her mission. But this power of the lowly (they, of all people!) will defy the strongest tyranny; this salt of faith will preserve the earth from corruption.

Who is it, then, that battles the despots of tyrannical "isms" (formerly the Nazis and now Mr. Ulbricht)? Who is it that unleashes the truth of faith upon the wolves and has the "right man on his side," even behind barbed wire or in the darkness of concentration camps, as in the case of the martyrs of the church who stood against Hitler? In such times the great pillars of the church, those who hold high office, are often pretty shaky. When it becomes a matter of hunger or fear of death, even the comfort of the well-educated quickly falls away like a worn-out robe. But there are, and have been, and always will be those who know that the attack is really against someone other than themselves. They know that his strength is made perfect in weakness and that he holds his shield above them.

One may always discover where Jesus is founding the church through his word and spirit by noting where his disciples are being called out of their former lives because an easy accommodation to the world (and also, of course, to a "pluralistic society") is no longer possible. It was no small thing for Abraham to be called away from homeland, fireside, and every familiar tie and to be sent out into the unknown. And it was no small thing that Jesus told those who put their hand to his plow not to look back to the dead they wanted to bury, the wives they wanted to marry, and the fields they still wanted to buy. To be sure, they received in return far more than they had left behind, and in the end they all knew that they had been given everything and that they had found the *one* costly pearl for which it paid to give up everything else. They knew in retrospect that God had not left them in the lurch and that it was through the gifts he gave them that they first experienced what life could be or what happiness was. But first they had to go through death and parting. First, relying on God's generosity, they had to throw away everything that had given meaning and content to their lives. First they had to be willing for the great operation to be performed on them; only then did they rise as new men.

Perhaps our own present-day Christianity, too, must go through that purifying fire. Perhaps all civil support for the church will be withdrawn and the pond of brackish water drained. Perhaps society (and not only the communists, but also the so-called free society of the West) will want to rid itself of this foreign body in its life. Perhaps it will try to sweat out the church by general indifference. Perhaps God really intends to give us a dose of this strong medicine. But that is precisely when the moment of promise dawns, for then that holy "remnant" by which God fights his battles will remain. Then the miracle of the church will confront us, because only then will it become clear that she lives from the word of her Lord, *only* from that word and from nothing else. Then perhaps that word will make use of a grandmother (as in Russia) to teach her grandchildren the catechism. Then secretly ordained priests will preach in catacombs. And while the great cathedrals are ruined or turned into garages, the torch of the word will be secretly passed from hand to hand until the moment comes when the great signal beacons will be rekindled and the city set on a hill will become visible to all.

The miracle of the church is that she always rises again out of every grave, whether it is self-prepared or dug by others. The rhythm of the time between Golgotha and Easter morning is repeated again and again in the church. In how many conceptual graves have the philosophers buried her! How many coffin lids have been closed on the word by false theologians and pseudo-Christian spirits of the age! But that word has risen again out of all corruptions and heresies, fresh as morning dew. No "idea" would have undergone that without going to pieces or suffering a sad, posthumous fame in the mausoleum of history books.

But by no means are we dealing with a mere "idea"; this is a matter of Christ risen and living. He knocks again and again on our doors when we have barred them against him. *That* is the miracle of the church.

That is why the church appears in the "Third Article" of the Creed, where the resurrection of the dead is central. *She* does not live; *Another* lives in her, Another whom all her wretchedness can neither silence nor imprison in his rocky tomb.

Since this Other lives in her and is among us, the church is not a monument to the past when this Other walked the earth. She is allied with the future, for she looks forward (as a wise or foolish maiden, awake or asleep) to him who will come "to judge the quick and the dead." The great of this world live under an "Exit" sign—and how clearly we can observe the often macabre departure of those who were once great and celebrated historical figures. The church's Lord, however, lives under the sign, "Coming soon."

Only from this perspective can we explain the most remarkable thing of all: the martyrs of this church did not merely suffer stiffly, silently, while they were torn away from a life that they, too, loved. They broke into songs of praise, whether they were in the arenas of Nero, facing the guillotine (as Gertrud von

LeFort's poem describes), or even in the cellars of the Russian secret police. They certainly did not suffer in order to honor the memory of the great Nazarene. They suffered because they were already ahead of the present in which their executioners lived; they heard the steps of the Coming One approaching from the other side. This is why an Orthodox priest could call out to the executioners before his death, "I salute you, dead men; I go to the living ones."

That was the source of their life. The man to whom the last hour belongs has no need to fear the next minutes. That meant that their hearts provided more than the mere stoic power to bear hardships; it also produced *joy*, expanding the narrow prison cell into a stage where the believer might see the fulfillment come.

Thus we are to love the church, even though she is only an earthen vessel containing the treasure of the gospel. We cannot say, "You don't appeal to me, your members don't appeal to me, and what you say offends me; therefore I keep away from you." It has pleased God to put his pearl in this wretched vessel and his treasure in this miserable, stony field. Whoever is offended by these unattractive receptacles gives up much more than just the institutional framework for something that he otherwise would have seen sympathetically and positively. A local congregation may be poor and somewhat sterile, but whoever despises it also loses the Lord who meets him in beggar's rags and whose humility no man may despise. The Lordship of Jesus is not adapted to golden frames; it is like a pearl that must be painstakingly sought among pebbles.

Heaven knows, that first church, the stable at Bethlehem, was no cathedral! And which of the bystanders on Golgotha would have imagined that that "sacred head, now wounded" bore a visage that would shine across the earth? At our death, when the faces of those we love will fade away like distant shadows, that visage will appear to us as a shield and comfort. Who would have guessed this when that god-forsaken cry broke from his tortured mouth and everything seemed to indicate that the last act of a tragedy was being played to its finale?

The glory of the church (am I stretching things if I say that now?) does not consist in her cathedrals, her thundering organs and her impressive assemblies. It consists in her being made holy by the word entrusted to her by Another. And when we pray for the church, we do not do it with the wish that she might outlast the ravages of time untroubled or even untarnished. We pray in the certainty that she is filled with the breath of the Holy Spirit, so that she dispenses bread and not stones from the pulpit, at the coffin, or by the sick-bed; so that her word does not congeal into a dead vocabulary, but becomes a spring of living water.

That doesn't have to happen in cathedrals and great churches. Perhaps the time for these places is past. I don't know. It can happen, however, in a murky cafe where a Salvation Army lassie talks with a bar girl; or it can happen where a driven, hounded man learns of Him who can loose his chains and breathe new life into his worn-out soul.

There are horrible Neo-Gothic churches that can almost make a tasteful person physically ill. But just sit there while a praying congregation surrounds you and its songs of praise rise to the artificial stone vaults overhead. Suddenly, everything is transformed. The earthen vessel becomes transparent, and is scarcely still there; the glory of the church blinds us to everything dubious in its appearance. For the glory of the church is not her *own* (the miserable Neo-Gothic is still all too apparent); it is the glory of the One who has come into the midst of his people.

That is the mystery of the holy, universal, apostolic church.

I BELIEVE . . . THE RESURRECTION OF THE BODY, AND THE LIFE EVERLASTING

> What is sown is perishable, what is raised is imperishable. It is sown in dishonor, it is raised in glory. It is sown in weakness, it is raised in power. It is sown a physical body, it is raised a spiritual body. If there is a physical body, there is also a spiritual body. —*I Corinthians 15:42–44*

How foreign these words "resurrection of the body" and "life everlasting" are to us! It makes no difference whether we are used to hearing them Sunday after Sunday or whether they are only a faint memory of statements we memorized as children. The great, or even so-called "ultimate" questions (such as the problem of whether there will be a last judgment and what will happen if there is) never come home to us or affect us as deeply as the little things.

In the morning, for example, much depends on breakfast's going right. We already feel faint tremors of premonition about a delicate task we must perform before lunch, or the anticipation of a lively party in the evening lifts our spirits. Even the newspaper belongs to this breakfast ritual. The front page carries something about a crisis in NATO, as well as an article about the deteriorating relationship between Peking and Moscow. That news is so important that it might change the face of the earth. It might lead to the tearing down of the Berlin Wall, for example, or it might mean that one day our planet will be blown up.

But the remarkable thing is that most people, when they pick up their papers, don't begin to read the front page, with its perspective on world history. They start with the local news: the charity ball at a downtown hotel, the four-alarm fire in the suburbs, the scandal in an executive's family, and the "earthshaking" remark made by Richard Burton as he dined with Earl Wilson at the Four Seasons. *That's* the kind of thing that sweetens our morning coffee so piquantly. Our lives are filled by the most trivial and the nearest-at-hand. The local news means more to us than the front page, and my pay envelope or my working conditions, in turn, mean more to me than the local news. In fact, the smaller a thing is, the more it means to me. The same thing is true with the so-called "great" of this world. Once, when I was a student, I was invited to the home of one of the brightest luminaries of our time. I had prepared myself for an excursion into the heights of humanity, but the illustrious company argued over the simple question of whether the grand old man might wear slippers for greater comfort, or whether he must continue to pay tribute to social convention and therefore remain properly and completely dressed.

It is good for us to remind ourselves from time to time of this order of values as it normally exists in our minds, because then a twofold surprise awaits us. The Bible, too, knows the insignificant and the everyday—hate and love and family squabbles, intrigues and orgies, sobs and laughter—yet the decisive impulses for everything that happens seem to come from a great distance.

The Bible talks about a prehistoric grasping for some sort of forbidden fruit, about Cain's murdering his brother, and about the flood. And right now we are discussing the "resurrection of the body" and "life everlasting" when this world's "Long Day's Journey into Night" reaches its goal. That raises a question, though. Is *your* and *my* life here, in this moment, to be determined by those primeval incidents, lost in the far reaches of myth, or by those promises of a future Beyond? "Forget it," we might say. "Between these first and last pages of the biblical *World Times* is the local news! That's where we live, and that's what concerns us. 'Let us eat and drink, for tomorrow we die' (I Cor. 15:32), and the bird of a cheerful breakfast in the hand is more important to us than a couple of resurrections in the bush." That's the way we think!

Now there is no doubt that Christianity bears a full measure of responsibility for the hold this distorted scale of values has obtained on all of us. Undoubtedly, Dietrich Bonhoeffer is fully justified when he reproaches many Christians for believing in a "life everlasting" as merely "a last escape into eternity." They are looking for a sort of metaphysical cabin in the sky or an evacuation route out of the misery of a life they can't handle. There is no doubt that a so-called "life everlasting" must seem to be an illusion of the weak, one that all sensible people who are up to their ears in this life would shrug off or even turn from in disgust. And there is no doubt that Karl Marx saw part of the truth when he said that the belief in a Beyond and a heaven in the future serves many people as merely an opiate which helps them out of their present predicament with the aid of a thin veil of smoke.

In reality, however, we are dealing with something completely different. We are dealing with the very realistic promise that our little life, as well as history as a whole, has a *theme* around which everything revolves; that the story of the world has been written by a hand sure of its goal. It means even more; it means that we cannot ascertain the possibilities which stand before us simply by noting the course of events as they present themselves to our human eyes; the Lord of history has at his disposal ways and means which we cannot even imagine. It means that he is a God of miracles and of surprises and that, in his name, we may be adventurers on a new level. To be sure, we know only the "theme" of the story God is writing about our lives: that he wants to lead us to his goal and bring us back from every far country to our Father's house. But we don't know *how* he does it, what roundabout ways he uses, and to what adventures he thus calls us. We have only the promise that we, like Israel, will reach the promised land if we, as God's pilgrim people, walk along behind the smoking pillar of fire (that is, if we hold to the theme which God has written over our lives) and if we don't let ourselves be led into some wilderness or be coaxed from the way by the fleshpots of Egypt. From the perspective of the last judgment we will be able to look back and recognize the necessity of everything that often seemed senseless and misleading at the time. Our experience may be like that of Moses (Exod. 33:23), who saw God passing by from a cleft in the rock, although he was permitted to look at God only from the back. He could see neither God's face nor the action of his hand.

But what good does this pious perspective do us *now?* We haven't come to that point yet; we are sailing toward it cheerfully (or maybe we are being harried) across the sea of everyday affairs. And certainly neither "life everlasting" nor the "resurrection of the body" are buoys or lighthouses which we heed on our journey, nor are they part of the breeze that drives us along.

We must ask ourselves why. Why is it that the goal and safe haven of life's journey for the people of the New Testament means so shockingly little to us—so little that hardly anyone bases his life on it or even takes it seriously?

There is a very simple, but immensely important, reason. The message of resurrection and everlasting life can become exciting to us only when we recognize it as the answer to a question which concerns us, and even profoundly motivates us, in other areas of our life. Ernst Bloch, the Marxist philosopher who has meditated and written so much about hope, once expressed himself on the matter in a very significant passage: "Nothing serves as an answer," he says, "which has not previously been asked. That is why so much that is clear remains unseen, just as though it were not there."

I would like to follow that with this question: Is the message about everlasting life also something "clear" in this sense, perhaps, which we have not noticed simply because no deep question has yet been asked in our life, and because God may have reserved this very moment of reading for lifting it out of its obscurity?

What could be the question that would demand "life everlasting" as its answer?

It is still fairly easy for a disciple of Jesus Christ to probe down to that question. We know that we have been loosed from chains which formerly held us as though they were welded fast. We know something of the relief from a conscience that no longer accuses us, because our guilt is forgiven and we have found peace of heart. Indeed, we know still more. When the little ship of our life threatens to capsize in the storm, *he* comes over the billows and stands by. And when we must die, he will be with us in our last hour.

Yet no matter how completely we may stand under his protection, we also know that the darkness is still there, grasping for us. Granted, we are on the victor's side; yet day after day we suffer the defeats that oppress us. We fall back into vanity, lying, and impetuosity, into all the things that often make us want to say the morning after, "That couldn't have happened because it shouldn't have happened." A disciple of Jesus Christ *shouldn't* backslide like that! Nonetheless, he *does!* That is precisely the question that results. Shall the One whose hand rests in ours, to whose star we look, and upon whose staff we lean, shall that One not lead us toward a goal where the onslaught of darkness is finally beaten back, where there is no more mourning and crying, where death no longer reigns, and where the dim mirror will be removed so that we can see Him directly, face to face? When we experience that deep split in our Christian existence and learn to know ourselves as pilgrims filled with a great passion for clarity who see the promised land of fulfillment only from afar, then that question whose answer is "life everlasting" wells up out of its obscurity within us.

But how about those among us who are not Christians? Do they also harbor this hidden question?

I think they do, even if it is of another sort. And here I must quote a "prophetess" whose name is seldom, if ever, spoken from a pulpit or mentioned in a book of this kind—Marlene Dietrich. Is there anyone who, by this time, hasn't heard her sing on radio or television:

> Where have all the flowers gone?
> Young girls picked them, every one. . . .

Then the song goes on to ask,

> Where have all the young girls gone?
> Gone to young men, every one. . . .
> Where have all the young men gone?
> Gone to soldiers, every one. . . .

246

> Where have all the soldiers gone?
> Gone to graveyards, every one. . . .
> Where have all the graveyards gone?
> Gone to flowers, every one. . . .

Thus the round of questions begins again; the circle turns back upon itself. One could ask the song's questions over and over while the shadow of the riddle grew larger around us and the voice of the singer wore thin.

But the song stops. Miss Dietrich makes her exit asking a question: "When will they ever learn? When will they ever learn?"

What an abyss yawns in that question! Can we ever learn what flowers, young girls, and young men are to be, when the game of life is abruptly broken off time and again, so that its round can begin all over—only to break off once more? Can we ever learn that everything which once loved and laughed and bore a live, softly whispered name will fade into the anonymity of the endless cycle?

No, we can never learn. And it is as though the famed chanteuse, like her voice, breaks on this question.

We sink back into namelessness, into that nothingness from which we come and into which we seem to fall again. But doesn't this sinking into namelessness involve precisely the inquiry after the one who has called me by name, declared me his possession, and summoned me to eternal life in fellowship with him? Doesn't this sinking into nothingness involve the question of him who has broken open the cycle and prepared a straight path to the Father's house for me, just as he burst open the grave on Easter morning? That is *one* grave from which more than merely flowers grew. Instead of having to ask, "Do you know where the flowers have gone?" we now have another question: "Dost ask who that may be? Christ Jesus, it is he . . ." [No. 150, *SBH*].

But could we comprehend who he actually is and could we gain the slightest intimation of what deliverance is and what new life, grounded in eternity, is like, if we hadn't previously been suffering under the throbbing circular idling motion of that wheel of fate which binds girls and men, flowers and soldiers to its grinding millstone, eternally pouring out and creating anew?

Goethe sensed the same question when he wrote: "The wave lifts us, swallows us, and we sink"; we are members of the "endless chain" of many generations.

I don't want to be misunderstood, of course. I certainly don't mean to say that when the wave pulls us down into nothingness we will immediately call out to Christ, that the religious question will then pop up "automatically."

The opposite is true. When Peter tried to walk on the water and then sank, he would never have called out to Christ if he had not known him before. And, after this wet, ego-deflating experience, Peter assured his fellow disciples quite definitely, "Previously, *before* he pulled me out, I didn't yet know who he really was. First I had to sink, to feel there was no bottom under me, so that then and *only* then I could prove him to be the rock on which I could stand. You have to face the void in order to recognize that he can snatch you out of nothingness, death, and hell. I had to experience being swallowed by the merciless elements in order to know his mercy, his heart, and his power."

Perhaps someone is thinking that it's time to call a halt now. I hear the question, "Are you trying to smuggle us into Christ and the lap of the church by a tricky maneuver? Are you trying to present Christ as the only possible answer to all the many vexing questions of life? Aren't there also other answers to these questions? Don't the Marxists, for example, have an answer? How about those utopians who dream of a kingdom of justice and peace? Haven't they, too, tried to give an answer in which they feed us with hopes of a gradual progress in the future?"

Indeed, I must concede that point. These other proposed solutions for our life's problems do exist. Therefore I understand the mistrust that one or another of you may feel about my point of view. I even share it and would like, for my part, to sharpen these critical questions still more. Why, then, do we mistrust such utopian ideas as the classless society? If I'm not mistaken, we harbor this mistrust because they simply postulate the exact opposite of everything that now oppresses us. Where there is social injustice, there shall be classless equality; where people are hungry now, all shall be completely filled. Isn't a hope of this sort actually, as Ernst Bloch says, often a mere "recoil against anxiety and fear," a reaction which is all too easy to explain on psychological grounds? In that case, then, don't we *have* to mistrust those finesses and subterfuges of our psyches?

This result seems natural. But then we must be ready to think this criticism through to its logical end and face the consequence: Couldn't life everlasting and Christ himself be products of that same sort of wishful thinking, too good to be true?

Naturally, I can't prove that Christ and the promise of life everlasting are different from those utopian dreams. But I can point out something that will make us pause and think. At any rate, it will not lead easily to drawing the conclusion that belief in the life everlasting is to be sought on the same level as those illusions we just mentioned.

Wherever the New Testament speaks of the Kingdom of God and life everlasting there are amazingly few "fanciful" elements. Fantasy is held tightly in check, and as a rule statements are limited to negative conclusions: There, in life everlasting, "they neither marry nor are given in marriage" (Matt 22:30). Again, "flesh and blood cannot inherit" it (I Cor. 15:50), and death will be swallowed up in victory (I Cor. 15:54). Basically, the Bible never talks about life everlasting as a condition that can be described; it simply makes the point that we shall be with the Lord and that we may see him face to face, although now his face is eclipsed by the inscrutability of our destiny.

That hope of being permitted to have him in his fullness would not be within our reach, had we not *already* received the down payment of his glory (as we said before) or if we had not *today* already experienced personally the meaning of the forgiveness of sins, the security of his love, the healing of mortal pain, and the new breathing space for our souls. But then, if we have experienced Christ, we know that he himself is always even greater than his greatest gifts. The pinnacle of promise is not what he *gives*, but what he himself *is* to me. Nothing shall come between us: that is life everlasting.

But we are still left with that troublesome phrase about the "resurrection of the body."[1] It sounds exceedingly rough and strikes us as all too physical. Even Luther said he was afraid that it would remind people of a butcher's shop. This overly physical idea has prompted Christians to cringe at the thought of cremation, since the obvious disintegration of the body into ashes would apparently prevent its reawakening.

In reality, however, the biblical concept of "flesh" does not mean the physical materiality of our body at all; it is a special quality. It is the expression for man's frailty, his inexorable passing. All flesh is "like grass" (Ps. 103:15); man is made of earth (and that means of the "dust") and will return to the earth (Gen. 3:19). And no deliverance spares us from the way of the grain of wheat in the earth, where it must die and turn to dust in order that it may then be awakened to new life. "What is sown is perishable, what is raised is imperishable" (I Cor. 15:42).

Here again the statements are cautious and very discreet. They limit themselves to metaphorical approximations. Everything will be completely "different" from what it is now; that is the core of what we are told. Here again, the view is narrowly concentrated on Him who not only causes the wind to pass over the grass so that "its place knows it no more," but who summons His creative word over the valley of the dry bones, and who holds a new and different life in reserve for us (Ezek. 37).

The tremendous, although very heathen, memorial to the bombing victims which stands in the Ohlsdorf cemetery in Hamburg shows only Hades and the somber ferryman, Charon, who carries despairing souls into the world of shadows. It shows only the pain of parting. But it is well that this powerful piece of sculpture stands in our city, so that we must press on beyond it in order to learn what Christ gives us. He turns our departing into a homecoming, receiving us on the sheltering banks across the dark underworld's River Styx. There, once again, the creative word, "Let there be . . ." rings out in a totally new way, calling us out of death into life, just as it once called the creation forth from chaos.

[1] The German text reads, "resurrection of the flesh." (Trans.)

Do we understand what this new word of creation at the End means? I can only try to approximate it by means of a parable, a little "experiment in thought." At some time or other we have all asked ourselves, "If it were possible, would I want to live my life over? Would I want to repeat it all over again?" Perhaps we are very active people who can't get enough of life and who would actually want to try the great experiment of existence once again. If we did, it would certainly be on the condition that we could do many things differently. Perhaps I would take up another vocation, or develop completely different approaches in my present vocation. Perhaps I would marry, or not marry, or even choose a different marriage partner. I would no longer depend on this or that person who has become inimical to me. I would demand more and different things from myself, now that I know my talents better and have an idea how much *more* I could have gotten out of them.

Beneath it all lurks the knowledge that I was intended to be something other than what I have actually become. In the heart of God, my image lives as something different from what I actually have made of myself. The father in the parable had this "proper" image of his son before his eyes and in his heart when with open arms he received the prodigal who had gone to ruin in a far country. That was why he loved him. He saw his "proper" image, and therefore he had compassion on the painful distortion of that image.

We live through the same process when, as disciples of Jesus, we learn what love is. Then we see the other person as God really meant him to be. We suffer precisely when something about him disturbs us (for instance, he may be a shady character), since God also suffers on his account. We suffer not only *because* God does, but also *as* he does, in the suffering of compassion. And then something remarkable happens to us. When we share the suffering of God, we are freed to be compassionate. Then we, too, see through the dirt with which the divine sonship of this dubious person has been encrusted and disfigured: we see the pearl lying in the dust—the pearl that was purchased at great price when He took the cross upon himself. Then our heart beats in time with the heart of God. That is an unheard-of liberation.

Since we also are so dearly bought, and since our image is kept and sheltered in the heart of God, his faithfulness will not end when we sink into the earth like a grain of wheat. Then his creative word will come to us anew, summoning us into his eternal presence. We shall be mysteriously changed, called out of our perishable life into a new existence beyond words, and yet we shall bear our identity, be recognized, and be called by the name which we received in this life—the same name by which God will acknowledge us in eternity. The "what" and the "how" of this continued life may escape all our efforts of thought and imagination, but we know the One who will prepare that place for us. *He,* at any rate, is no riddle to us, for we have already looked into his heart. His arms encompass time and eternity like giant parentheses; there is none other and nothing else beyond him. The boldest reconnaissance efforts of the human spirit and the most extravagant metaphysical systems fail to draw those parentheses into the field of study. Speculations of that sort simply end in the blind alleys of fantasy. The surprising thing is that the parentheses around this world and the world to come are much too close for the philosopher's telescope to find as it sweeps the reaches of space. They are in Him who is with us when we are gathered in his name; in Him who tells me, "Fear not; only believe"; in Him who comes to me at the altar in bread and wine and who, as Luther put it, "lies as a child in Mary's lap, although the universe cannot contain him." His arms are the parentheses encompassing time and eternity, this world and the next.

Do we understand, then, what it means to say that these mysteries are hidden from the wise and understanding and that we must become children in order to comprehend what holds the world together at its inmost core? Whoever is close to that Heart in prayer and trust knows that the dust (which both blinds him and dirties him) has already been removed. When the powers of death and despair clutch at him, he is given a sovereign calmness by that future world with whose life he is already allied. As Ernst Juenger once wrote in *Radiations,* "Here even the least of men is given the point where he comes in contact with the whole business, and not just a part. From that point flows unheard-of victory and even the power to rule. In situations where the cleverest fail and the most valiant devise an escape, you sometimes see a person quietly giving the right advice and doing the right thing. You can be sure that he is a man who prays." And the philosopher Peter Wust sums up his own work when he says, "The great things of existence are given only to those who pray." Those who pray, however, are always those to whom the future world is near.

Actually, our view of that world is blocked: "Foolish the man who turns his dazzled eyes that way." But we really don't look that way at all! We look only to the heart of someone who is here for us now, in this moment, and who will not let us fall, even when we one day cross the Styx. In fact, should I escape to the uttermost part of the sea, he will still be there; he will even be in the hell of my despair (Ps. 139:8).

I do not believe in the life of the world to come, then, because I look into eternity and let my imagination play around with golden streets and crystal seas. I believe simply and solely because I am already the comrade of him whose faithfulness to me will never end. His hand gives me confidence to walk into the dark, even into the "inconceivable" and "totally other" world to come. For then he alone will not be different or strange to me; I will recognize him again as the one whose voice has long been as familiar to me as a shepherd's voice is to his sheep.

One of my dearest students lay on his deathbed, and I spent his last nights with him in his hospital room. Time after time, as he lay gasping for breath, enduring frightful bodily torment, he desperately reached for my hand. Suddenly in the morning stillness the bells in a nearby Catholic church struck six. Then he brightened and said, "Do you hear the Easter bells? He is calling me now. Look, now I am rising!" In his extremity, the ordinary little bells, which were just ringing in a normal day on earth, became a signal for him from the Lord of Easter. He had trusted him in life, and now the Lord brought him up out of the fearful valley of the shadow of death.

As the Lord performed this miracle and let him hear the Easter bells (where there really was only an everyday clanging), he once again turned water into wine and gave marvelous satisfaction with a few loaves of bread. The dying man knew that his Lord would also transform *his* wasted, pain-racked body, keeping it forever in a new and altered form. Dreaming, removed from all earthly need, carried over into that totally other world, he already greeted me from the other side. It was as though he had left me behind in the mortal world and was turning to wave to me in the name of the Lord who receives both the living and the dead. "If we live, we live to the *Lord*, and if we die, we die to the *Lord*."

That was the moment when I grasped the meaning of the "resurrection of the body." A glimmer of transformation already flickered over those features contorted with pain. The "grim reaper" wasn't slinking around—you could tell that in your bones. It was the risen One who stood there ready to escort his faithful servant on that dreamlike journey. I felt what that godly man Johann Albrecht Bengel had expressed so quaintly two hundred years before: "When a pilgrim enters that better world, the door opens and a little breath of heaven always sweeps over those most closely involved, strengthening them until their turn for the good journey arrives." Did you catch that? There is no talk about that grim reaper who seizes us with bony fingers; instead, we hear of a "good journey."

I must stop here and put aside the many thoughts which still clamor for expression. These images of the experience of transformation should stand at the end of our meditations, even if they themselves are mere pointers and indications from the world to come. They can help us and affect us only when they become pointers to him who already stands waiting for us, not only at the cradle and the grave, but also between them in the world of offices and assembly lines, shipyards and evening parties. He asks us, as he asked the rich farmer in the parable, "The things you have prepared, whose will they be?" (Luke 12:16 ff.). Who will you be when you must go alone through the lonesome, narrow gate of death without anything to take with you? Are you one of those who merely build castles in the air as they pursue success,